How to Garden

How to Garden

Exactly what you need to know—and only what
you need to know—to grow all kinds of flowers,
vegetables, trees, and shrubs successfully

Jerome A. Eaton & Carroll C. Calkins

ILLUSTRATIONS BY LINDA LAKE

ALFRED A. KNOPF   NEW YORK

THIS IS A BORZOI BOOK
PUBLISHED BY ALFRED A. KNOPF, INC.

Grateful acknowledgment is made to the following
individuals, firms, and organizations for permission to
use the photographs found on the pages indicated:
All-America Rose Selection: p. 105.
Thomas H. Everett: pp. 142, 145, 149 (both), 166 (both),
167 (both).
David Hampfler: pp. 3, 12, 36, 46, 48, 60, 62, 69, 70, 71,
75, 80, 82, 83, 93, 96, 99, 106, 111.
Stokes Seeds, Inc., Buffalo: p. 133.
Union Carbide Corporation: p. 163.
The frontispiece (facing title page) shows the five basic
flower forms of tulips (from left): parrot, lily-flowered,
double-flowered, cottage, and (in the center) Darwin.
Manufactured in the United States of America

Contents

How to Garden

⚼|Introduction|⚼
The Fallacy
of the Green Thumb

Rooted deep in the folklore of gardening is the idea that people for whom plants perform well are blessed with some special sensitivity to the forces of nature. They are said to have a "green thumb." But the idea that some people are born with the ability to grow plants well and others are not is nonsense.

It's true that some people are more interested in plants, more observant, and more attentive than others. These are the people who always have "good luck" with their plants. Actually, about the only time luck is involved with gardening is when it rains on the day you need it. All the rest is a matter of understanding the plant's basic requirements for light, temperature, soil, nutrients, and water. Plants that get what they need will thrive. Those that are deprived will languish. Fortunately, there's usually time to take corrective action. It is as simple as that.

One of the challenges of gardening is learning what the various kinds of plants need in order to grow well. Another challenge is selecting the plants best suited to the conditions of your garden. Fortunately,

there are lovely specimens that will thrive in every conceivable environment. There are plants for the desert, the bog, the jungle, and the arctic wastes; for acid soil and alkaline, for sunny places and for shade. If you choose the right plants for a given situation, and understand and fulfill their needs, your garden is sure to be a success. Success, for a gardener, is enjoying the natural response of the things you grow to the proper conditions you have provided.

This book is a guide to such success. It is clearly divided into specific subjects logically arranged for easy reference.

We have described trees, shrubs, annuals, perennials, bulbs, and other kinds of plants that are most suitable for home gardeners. Although we have been selective, including only the easiest-to-grow and most rewarding plants in each category, there are hundreds of recommendations, and you will be sorely tempted to try many of them—perhaps more than you should. Restraint is a virtue that is usually acquired the hard way. Keep the following thought in mind and you will save yourself a lot of labor and disappointment: *The best garden is slightly smaller than the largest that can be easily cared for. If you let the balance tip the other way, and maintenance becomes* an enormous chore, the joy of gardening will be diminished and the fruits of your labor will be flawed.

The success of a garden of any size depends on the gardener's understanding of how plants best adapt to a given situation. The plants in this garden both contrast and blend well with one another.

❧ |1| ❧
What All Plants Have in Common

All flowering plants are essentially the same. They have roots, stems, leaves, flowers, and seeds, even though these may be so varied in form as to be unrecognizable. Each part is vital, and if you understand what it does, you will be better able to give your plants the care they need.

The roots hold the plant in place and take up necessary substances from the soil: water, nitrogen, phosphorus, potassium, and trace elements such as zinc, manganese, and boron. Roots do not manufacture food. By the process of osmosis, they simply take up liquid that is suspended between the particles of soil and start it on its upward journey.

The stems are the conduit through which the liquids from the soil are passed on to the leaves and through which the nutrient manufactured by the leaves is then circulated to all parts of the plant. The stems provide the framework that supports the plant, and the stems of some plants, particularly trees and shrubs, also have the capacity of storing food for later use.

The main purpose of the leaves is to convert the chemical elements of air and water into nutrients that the plant can use. This complex transformation of energy—called photosynthesis—is the basis of all plant growth. It can only take place in sunlight (or in the proper artificial light) and only when the leaf contains the green pigment chlorophyll. (Plants with leaves that are red or yellow during normal growth actually have the necessary chlorophyll but it is obscured by the other colors. The reds and yellows that appear on the foliage of some green plants in the fall indicate the loss of chlorophyll that takes place as dormancy approaches.)

Photosynthesis is affected by the weather. It is more efficient when the temperature is above 60° F., which is why most plants do not grow so fast when it is cold.

The leaves give off oxygen in the form of water vapor and take up carbon dioxide. In this regard they are considered effective air conditioners.

Because the leaves depend on the roots for water and the materials with which to make food, any damage to the roots will be reflected in the appearance of the plant. If you should damage or remove some of the roots in transplanting, some of the top growth should also be removed to maintain the necessary balance between the two, as explained in chapter 16.

For the gardener, the flowers on a plant may be the ultimate goal. From the point of view of the plant, they are just an intermediate step on the way to the all-important production of seed. The intricacies of seed production are best left to the botany books. Suffice it to say here that a pollinating agent—the wind, bees, butterflies or moths —transports pollen from the tip of the stamen to the sticky tip of the pistil. Thus fertilized, the seed will begin to develop in a seed case, in a cone, or within a fruit. All the energy of the plant is directed toward producing seed, because only plants with a strong capacity for procreation can continue to survive.

When the seed of a flowering plant has ripened, the cycle of growth is complete and the plant begins to die or become dormant. You can prevent the production of seed and prolong the season of bloom by snipping off the spent flowers. With some plants, such as pansies and roses, this will add an extra month of color to your garden.

Most flowers are self-fertile. This means that the male part (stamen) and the female part (pistil) are on the same flower. But in some species the male and female parts are on separate flowers, and in still others they are on completely separate plants. For these last, if the female plant is to pollinate and produce seed there must be a male of the species within 500 yards or so. This is important to know if you are buying such plants as the holly, because the berries, which contain the seed and for which the plant is usually grown, cannot be produced without pollination. The nurseryman will

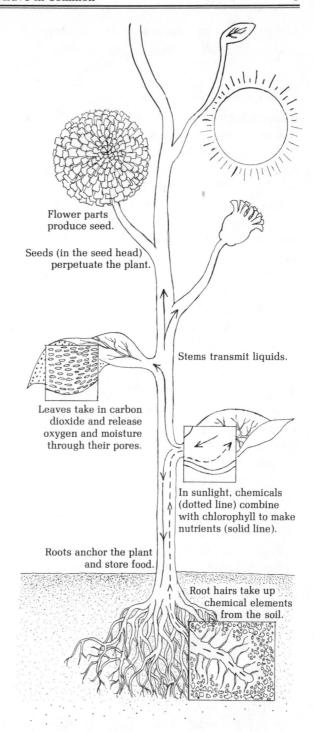

Flower parts produce seed.

Seeds (in the seed head) perpetuate the plant.

Stems transmit liquids.

Leaves take in carbon dioxide and release oxygen and moisture through their pores.

In sunlight, chemicals (dotted line) combine with chlorophyll to make nutrients (solid line).

Roots anchor the plant and store food.

Root hairs take up chemical elements from the soil.

usually tell you which sex you are buying and remind you of the need for the other.

What's in a Name

Nomenclature is another attribute that all plants have in common. Every plant has a botanical name that serves to distinguish it from every other. These names are in Latin, which is still the nearest thing we have to a universal language. Thus the name *Betula papyrifera* is understood by gardeners in Russia, Germany, Iran, and Japan to mean the paper-barked birch.

Not only does the Latin name serve internationally, but locally it is often the only way you can determine exactly what plant you are getting in a nursery, ordering from a catalog, or discussing with a friend. Take the name "bull bay," for example. This is the accepted common name for *Magnolia grandiflora*, a broadleafed evergreen flowering tree 60 or 80 feet high. It is also the name used for *Persea borbonia*, a similar tree about half that size. Only if you use the botanical name can you be sure of avoiding confusion. Consider, too, the name "sweet bay." This is used for another magnolia, *Magnolia virginiana*, a half-evergreen tree with fragrant flowers, and also for *Laurus nobilis*, the evergreen tree from which wreaths were made in ancient times for winners of the Olympic Games. In short, there is good reason for botanical names.

The binomial system of nomenclature, as it is called, was devised by the Swedish botanist Carolus Linnaeus. Each plant has a name with at least two parts. The first part indicates the genus, the second part the species. In the example above, *Betula* is the entire birch genus, and *papyrifera* is the paper-barked species; there are several

The many fern species include kinds adaptable to shade or sun as well as to moist or dry locations. Their distinctive fronds make an interesting contrast with the foliage of other plants.

other species in the genus, such as *B. nigra*, the black birch. A plant name may also have a third part to indicate a variety of that species. *Betula papyrifera grandis*, for example, is paper birch with large leaves. *B.p. minor* is a shrub form. The name of a plant in a genus such as *Rosa* that has many hybrids and selected varieties may include varietal names such as 'Peace' or 'Harrison's Yellow'. As in these two examples, such varietal names are usually enclosed in single quotation marks.

The Latin names often provide useful clues to the qualities and characteristics of a plant. *Alba* means white, *rubra* means red, and *nigra* means black. *Siberica*, *chinensis*, and *alpinus* indicate the native environment and imply something about hardiness. Shape or size is revealed by such terms as *macro* for large, *micro* for small, *brevis* for short, and *longus* for long.

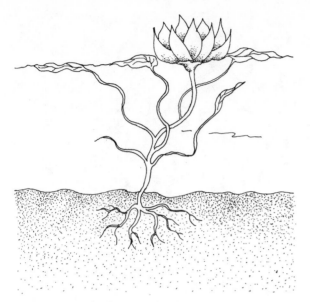

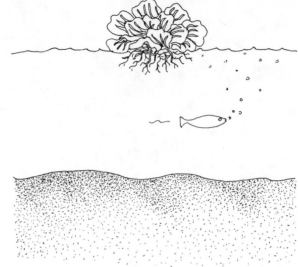

Water lilies root in the soil and send their leaves and flowers up to float on the surface. Normally they grow at depths
of from 1 to 3 feet, but this can be adjusted if plants are
rooted in movable containers.

Water lettuce (*Pistia stratiotes*), roots and all, floats on the
surface and derives nutrient from the water alone. In
sunny locations clusters of plantlets will develop, which
can be easily separated to avoid crowding.

You can have a lovely garden without knowing any botanical names, but they are certainly nothing to be afraid of, and they can
be helpful.

A Few Interesting Exceptions

Mosses, ferns, aquatics, epiphytes, and
parasites are plants that have developed
some unique methods of survival. If you
plan to grow any of these, you will need to
know a little about them.

The mosses and ferns you will certainly
recognize. The aquatics include the water
lilies, lotus, cattails, and similar water
plants. Epiphytes include the orchids.
Mistletoe is an example of a parasitic plant.

Mosses, unlike most other plants, are
difficult to start from scratch. They grow
mostly in acid soil, in moist and usually
shady places. Where the conditions are

right, the moss will simply appear. If you
are fortunate enough to have moss establish itself in your garden, relax and enjoy it.
It is attractive on its own and is also an
indication that most garden flowers would
be unlikely to do well in that location.

Mosses cannot be started from seed
because they reproduce by means of minute
spores. The spores can be started under
laboratory conditions, but this is hardly
practical for a home gardener. They can be
successfully transplanted only if the garden
situation is similar to their setting in the
wild.

Ferns also reproduce by means of
spores, and they too will appear when conditions are right. But they have a more
typical root structure, are sold in nurseries,
and can be transplanted. They will do well,
however, only if they have exactly the conditions they need, which are much like

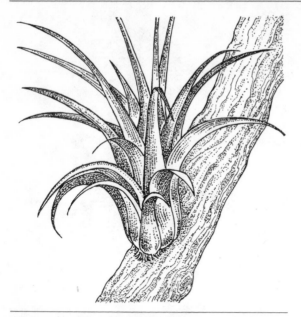

Epiphytes, such as this bromeliad, anchor themselves to other plants. Unlike parasites, they take nourishment not from their host, but from air and water and from the debris that collects where they are anchored.

Parasites actually root on and sap nourishment from other plants, thereby diminishing the strength of their host. But many, like this mistletoe, do no serious damage and can embellish an ordinary tree.

those required by the mosses. Mosses and ferns are companion plants in nature and are equally compatible in the garden.

Some aquatic plants, such as water lettuce (*Pistia stratiotes*), float on the surface and grow beautifully without any attention. Others, such as the water lilies, have a somewhat more conventional growth. Their roots grow in the soil at the bottom of a pond, and long stems lead to the floating leaves that support the flowers and the seed that will develop.

The most glamorous of the plants with unusual life-styles are the epiphytes, which include some orchids, ferns, and bromeliads. "Epiphyte" literally means "growing on"; these plants grow on other plants. They use the host only as a perch. They take no nutrient from it. An orchid may root itself in the moss and decayed leaves caught in the fork of a tree, but it does not

penetrate the bark. There are also plants that get nutrient from rainwater and from the air itself. A good example is the bromeliad called Spanish moss, which can grow on a telephone wire.

Parasites, on the other hand, which include mistletoe and various fungi, do take nourishment from the host plant and can do it harm.

Although not unusual in the way they grow, the cacti have developed a unique life-style. Some roots spread wide and shallow to capture as much of the limited moisture as possible. The stem is often a flexible reservoir that expands greatly to hold water, which is then used gradually as needed. The leaves, through which water is released to the atmosphere, present a minimal surface to reduce the rate of expiration. Some leaves have, in fact, become spines, which also serve to protect the plant.

❧ | 2 | ❧
Plant Hardiness
and Getting to Know Your Garden

Every plant is dependably hardy in its native clime. But in the quest for variety in flower, foliage, and form for their gardens, plantsmen have introduced thousands of specimens from one climate to another.

With this tide of plant migration has come the bugaboo of questionable hardiness and the need for some method of indicating which plants are hardy enough for which climates.

Some countries are blessed (or cursed) with only two or three different climates. In this country, however, seven major climate zones have been defined by the United States Department of Agriculture, and each of these has been divided into two subdivisions, for a total of fourteen.

The subdivisions provide a degree of refinement that is unnecessary for a book of this kind. The version of the USDA map provided here includes only the seven basic hardiness zones. The plant lists in this book are keyed to these zones. The zone number indicates that the plant is hardy throughout that zone, and, of course, the warmer zones.

Look at the map to see which zone you are in. Say you live in St. Louis, which is about dead center in Zone 5. The average annual minimum temperature in this zone is 5° to 10° below zero. You probably have a pretty good idea as to whether or not this is true in your garden. If the temperature where you are has never been down to zero, your garden is in the next warmer climate zone (Zone 6) no matter what the map shows.

By the same token, if you live near the northern edge of a climate zone, your garden may actually be in a colder climate. If you live near the southern boundary, you may, in effect, be in the warmer zone. The best way to get the facts about the temperature in your garden is to use a high-low recording thermometer and note the average minimums for a few years to establish a norm. While this may seem like a lot of bother, it can help you avoid the unfortunate mistake of planting trees and shrubs that are doomed to perish in your garden.

Temperature is only one aspect of climate. Rainfall, humidity, light intensity, and air pollution also influence plant growth. But these vary so widely that they cannot be dependably delineated on a map.

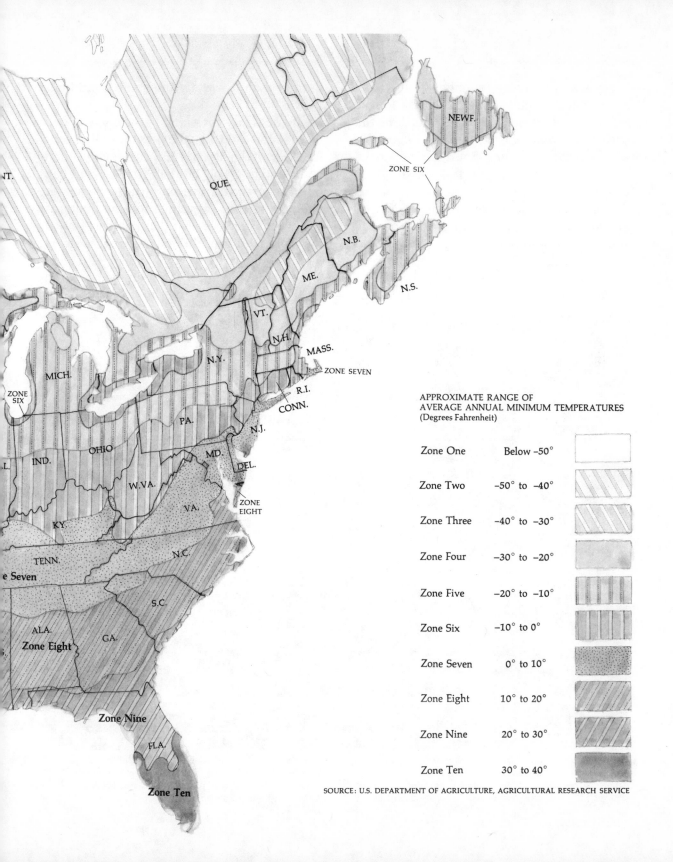

ZONE SIX

ZONE SEVEN

APPROXIMATE RANGE OF
AVERAGE ANNUAL MINIMUM TEMPERATURES
(Degrees Fahrenheit)

Zone One	Below −50°	
Zone Two	−50° to −40°	
Zone Three	−40° to −30°	
Zone Four	−30° to −20°	
Zone Five	−20° to −10°	
Zone Six	−10° to 0°	
Zone Seven	0° to 10°	
Zone Eight	10° to 20°	
Zone Nine	20° to 30°	
Zone Ten	30° to 40°	

SOURCE: U.S. DEPARTMENT OF AGRICULTURE, AGRICULTURAL RESEARCH SERVICE

Every garden has a number of so-called microclimates that offer both challenges and opportunities. Snow melts early in the spring in various warm spots and lingers for weeks in the cold ones. South-facing slopes are warmer than those that face north. Windy places are colder and less humid than sheltered places. An area protected by the south-facing ell of a house can be 20° warmer in winter than the opposite exposed corner facing north. This range of temperatures and conditions provides opportunities for a wider selection of plants for your garden than if exactly the same conditions prevailed throughout.

If you study your land carefully, you can create the setting that best suits your fancy and the needs of your family—and your budget. For outdoor living you can build a terrace or deck, either shaded or open to the sun. For recreation the facilities might be as simple as a flat stretch of lawn for croquet or badminton, or as elaborate as a tennis court or a swimming pool with bathhouse—or both. And for their beauty, and their function, there can be plants, in be-

What seems to be a problem can often be turned to a gardener's advantage. This boggy, low-lying area was made into an informal pool set among a variety of attractive plants—candytuft in the foreground, a clump of day lilies across the pool, and a planting of species geraniums— that thrive in moist places.

Here, a south-facing sun pocket was used for plants too tender to grow safely in the open. In the foreground at left is *Cotoneaster salicifolia*, the tree is *Caragana arborescens* 'Lorbergii', artemisia billows over the walk, and in the foreground corner is *Perilla frutescens*.

wildering variety. Bewildering, that is, unless you learn to "listen to the land" to find out what it calls for.

As we have explained above, within the overall climate of an area, every individual piece of property has its own range of small climates or microclimates. Once you have learned by observation where these areas are, you can avoid putting tender plants in cold pockets, and you can use a heat trap, such as a south-facing wall, to provide a longer season of bloom.

To know the nature of the land is to know that there are no "problem conditions." There are only "conditions," and for every one there are plants that will thrive. The problems are created when we try to grow plants in one place that are best suited for another. All plants do best and are easiest to care for when they grow under the conditions that are most nearly natural to them.

If there is a low wet place, consider it an opportunity to grow some interesting bog plants. If there is a windy hillock, this is the place for plants such as pines or junipers that make lovely sculptural forms under the buffeting of the wind. If there is a hot, dry, sandy place, there are succulents that will thrive there.

First, there is the soil to consider. With a long narrow trowel, you can dig and probe to see if the topsoil is composed mostly of sand, humus, or clay. In areas where trees and shrubs will be planted, dig a test hole to see how deep the topsoil is and whether or not the subsoil drains well. If a hole holds water for more than a day, the drainage is not good. And, of course, you will want to check the soil for its acid-alkaline balance in places where plants will be set out. (See chapter 3.)

It's important to know the patterns of sun and shade on the ground throughout. If you want a vegetable garden, it should be where the sun shines longest. Rhododendrons and azaleas, and many other lovely plants, do best where there is dappled shade all day, or where there is a little direct sun and shade for the rest of the day. Some plants, such as ferns, do beautifully in deep shade.

The shape of the land is important too. A south-facing slope gets more sun during the day than a north-facing slope. On a steep slope, rain or irrigation water will run off faster than it can soak in (unless the soil is very sandy). This is an appropriate place for plants that can withstand drought. Another opportunity afforded by a steep slope is the use of a woody ground cover, such as a low-growing juniper, that will break the impact of water on the soil and hold it in place. A rising slope presents more surface to the eye. A slope that rises from a viewing point, such as a large window or a terrace, is an excellent place for the display of favorite plants.

It is not necessary, nor is it possible, to get to know immediately all that your land has to offer. You can quickly determine where to set out the major plantings of trees and shrubs, and where to put the things that need the most shade and most sun. But the refinements and pleasures of finding just the right plant for a particularly challenging microclimate can go on for years.

With the change of seasons, particularly in northern gardens, the patterns of sun and shade also change. The patterns change too when deciduous trees drop their leaves.

The best way to record the variations in temperature, sun, and shade as well as any variations in the soil in your garden is to make notes in the garden and transfer them to a plot plan laid out on graph paper at a scale of, say, 3 feet per ¼-inch square. But if keeping notes and making a plot plan for a graphic representation of the microclimates in your garden seems like more of a project than you want to take on, merely an understanding of the possibility, and an awareness of the variables, will help you avoid the kinds of mistakes that so many gardeners make.

The most common mistake results from a perfectly understandable enthusiasm for a particular plant. A gardener might say, "I just love roses, and the first thing I'm going to do is plant a rose garden." Well, unless there is a place with good subsurface drainage, good air movement, and at least five hours of full sun a day, it would be better to get the roses from a florist. Or no matter how much one might be enamored of rhododendrons, they won't grow successfully without acid soil, lots of moisture, and some shade.

Nature, in its abhorrence of a vacuum, has created plants for every conceivable situation. Once you understand the conditions that prevail in your garden, you can take advantage of a secret that has long been shared by all great gardeners: it is better to take advantage of natural forces than to try to work against them.

☆|3|☆
Understanding the Soil

In gardening the importance of the soil is obvious; it lies at the root of the matter. Good growth, in general, indicates good soil, and where growth is sparse and scrawny the soil is probably poor in quality or too shallow to support good root development. The better the soil, the wider the range of plants that it will grow successfully. On the other hand, no soil is so poor that something will not grow on it.

Good garden soil is said to be friable (easily crumbled) and to have good tilth (which means that it has been well crumbled by cultivation). The soil that can most readily have these qualities is loam. Loam is a well-balanced mixture of sand, silt and clay, and humus, which are the basic elements of all soil.

The sand in the soil helps maintain open space for air to enter and water to drain through. The silt and clay hold nutrients that can be released to the roots. The spongy humus gathers clay particles, by molecular attraction, to make the microscopic crumb structure necessary for friable soil. It also serves as a reservoir that can retain and release water, and when not saturated with water this organic material also helps increase aeration of the soil.

Aeration is vitally important. Without sufficient air as well as warmth, moisture, and the humus upon which they feed, the microorganisms with which the soil is literally alive cannot function. There are many billions of these minute organisms in a single handful of soil, and through complex chemical interaction, they convert plant food to forms that can be taken up by the roots. Without this action the elements necessary for plant life are unavailable even if they are present in the soil. It is no exaggeration to say that the main purpose of improving garden soil is to improve the environment for the microorganisms upon which all plant growth depends. The bacteria, fungi, enzymes, algae, protozoa, earthworms, insects, and other living organisms in the soil are at their most efficient when the temperature of the soil is about 60° F. This is a primary reason why plant growth slows down as the temperature drops.

The inorganic or "chemical" fertilizers, however, are immediately available to plants and do not need breaking down.

The upper layer of soil, called topsoil, is usually the best. It has more humus, from decaying roots, and is usually darker in color than the subsoil that lies below. The subsoil usually contains more clay. The next level is hardpan, which is often impermeable. If the hardpan is near the surface the soil drainage will be poor.

Although it calls for considerable spadework it is a good idea to dig a hole 2½ to 3 feet deep in a planting area to see the profile of the soil. At this depth you will doubtless get to the subsoil and possibly to the hardpan. Most plants will do well if the topsoil is 1 foot deep and the subsoil adds another foot or so of potential root area. Where there is less than this depth of soil, dig a hole twice the size of the root ball of a new plant and fill it with topsoil.

You can use the hole you dug in the ground to check drainage, too. Fill it with water and see how long it takes to empty. If it takes only an hour or so, you can grow plants that require good drainage. If the water stays for 24 hours you will have to break through the hardpan with a pick, crowbar, or posthole digger, or lay drain tile to provide drainage.

If water seeps into the hole, the water table is so near the surface that planting in raised beds or containers may be the only way to grow plants that require good drainage.

Never work the soil when it is wet. This compacts and compresses it so much it cannot readily admit the air so important to the growth of soil bacteria.

Evaluating Soil Structure

To check the structure of the soil, drop a shovelful on a concrete surface. If it does not hold together at all, it is too sandy and will not hold water or nutrients. If the soil breaks into small pieces of consistent size, it has a texture in which roots will thrive. If it breaks into large chunks or stays in a lump, humus and sand should be added to make it more friable.

A pinch of soil rubbed between the fingers can also reveal a lot about its make-up. Sand feels gritty, silt smooth, and clay sticky. If the soil makes a string when rolled between the fingers, the clay content is high.

The cureall for poor soil structure is humus. This can be any spongy, partially decomposed organic matter such as compost or peat moss. It adds body to sandy soil so that it will retain water, and in clay soils it creates much-needed air space. For container plantings, vermiculite and perlite are also useful for creating air space in soils that are too tight and sticky. Mulching, which has other attributes, as explained elsewhere, is also helpful in maintaining

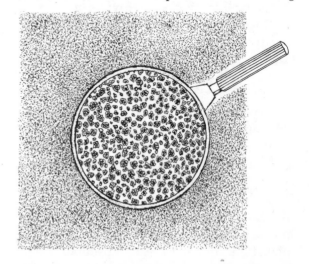

Sand consists of hard, nonabsorbent bits of mineral, surrounded by air spaces. Water drains through it very quickly, carrying away nutrients.

the quality of the soil. It keeps the rain from compacting clay and from leaching nutrients out of the root area in sandy soil.

The Acid-Alkaline Balance

Most plants do best in a soil that is neutral —that is, neither acid nor alkaline in composition. There are a few excellent shrubs, however, such as rhododendron, azalea, pieris, and leucothoë, that thrive only in acid soil. Others, including lilac, wisteria, clematis, and most vegetable crops, perform best in alkaline soil.

The measurement of alkalinity and acidity is expressed as pH ("power of hydrogen"). On a scale of 1 to 14, 7 is neutral. Lower numbers indicate acidity, higher numbers alkalinity. The range for garden soils is from about 4 (the most acid) to about 8.5 (the most alkaline). A simple soil-test kit which you can buy will give you a dependable pH reading.

An acid soil can be made more alkaline by adding ground limestone. To raise the pH from 5.5 to 6, add 4 pounds per 100 square feet (an area 10 feet by 10 feet). To raise it from 5 to 5.5, use 8 pounds per 100 square feet.

An alkaline soil can be made more acid by adding elemental sulfur. To lower the pH from 7.5 to 6.5, use 2 pounds per 100 square feet.

Another way to increase acid content is to spread a 50-pound bale of peat moss over 1,000 square feet of ground and dig it in to a depth of 4 to 6 inches.

For a complete soil test, to reveal possible deficiencies as well as the acid-alkaline balance, send a sample of soil to your county cooperative extension agent or to the department of ornamental horticulture in land-grant colleges.

Composting

Composting is the process of reducing organic matter, such as leaves, grass clip-

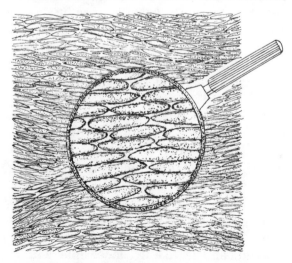

Clay is composed of layers of closely packed, overlapping plates of mineral material. Water travels slowly through clay, and so it stays wet for long periods.

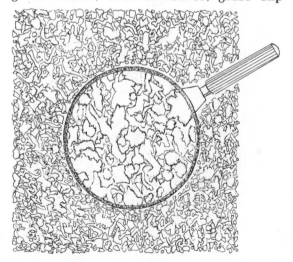

Humus is a spongy substance that forms from the partial decay of organic matter. This permeable material retains water and nutrients well and releases them readily.

pings, and other vegetable materials of all kinds, into smaller pieces called humus.

The actual breakdown is done by bacteria and other microorganisms in the soil. To carry out this process, they must have moisture, oxygen, and nitrogen. If the compost pile is too dry, there will be no bacterial action, and if it is soaked with water, the action will stop for lack of oxygen. The nitrogen must be added as extra food for the hard-working bacteria.

A moist, well-aerated pile of organic material can be reduced to good compost in about two months in warm weather. In cool weather the process will take five or six months, and when the temperature is freezing the process stops completely.

Don't think that composting must be smelly and unsightly. It is, in fact, a clean and odorless way of disposing of vegetable matter. Do not, however, put meat scraps or other garbage on a compost pile.

The secret of odorless and efficient

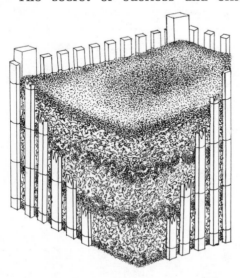

To build a compost pile, alternate 9-to-12-inch layers of organic material with 2-inch layers of soil. A depression should be made at the top to collect water. Container walls should be at least 50% open for air circulation.

composting is to provide plenty of oxygen for the soil bacteria. For this reason compost should never be put in a pit below the ground. Not only should the pile be above the ground and well ventilated, but a working pile must be turned every two weeks to aerate it more completely. This requires some labor, but the humus is well worth it.

The time to use the compost is while the vegetable matter is still crumbly from partial decomposition by bacterial action. If left too long in the pile, the material will turn to a dark fine-textured humus that looks good but has disintegrated too far to be of any value.

Compost at the crumbly stage has some value as a plant food, and when dug into planting areas it is a useful means of returning to the soil some of the nutrient that was extracted by the growing plants.

Its greatest value, however, is for mulching and soil conditioning. For optimum effect a mulch should be at least 4 inches deep. This depth of loose material serves to insulate the soil, conserve moisture, and control weeds. The weed seeds in the soil cannot easily grow through the layer of mulch. Most of the seeds in the compost itself have been killed by the heat of the process.

Compost is particularly valuable as a soil conditioner. Its fibrous content will lighten the texture and improve the drainage of heavy claylike soils, and will also increase the water-holding capacity of light sandy soils.

Put the compost pile in a place that gets a few hours of sunshine, is somewhat out of sight, and is readily accessible with a wheelbarrow. The pile can be unsupported, or for a neater appearance, can be contained as shown in the illustration.

✄ |4| ✄
What You Should Know About Planting

There is no great mystery about planting. It is simply one of a series of steps that starts with a specific need.

Before you start thinking about digging a planting hole, you have to decide where you would like to put the plants, and for what purpose.

Perhaps you think it would be nice to have a little flowering tree at the turn of your entry walk. Or a handsome large shrub would be refreshing to see out the bedroom window when you get up in the morning. Or it would be a pleasure to have some fragrant plants beside the terrace. Or you may want a windbreak and some kind of screen planting to block the view of the neighbors' back porch.

Once you know the purpose, the next step is to consider the conditions of the site and seek out the kinds of plants that will thrive in those conditions. Fortunately, the world of plants is large enough to offer candidates for almost any situation.

As said before, it is much more practical to choose a plant to suit the conditions of the site than to try to make the site accommodate the needs of the plant.

And, of course, it never pays to plant trees or shrubs that may not withstand the coldest temperatures in your garden.

Digging the Hole

When you have the plant you want and know where you want to put it, it is time to dig the hole.

The less time the roots of a plant are exposed the better. The hole should be dug before the plant is brought to the site.

A planting hole should be about half again the diameter of the root ball. If, for example, the root ball is 18 inches across, the width and depth of the hole should be about 30 inches. This will allow about 6 inches of space all around for new soil.

If the planting area is in a lawn or grassy place, remove the turf to a depth of 2 to 4 inches and put it aside. A spade is the best tool for this purpose. Use it vertically to make a series of parallel cuts about as far apart as the width of the spade. Slide the spade under the roots between the cuts, and lift the strips of turf. These strips will be useful after planting.

In digging the hole you will first encounter the topsoil, which is darker in color and contains more organic matter than the lighter subsoil beneath. The layer of topsoil may be just a few inches deep, or it may go down for a foot or so. Put the topsoil in a separate pile. It will be used again when the hole is refilled.

When the hole is dug, fill it with water to test the drainage. If the water stands in the hole for more than four hours, the drainage is not good enough for most plants. If this condition prevails, you have four choices: select a plant that will grow in a boggy situation; provide drainage for the hole; choose a new site for the plant; or plant in a raised bed.

First try breaking down through the subsoil with a crowbar. Sometimes it is an impervious layer of clay or shale with well-drained gravelly soil beneath. Further

testing will reveal whether or not there is drainage under the subsoil.

If water stands persistently in the hole, the only sure way to move it away is with drain tile leading from the bottom of the hole to a lower place where the water can escape. This is only possible on sloping ground, and, at best, is a considerable chore. If, however, you really want to have a specific plant in a certain place, this may be the only way to do it.

You may have heard that the way to provide drainage in a hole is to dig deeper and put in a foot or so of gravel. This is nonsense. The gravel cannot move water out of the hole. In fact, it can do just the opposite. The hydrostatic pressure of water in the surrounding soil can force water into the gravel area where the resistance to movement is less.

If you live where there is a prolonged

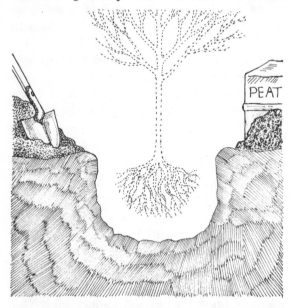

Separate the dark-colored topsoil from the lighter subsoil. Make the hole half again the size of the root ball of the plant you are setting out. This may seem like a lot of extra digging, but it is worthwhile.

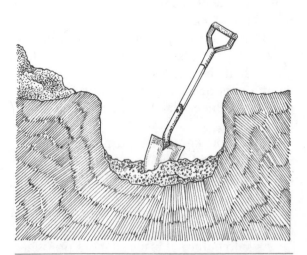

Mix equal parts of topsoil and peat moss, add fertilizer as recommended, and fill the hole about one-fifth full with this mixture. This is the area where nutrient is needed most by the feeder roots that develop there.

rainy season, keep in mind that the water table will not be the same all year. A hole that drains well in July may be filled with water in November.

If it proves to be impossible to attain good underground drainage, you can resort to planting in a container or a raised planting bed.

Preparing the Planting Soil

Make as accurate an estimate as you can of the amount of soil it will take to fill in around the root ball.

The main ingredient will be the topsoil. Put aside a little less of this than you think it will take to fill the hole after the plant is put in place. If there is not enough topsoil for this, you can add some of the subsoil. You might also consider bringing in some more topsoil from elsewhere on your prop-

erty. To complete the planting soil, add peat moss or compost in the amount of about one-quarter the volume of the topsoil and mix it all together thoroughly.

Add to the soil mixture a cupful of a slow-release fertilizer for each bushel of soil. (A bushel basket measures about 12 inches high and 16 inches across.)

In estimating the amounts, keep in mind that it is better to have too much of this mixture on hand than too little. You can always find a place in the garden to use some good enriched planting soil.

Putting the Plant in Place

The best time for this job is on a cloudy or drizzly day when the plant will lose the least possible moisture through its leaves during the process of transplanting.

The first step in setting the plant in

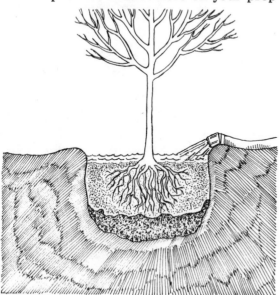

Set the plant in the hole so that the soil level relative to the plant will be the same as it was in the nursery. A change of color marks the original soil level on the trunk. Add soil and water slowly to avoid air pockets.

Immediately after planting, cut back at least one-third of the top growth to keep it in balance with the root area, which was reduced during transplanting. Build a rim of soil to keep water from draining away from the root area.

place is to establish it at the same height relative to the surrounding soil as it was in its previous location. On bare-root plants this level is evidenced by an obvious difference in color on the stem. On balled and burlapped or container-grown plants the established soil level is also obvious. The difference between bare-root and balled and burlapped plants is illustrated on page 24.

The step-by-step details of planting are clearly shown on the preceding two pages.

Lay a straightedge, such as the handle of a rake, across the hole as a point of reference to help in setting the plant at the proper height.

Make a mound of soil in the hole and sit the plant firmly on it. The mound can then be raised or lowered until the plant is at the proper level.

It may be necessary to lift a tree or shrub in and out of the planting hole several times to establish the proper soil level. Always lift the plant by its root ball, not by the trunk or stem. Lifting by the trunk puts all the weight of the soil on the roots, and some of them may be torn away. This can impair the ability of the plant to re-establish itself after it is placed in its new location.

If the root ball is too heavy to handle alone, use a strip of burlap as a sling under the root ball so two people can work together to lift it in and out.

When finally positioned firmly on the mound of soil, the plant should be an inch

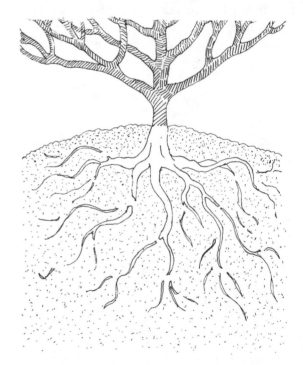

In cold climates a mulch should be used not only to reduce evaporation during the growing season but to prevent root damage caused by alternate freezing and thawing.

On sunny days the top few inches of frozen soil can melt. At night, or on colder days, that area can freeze again, expand, and rise, until the plant is torn from its lower roots.

or two higher than its proper level, because it will settle when the root area is soaked with water—as it should be after planting.

Before filling the hole with the planting soil, cut away any obviously damaged or broken roots cleanly with sharp pruning shears. If the root ball is wrapped with burlap, simply untie the top and leave the burlap in place. When covered with soil it will soon rot away.

Fill in around the roots with the prepared soil. Tamp the soil down thoroughly with the end of a 2-by-4, or tread it with the feet to establish firm contact between the soil and the roots.

When the hole is about half-filled with soil, soak it thoroughly with water to settle it further. Then continue filling and tamp-

Four to 6 inches of pine needles, hay, or wood chips will keep the surface from thawing and prevent damage. Remove the mulch in spring so that the sun can warm the soil.

ing until the soil level is even with the surrounding area.

To hold water in the root area, make a reservoir with a raised rim around its perimeter. This is where the sod that was cut into strips comes into use. Simply stack the strips in a circle to make the sides of the holding basin. You can also use soil for this purpose, but the sod holds more firmly and is less likely to wash away in a heavy rain. When the holding basin is finished, water thoroughly again.

A 4-inch covering of your favorite mulching material, extended just beyond the root area, will reduce the loss of water from the soil by evaporation. An occasional sprinkling of the mulch will also help to raise the humidity around the plant.

No matter how careful you are when planting, there will be some damage to the hair roots that take up moisture and nourish the plant. Anything you can do to reduce the rate of transpiration through the leaves until the feeder roots are reestablished is all to the good. Frequent application of a fine spray of water is helpful. You can also cover shrubs with damp burlap for a day or two. Anti-desiccant sprays are often used to prevent water loss through the foliage, particularly on evergreens. And, in all cases, the branches should be cut back somewhat to keep the top growth in better balance with the reduced efficiency of the root system. Cut back the branches of shrubs and trees that are up to 6 feet tall by about 10 percent. Cut the branches of taller trees back by about 25 percent.

The loss of large trees and shrubs when they are transplanted can most often be traced to the gardener's reluctance to cut the top growth back as severely as necessary. Although this pruning does alter the

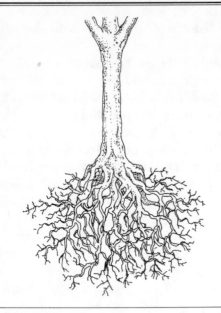

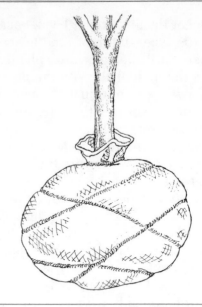

The term "bare-root" refers to plants which are sold during their dormant season when the roots can be safely bare of soil (above). Only deciduous trees and shrubs are sold this way. Roses are the most familiar bare-root nursery plant, although they are also sold in soil-filled containers. The roots of balled and burlapped—"B and B"—

plants are covered with the soil in which they grew and then wrapped in burlap (above). Evergreens and some deciduous plants are sold this way. Burlap need not be removed before planting, as it will rot away, but a plastic, tarpaper, or metal wrapper should be cut away.

appearance of the plant, it is a necessary sacrifice to maintain a workable balance with the reduced size and efficiency of the root system.

To reduce the risk inherent in the transplanting of a tree or shrub it is important to provide an adequate supply of water during the growing period for the first 18 months in its new location. After that the root system should be well enough established to supply the needs of the plant without any more attention than normally required for other plants in the garden.

By "an adequate supply" we mean that before the soil in the root area dries out completely it should be thoroughly watered again. If you have any doubts about your understanding of the principles of watering, there's more on this subject in the next chapter.

Some tall plants will need staking to keep them from rocking back and forth in the wind and breaking off the feeder roots.

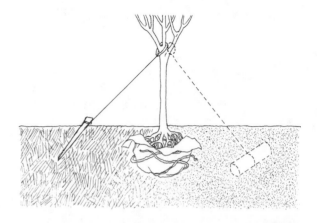

One to three guy wires staked at equal intervals around the trunk may be required for support. Use rubber padding on the branches to avoid chafing the bark. The guy wires can be anchored to a peg or a buried log.

❧ |5| ❧
Watering, Feeding, and Weeding

A garden hose in the hands of someone who does not clearly understand how water moves in a plant—and in the soil—should be considered a dangerous weapon. More damage is done to plants by improper watering than by any other means. This can be avoided by understanding when, where, and how to apply it.

When to Water

A plant can be safely watered when the soil around the roots begins to dry out. If you aren't sure, you can tell by digging into the soil with your finger or a trowel.

Watering becomes urgent when the soil is dry and the leaves of a plant, be it a garden flower, a house plant, or a shrub or tree, begin to show signs of drooping or wilting. It is the water in the leaves that keeps them filled out.

Now here is where confusion may arise. Leaves may also show signs of wilting when the soil is wet. The wilting indicates the same problem, lack of water in the leaves. But the cause is not too little water in the soil, but too much. If the soil is filled with standing water, there is no space for the oxygen necessary for the function of the root hairs, which take moisture from the soil and transmit it to the plant. Wilting, then, can be caused by either too little or too much water, and it is easy enough to tell which of these extremes is the problem by feeling the soil.

Watering can be done anytime during the day except late in the afternoon when the leaves might not dry before nightfall. Wet leaves at night are vulnerable to fungus diseases. And, of course, watering can be done without wetting the leaves.

How soon the soil will dry after a watering depends on the makeup of the soil, the plant's rate of growth, and the drying effects of heat and wind. Mulching, where practical, helps retain moisture in the soil.

Sandy soil retains little water and dries out quickly after watering. Clay soils and soils with lots of humus hold water much longer. A fast-growing plant such as an annual will take a given amount of water from the soil much faster than the slower-growing shrubs. Wind and hot weather take moisture from the soil (as well as from the plant itself) and create the need for more frequent watering.

Where to Water

There is only one place to put water, and that is where the roots are.

Any water applied outside the root area is wasted. Even more obviously wasted is the water that runs off the surface and doesn't get into the ground at all. The runoff you see on sidewalks and gutters is a total loss, and if it is muddy it is taking valuable topsoil with it.

Water and nutrients can be taken in only by the tiny root hairs that develop near the end of each root. Most of these feeder roots are at the perimeter or dripline of the plant, and this is where most of the water and plant food should be applied.

The larger the plant, the farther the feeder roots from the stem. In watering a large tree, for example, very little of the water applied at the base of the trunk will find its way into the tree. And, of course, the feeder roots on deep-rooted plants are much farther down than those on shallow-rooted ones. The illustrations will give you an idea of how water penetrates different kinds of soil and how long you may have to water a given plant to saturate the root area.

Roots cannot seek out water, but they will thrive where there is water. To promote the extension of a root system, saturate the soil somewhat beyond its immediate perimeter.

How to Water

The key to proper watering is an understanding of how water moves through the soil. It goes down, to be sure, and it moves laterally; but in very specific ways.

Water does not move down into the soil

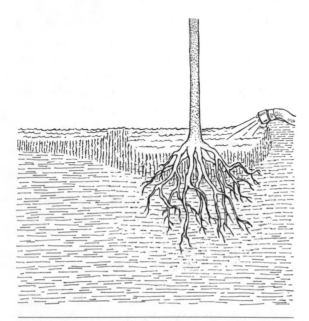

Given the same rate of flow, water moves differently in different kinds of soil. In clay soil the water will run off be-

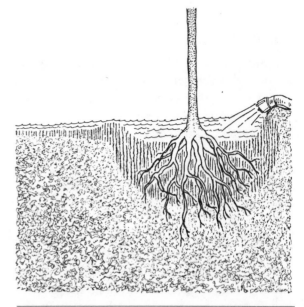

fore it penetrates very deeply. In loamy soil the water penetrates to a moderate depth before it runs off. In sandy soil

until the surface is so completely saturated that it can hold no more. Then the water that cannot be held at that level moves down to saturate the next level before it can go deeper. The only control you have, in a given kind of soil, is how deeply you saturate it. As indicated previously, you should water deep enough to saturate the root area, particularly around the feeder roots.

As water moves down from one saturated area to the level below, there is space for oxygen to enter and no danger of suffocating the root hairs (and soil bacteria) that require oxygen to live. Suffocation or "drowning" is a danger only when water does not move on down and stands for days in the soil.

Water goes straight down through the soil with relatively little lateral movement. It must be applied evenly over the entire spread of the root area if all the roots are to be reached. In a planting bed, container,

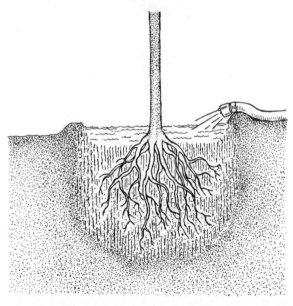

the entire root area may be saturated before it overflows the reservoir, but the water can also drain away quickly.

or pot it is easy to flood the surface over the root area. In the open ground, particularly on a slope, some kind of reservoir must be created to hold the water in place until it soaks down into the ground.

Runoff is wasteful, so don't apply water faster than the soil can take it in. And don't apply it too hard. A strong jet of water can slice away the topsoil and expose surface roots.

Soil soakers of canvas or perforated hose apply water gradually along their full length. Hose-end bubblers or soakers can be used to break the force when watering individual plants.

There are a variety of sprinklers to cover lawns and other large areas. They seldom apply water evenly over the area they cover. You can check this by setting coffee cans at 3-foot intervals in a line from the sprinkler to the edge of the spray pattern. This will indicate how you should move the sprinkler from time to time to even out the application. It will also tell you how long it takes to put down an inch of water. Then if you dig down with a trowel you can see the penetration per inch of applied water and adjust the length of time you water according to the depth of the root area.

There are underground sprinkler systems with plastic pipe and fittings that can be put in without professional help or special tools. For an out-of-the-way vegetable garden or cutting garden, the pipe and fittings do not have to be buried and are thus even easier to install.

Components of Fertilizer

When it comes to encouraging the maximum development of a plant, food is the primary

Nitrogen (N), phosphorus (P), and potassium (K) interact to promote plant growth, although each has its greatest effect on a specific aspect of development.

ingredient, just as it is for animals and man.

All plants need nitrogen (N), phosphorus (P), and potassium (K), and these are the constituents of a complete plant food. There are also many necessary trace elements, so called because they appear in quantities too small to measure meaningfully. These include boron, manganese, zinc, and iron, among others. They are a part of every complete fertilizer, be it dry or liquid, organic or inorganic (more about the latter classifications will follow). In some areas where certain trace elements are known to be lacking in the soil, they are also included in the fertilizer, as is indicated on the bag.

Most garden soils contain all of the elements needed for plant growth. But before these materials can be taken up by the roots, they must be dissolved, because plants can take them up only in liquid form.

This is a slow process. The humus and other organic materials that supply nitro-gen, for example, must be broken down by microorganisms in the soil to render first ammonia, then nitrates, and finally the nitrate solution that is the only form in which a plant can take up nitrogen. The other elements require a similar slow, though less complex, breakdown before they become available to the plant in liquid form.

This process applies to organic fertilizers such as manure. Chemical fertilizers, however, are available to the plant as soon as they are dissolved in water.

On the fertilizer container the three basic elements are always listed in order, with a percentage indicated for each element. A 10-5-10 fertilizer, for example, has 10% nitrogen, 5% phosphorus, and 10% potash.

In terms of actual plant food, this means that a 10-pound bag of fertilizer has 1 pound of nitrogen, ½ pound of phosphorus, 1 pound of potash, and 7½ pounds of filler. The filler is usually an inert substance in granular form. It has no nutrient content but has some value as a soil conditioner. All of the elements work together to promote plant growth, but each has its special characteristics. A "complete" fertilizer has all three elements; a "balanced" fertilizer has them in equal parts.

Nitrogen tends to induce the development of the proteins that promote cell growth. This is evidenced by the growth of sturdy stems and rich green foliage. Heavy applications of nitrogen, such as in a 20-5-5 formulation, can force green growth at the expense of flowers and seed. If too much is applied, it creates a strong solution that will damage the root hairs so they can no longer transmit liquid from the soil to the plant, and the plant will then wilt.

Since nitrogen is the least stable of the elements in plant food and tends to leach down into the subsoil, periodic applications are required to keep it in the root area of shallow-rooted plants.

Phosphorus or phosphoric acid helps most in the ripening of stems and seeds. In both its natural and manufactured form, it is converted slowly to liquid form and is unlikely to do any damage to the plant even if a little more is applied than recommended.

Potassium, or potash, combined with the other two elements helps to form starch and fleshy fruits, and to encourage healthy growth that is less susceptible to disease. It is particularly important to vegetable root crops such as carrots and beets. Potash is also stable in the soil and is released slowly.

How to Apply Fertilizer

The question of when to feed depends on the plant and its environment. At one extreme are houseplants that, in general, can be safely fed every two weeks because of the relatively small root area in the container and the constant leaching out of plant food by the necessary watering. At the other end of the scale is a mature tree that has such a vast and efficient root system that it can go for its lifetime without feeding.

Many shrubs and small trees, however, will benefit from an annual feeding. This should preferably be in the early spring before new growth starts.

In climates where there is little rainfall and thus no danger that the nutrients will wash out of the root area soon after they are applied, shrubs and trees can be fed in the fall. This must be done at least six weeks before the first expected frost in cold climates to allow time enough for the new soft growth to harden sufficiently to withstand freezing.

It is always a good idea to add fertilizer when new plants are set out. And, of course, all fertilizers must be watered in when they are applied to move them down into the root area.

Lawns should be fed with a high-nitrogen plant food at regular intervals during the growing season, because the top growth is constantly being cut back and is expected to renew itself.

Except as noted above, plant food can actually be applied at any time. The plants take it up only during periods of growth, and plants begin to grow, in cold climates, only when the soil begins to warm. The point is that no matter when fertilizer is applied, it has an effect only when the plants are in active growth. It is best to have food available when the plants first

After breaking up the surface of the soil so that it will freely admit water to the roots, apply dry fertilizer in amounts recommended on the container. Water slowly to carry the nutrients evenly to the root area.

begin to grow, because the growth that is lost in the initial surge may never be compensated for.

The amount of fertilizer to apply depends on the plant and, more specifically, on the analysis of the plant food. The higher the percentage of nitrogen, phosphorus, and potassium, the less is required for a given application. A 20-10-20 formulation, for example, has twice the strength of a 10-5-10. Read the instructions on the bag and follow them carefully. Applying more plant food than required is always wasteful and often harmful.

Dry granular fertilizers are usually mixed into the soil prior to or at the time of planting. They can also be spread on both sides of a row of plants, or all around individual plants, or worked lightly into the soil (to avoid disturbing the root area), and then watered in.

Liquid fertilizers are sprayed on with a hose-end attachment, or mixed in a watering can and sprinkled on the foliage and around the base of the plant.

The Organic-Inorganic Question

No other aspect of gardening is so fraught with controversy. There are those who claim that only organic fertilizers—that is, those derived from plants or animals—should be used. These organic gardeners believe that plants fed with tankage, sewage sludge, hoof and horn, blood meal, fish fertilizer, compost, and the like will not only be healthier but also in the case of fruits and vegetables be more nutritious and have better flavor.

Inorganic fertilizers are either mineral or man-made, and the gardeners who use them believe that a carrot, cabbage, potato,

To spread fertilizer over large, open areas a mechanical spreader—which can be rented—should be used. Water the fertilizer in with a sprinkler. On sloping areas, water intermittently to minimize runoff.

Liquid fertilizer is the quickest-acting and can be applied to the entire plant, as well as to the soil, with a watering can, hose-end applicator, or portable sprayer attached to a tank.

petunia, or pyracantha cannot tell whether the solutions it takes up through its roots were derived from organic or inorganic sources. The chemical facts are with the proponents of the inorganics. The chemical solutions that the plants can actually take up are identical, no matter what they came from. As for flavor of a given variety, this is strictly a matter of genetics. The kind of fertilizer used has no effect.

There is no doubt that many organic gardeners can point with pride to crops of every kind that are superior to those of their neighbors who use only chemical fertilizers. But it is our belief that this is due more to the composition of the soil in the organic garden than to the source of the fertilizer.

As explained in the chapter on soils, the health and welfare of all plants are largely dependent on the health of the microorganisms in the soil. The soil bacteria thrive on humus, and they need lots of oxygen. Most organic fertilizers contain more humus than the inorganics, and this increases aeration of the soil.

We must also realize that every self-respecting organic gardener adds compost to the soil—compost being an unexcelled medium for the development of microorganisms. He also uses a thick mulch of organic material over the surface of the soil. This mulch prevents soil compaction, conserves water, and keeps down weeds, all of which help produce more and better plants.

If gardeners using chemical fertilizers add the necessary humus to the soil and use mulches to the best advantage, they will do just as well as organic gardeners.

Some fertilizers release their nutrients much faster than others. The fastest-acting are those in liquid form. Use them when a plant needs a quick shot of energy. The slowest-acting are pelleted materials designed to release their nutrients gradually over a long period of time. They are most often used as a source of nitrogen for lawns or when planting a large tree or shrub.

Weeding

A weed, by definition, is any plant that grows where it is not wanted. Alfalfa is a valuable crop in an alfalfa field, but would be a bothersome weed in a strawberry patch. Grass is what you want in a lawn, but it's a weed between the paving stones on a terrace.

A few weeds can be tolerated, and some gardeners can tolerate quite a few, but when weeds become so numerous or vigorous that they threaten the appearance or the health of desired plants, it is time to take action.

Weeds can be removed by pulling, by hoeing, or by applying a herbicide. Pulling is fine when there aren't too many and when there's no danger of dislodging the roots of adjacent plants in the process.

Hoeing is effective, but with a conventional hoe there's the danger of cutting too deep and damaging favored plants. A scuffle hoe, which cuts just below the surface, is easier and safer to use.

When weeding, pull a bushel basket along with you and put the debris in it as you go. Then, when you are through weeding, you are through. There's no need to go back over the same ground and pick up anything. There is also less chance of spreading the seeds and starting a new crop as the weeds are pulled.

Chemicals to eliminate weeds are effective for pathways or terraces, but they must be used with care. If a spray is used it can drift onto nearby ornamentals, and if the ground above the roots of trees or large shrubs is saturated with a herbicide, it can leach down onto the root area and damage or kill the tree or shrub. However, if applied in strict accordance with the manufacturer's instructions, herbicides can be useful. They are particularly valuable for getting rid of such undesirables as poison oak or poison ivy. Spray the material on carefully, or paint it on the leaves with a long-handled brush.

On lawns, the days of cutting out each dandelion or crabgrass plant by hand are happily over. Manufacturers who specialize in lawn products have selective granular herbicides that will eradicate a variety of broadleaf weeds and certain undesirable grasses without injuring the lawn itself.

These materials are applied dry with a simple mechanical spreader, and there is no risk of their drifting onto other plants.

There are also weed-and-feed formulations that combine the herbicide with fertilizer so both chores can be handled in one application.

Mulching to Prevent Weeds

A near-magical method of weed control that also offers valuable side benefits is the application of deep mulch. This can be done on vegetable gardens, flower beds, borders, foundation plantings, or any other place where there is bare soil to be covered.

An effective mulch excludes light, and thus keeps weeds from developing but lets in the air and water necessary for plant growth. A good mulch also has enough bulk to stay in place without shifting or blowing away.

Compost is an excellent mulch. Many by-products are also used; they vary with the locality. Peanut shells are popular in Georgia and Virginia. On the East Coast, oyster shells or salt hay is used. Cocoa hulls, bagasse, tan bark, and granite chips are other regional favorites. Wood chips from tree prunings are available in most places, as is pea gravel.

A covering with any of these materials 2 inches deep will keep down all but the most persistent weeds, and these can easily be pulled by hand. And, as mentioned elsewhere, mulching provides the further advantages of preventing compaction by rainfall, retaining moisture, and stabilizing the temperature of the soil.

Some materials, such as sawdust, wood chips, and peanut hulls, have a high cellulose content. The microorganisms in the soil that break these mulches down gain much of their energy from nitrogen and thus denitrify the soil when such materials are applied. To compensate for this, add a high-nitrogen fertilizer, such as a 10-5-5, with the advent of the growing season. Apply in the amounts recommended in the instructions on the bag.

Peat moss is often recommended as a mulch. Its main drawback is that it gets so dry during a short period of drought that it becomes virtually impervious to water. If you do mulch with peat moss, roughen up the surface periodically so that it will allow the rain or applied water to penetrate. Peat moss is far better as a soil additive to increase acidity or organic matter in soils where required.

⊱ |6| ⊰
Choosing and Using the Best Trees

The overall style and character of your garden is determined more by the trees and shrubs you choose than by any other plants. Not only are these the largest elements, they are the most expensive, and it pays to select them with care.

Sometimes there's a question as to whether a plant is a tree or a shrub. Privet can grow 20 feet tall or more, although it is considered a shrub. But, in general, trees tend to have a more distinct head of foliage held well above the trunk, or trunks, which are heavier than the limb structure of the shrubs. And, of course, most trees are larger than shrubs, and because of their size and visual impact they should be the first elements selected in developing a new garden.

In their natural settings, trees range in size from a 15-foot Japanese maple to a 400-foot redwood, but for garden purposes they can be categorized as small (up to 20 feet or so) and large (to about 60 feet).

Consider what trees can do for a garden: They provide cooling shade, and when planted to shade a roof or the side of a house from the sun they can do wonders in reducing the temperature inside. They also provide shelter from the wind and can screen out unwanted views. Deciduous trees can create a bold design of branches against the winter sky. There are trees with showy bark and trees with magnificent color in the fall. Some are noted for their flowers, or for their fruit or nuts, and all offer refuge and food for birds.

If trees are not planted with forethought, there can be disadvantages too. If a tree is set in an inappropriate place its roots can crack sidewalks, interfere with drainage lines, and diminish the strength of other plants within its range. Branches can break off and damage a roof; leaves, twigs, stems, and fruits can create problems of maintenance; and deep shade can darken a room. All of these potential problems can be avoided if you understand the natural habits of the trees you choose and plant them accordingly.

A tree can be considered an investment, and it pays to buy as big a one as you can afford. Its impact on the landscape will be immediate, and you won't have to wait so long for it to provide the maximum amount of the shade, flowers, or fruit for which it was planted. But if you can't afford a big tree, plant a small one.

You have heard people say, "There's no sense in planting a small tree—it will grow so slowly that I'll never live to see it mature." But even the smallest tree can be a point of interest, and, looking back, one realizes that a ten-year span goes by very quickly. The thing to do is plant the trees you want, of any size, this year. Don't put off the planting until next season. Our purpose here is to make it as easy as possible to choose the trees that will give you the most of what you want in your garden.

The rest of this chapter is a descriptive list of desirable trees, subdivided into flowering trees, fruit trees, other deciduous trees, and evergreens. Within each subdivision the trees are listed alphabetically. We have included only a small fraction of possible ornamental trees, but these are the ones that in our opinion are the easiest to grow and are most useful in the landscape. Unless there are specific directions to the contrary, requirements for water, soil, and fertilizer have been covered in earlier chapters.

Flowering Trees

Cherry, Japanese weeping (Prunus subhirtella pendula). The popularity of this small exotic (10 to 12 feet tall) attests to its beauty. The species is grafted onto an upright trunk, usually of a hardier kind, and the branches, covered with pale-pink flowers in early spring, cascade to the ground. Plant this specimen in full sun and well-drained soil. Zone 5.

Crabapple, Japanese flowering (Malus floribunda). Among the attributes of this handsome tree is the unusual development of its flower and fruit in early May. The flower buds develop a deep-red color and then, as they open, reveal petals of pink that turn white as they mature. After this engaging spring show, the small cherrylike fruits gradually redden and remain for a few weeks until the birds take sufficient notice. The tree will adapt itself to many garden locations but requires sunlight to flower and fruit successfully. It grows to about 25 feet tall. Many other crabapple species and hybrids in a variety of sizes and with different flowers and berries are available at most large nurseries. Zone 4.

Crape myrtle (Lagerstroemia indica). The profuse clusters of showy flowers in late summer when few other trees are in flower make this a most useful small tree. The flower petals have an interesting crepelike texture and range in color from white through unusual shades of pink and red. The tree usually has multiple trunks, and when small it looks like a shrub. As it approaches its maximum height of about 25 feet it becomes more treelike. It does best in full sun but will tolerate some shade. Zone 7.

Dogwoods: flowering dogwood (Cornus florida), **cornelian cherry** (C. mas), and **Japanese dogwood** (C. kousa). Whenever dogwood is mentioned it is the flowering native, either white or pink, that first comes to mind. As the flowers unfold in midspring and literally cover the flat sprays of branches it is easy to see why this is such a popular medium-sized flowering tree. Technically, these showy flowering parts are bracts (small leaves), not flowers. The shining red berries are decorative in the fall.

Cornelian cherry is of similar size and is also useful for early-spring bloom. The tiny yellow flowers are literally massed on the branches and from a distance create the effect of a sulfur-yellow cloud. Flowers are followed by bright-red cherry-sized fruit, which are edible, although seldom eaten.

The Japanese dogwood earns its place in the garden with a prodigious display of bloom, which is particularly welcome because it appears late, after most of the other tree-borne spring flowers have come and gone. The white bracts with their interesting pointed shape turn a rosy pink as they fade.

All three of these useful medium-sized trees are tolerant of a wide range of garden conditions, with the exception of extreme dryness. They are susceptible to borers, which can be detected by frequent casual examination.

C. florida and *C. mas*, Zone 4; *C. kousa*, Zone 5.

Franklin tree *(Franklinia alatamaha)*. In addition to having an interesting upright form, usually with multiple trunks, the Franklin tree bears its creamy-white flowers with yellow centers in late summer when few if any other trees are in bloom. The plant is unusually adaptable. It tolerates moist soil and will produce flowers in light shade. They grow to about 20 feet. Zone 5.

Golden chain tree *(Laburnum vossii)*. This medium-sized tree reaches its usual 25-foot height in about ten years. Its rather narrow form is accentuated by the long pendulous clusters of yellow flowers. The cloverlike leaflets give the tree a delicate look, until they drop in the autumn. It will grow in a wide range of soils, but to thrive and flower successfully it needs full sun and good drainage in the root area. Zone 5.

Golden rain tree *(Koelreuteria paniculata)*. True to its name, the golden rain tree pro-

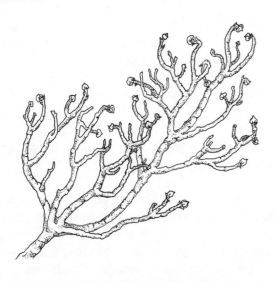

Leaf-drop in deciduous plants marks the end of the season of active growth and the onset of dormancy. On this dogwood, buds for the next season's growth have formed.

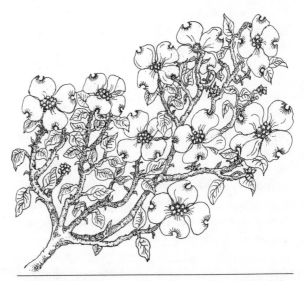

Shown above is the same branch in early spring of the following year, in full flower with leaves just beginning to show.

Because trees and shrubs—
together with man-made objects
—establish the basic form of a
garden, plants should be set out
with an eye to their ultimate
size and shape. On the left is a
Magnolia virginiana and on the
right a flowering dogwood, both
of moderate size. The spring
bulbs act as accents of color and
fragrance.

duces a prolific show of pendant yellow flower clusters. It offers the advantages of blooming in midsummer, which is a welcome time for a flowering tree. It is not, however, a distinguished tree in any other regard; before and after flowering it recedes into the background. It will grow in almost any soil, and if it gets adequate water during the summer months it will grow to a height of 20 to 30 feet in a few years. If pruned to shape when young, it will develop a compact form less susceptible to wind damage than the long-branched natural shape. Zone 6.

Hawthorn, Washington (*Crataegus phaenopyrum*). For a small tree, this one is a prodigious performer. It has rose-colored blossoms in spring and a canopy of rich green leaves in summer, and in winter the dense network of twiggy branches etches a handsome pattern on the background of sky or snow. A further bonus, if not devoured by the birds, is the display of small red fruit that appears in the fall. The thorns are sharp, so plant it well away from foot traffic. It grows 10 to 12 feet tall. Zone 4.

Magnolia, saucer (*Magnolia soulangeana*). This is one of the showiest of all the magnolias. It is literally a mass of color in early spring when the large creamy-white flowers, suffused with purple, unfold in the bare branches before the leaves begin to appear. When the deep-green foliage does come out, it clothes the tree fully and makes it a favorite place for a variety of birds. Even in winter it's attractive, with its grayish bark, and furry flower buds accentuating the tips of the branches. It grows to about 20 feet tall and 20 feet wide and does well in both dry and damp soil. Zone 5.

Magnolia, sweet bay *(Magnolia virginiana).* Grown especially for its extremely fragrant white flowers that bloom in early summer. While exceeding 40 feet in height in the South, it grows more like a shrub in the North. In either case its structure is usually narrow. Zone 6.

Scholar tree *(Sophora japonica).* Outstanding for its wide-branching limb structure and profusion of yellow pealike flowers in mid- to late summer, at a time when few other trees are in bloom. Height and width are about 35 feet. Zone 4.

Shadbush or **serviceberry** *(Amelanchier canadensis).* An airy display of white flowers lights up the slender branches of this elegant tree in early spring. While it can grow to 45 feet tall, it usually attains about 20 feet and is most often seen at the edge of a woodland. A native of the Northeast, it will do well in any area where the winter temperature drops below freezing. Small red applelike fruits develop in the fall and persist until other bird food gets scarce in early to mid-winter. Shadbush is adaptable to a variety of soil conditions and has no serious insect or disease problems. Zone 4.

TREES

One or two magnificent trees can dominate an entire garden. On any site where there are existing trees, it pays to save as many as can be attractively accommodated. They can create an environment of dappled shade where other woodland plants will thrive. But if trees are crowding one another, or if shade is too dark, don't hesitate to cut down the offenders.

Silk tree *(Albizzia julibrissin)*. The early-summer display of pink flowers the size and shape of powder puffs makes this a distinctive flowering tree. The horizontal branching pattern and flat apple-green leaflets add to its appeal. It does not blend well with other trees and is best used standing alone on a lawn. With its low spreading shape it looks particularly at home planted near a house of contemporary design. It grows to a height of about 20 feet and a spread of 30 feet. Zone 6.

Silverbell *(Halesia monticola)*. The pendant white flowers on this small tree add a bright note to any spring garden. The flowers are evenly spaced on the branch and can be seen individually. They stay in bloom long enough to make it worthwhile to put this plant front and center. Because it responds so well to deep rich soil, it also pays to create this condition if necessary by adding peat moss, leaf mold, or compost in the planting hole. Dig the hole at least 3 feet wide and 3 feet deep and mix the humus in well. Silverbell flowers best in full sun and grows to about 15 feet high. Zone 5.

Sorrel tree *(Oxydendrum arboreum)*. This native American, outstanding for its deep-red fall color, also has pendant white flower clusters in midsummer when few other trees are in bloom. For years the sorrel tree's garden use has been rather limited, but as the existing specimens gain size and visibility, its excellent qualities have become more evident and its popularity has increased. It has few pests, and although it can grow to 50 feet tall, it often stays in the 30-foot range for years. When grown in a garden with space around it, it develops a broader head than in the wild. Zone 5.

Stewartia *(Stewartia pseudo-camellia)*. The branch structure alone would justify planting this small tree. But add the interest of the bark, which peels away from the trunk, and you have a superb subject for the winter landscape. The bright-green leaves are a welcome attraction in spring. Then, after amply proving its worth, it produces a bonus: hundreds of single 3-inch camellia-like white flowers with orange stamens. It will eventually grow to 40 feet tall but seems to stay for years at 10 to 15 feet. It is tolerant of some shade and requires no more than 10 feet of ground space, making it useful in gardens of modest size. Zone 5.

Fruit Trees

While it is not practical for home gardeners to produce fruit as commercial growers do, with their complex pruning and spraying schedules, it can be worthwhile to plant a few fruit trees if there is space available. Even if the trees produce marginally, the fruit is welcome. Fruit trees also qualify as flowering trees, although their period of bloom is generally shorter than that of the trees listed above.

Dwarf trees are the best choice. These are standard trees grafted onto a dwarfing rootstock that serves to reduce their size to one-half or one-third the normal size. Their fruit is the standard size and the crop is proportional to tree size. The following choices for varieties to try are based on the flavor of the fruit, adaptability to various climates, ease of culture, and availability. These trees are all self-fertile; they do not require another tree for pollination. *Peaches*: Burbank; July Elberta. Zones 5 to 8.

Apples: Red Delicious. Zones 5 to 8.

Pear: Duchess. Zones 5 to 7.

Tart pie cherry: North Star. Zones 4 to 8.

Other Deciduous Trees

Birch, white *(Betula pendula).* There are several species of birch, with either white, off-white, or exfoliating (peeling) bark. This white birch, with its drooping branches, is a favorite tree for almost any setting. The distinctive coloration does not begin to develop until the trunk is about 2 inches in diameter.

Although they make handsome single specimens, they are often planted in clumps of three or five for a more dramatic effect. They tolerate some shade and can take moisture in the root area.

Leaf miner is a problem and to hold it in check, the trees should be sprayed with Sevin carbaryl or diazinon when the leaves first come out and again when they are almost fully developed.

White birch seldom grows more than 25 feet tall, with a trunk 6 to 8 inches in diameter. Hardy through Zone 3.

Gum, sweet *(Liquidambar styraciflua).* This American native, along with the oak and maple, helps to produce the colorful fall foliage that people from all over the world come here to see.

It's a stately tree, 50 to 100 feet tall, of pyramidal form and with star-shaped leaves. In the fall, the leaves range in color from pale yellow to deep mahogany and maroon. It also bears burr-like seed pods that make handsome ornaments when used in Christmas wreaths.

The tree has a long taproot and is difficult to transplant. It is best to buy container-grown specimens. Sweet gum grows well in dappled shade and will also do well if planted close to a pond or stream. Hardy through Zone 6.

Maple, cut-leaf Japanese *(Acer palmatum dissectum).* This elegant small tree can be counted upon to develop an interesting branching pattern that is clearly revealed in winter. When densely covered with foliage, it has a unique asymmetrical form. It grows 5 to 8 feet tall and is wider than it is tall. The individual leaves are also of interesting design and display lovely changing colors, from the cool greens of spring to warm autumn tints. The tree will tolerate both damp and dry situations and thrives in partial shade or full sun. Zone 5.

Maple, sugar *(Acer saccharum).* This is one of the most striking of all trees for autumn color, with foliage of vibrant yellow to orange-red. Keep in mind, however, that lawn grass does not do well under this tree because of its dense shade and shallow root system. It grows to about 40 feet with a spread of 30 feet or more. Zone 3.

Oak, pin *(Quercus palustris).* A handsome tree of rather formal mien with a symmetrical pyramidal shape and branches angled slightly downward. The leaves turn leather-brown in fall, and some hang on all through the winter. It tolerates wet soil conditions. It grows to about 25 feet and 15 feet wide. Zone 4.

Willow, weeping *(Salix babylonica).* With its slender, pendulous branches, this willow can be confused with no other tree. Its distinctive weeping form has long been a favorite with artists both in the Orient, where it originated, and here, where it was brought by early settlers.

TREES

Willows are among the first trees to leaf out in the spring and among the last to lose their leaves in the fall. They do best when the roots are constantly moist, and in this condition will reach a height of 20 feet in 2 or 3 years, and 50 feet in 15 years or so.

Willow branch tips often touch the ground, creating shade so dense that nothing will grow under the tree. Willows are brittle and tend to split in wind storms, so it is best to train a tree to one strong trunk. Hardy through Zone 4.

Evergreen Trees

Acacia *(Acacia decurrens)*. This lovely tree and its many ornamental cousins are treasured for their clear yellow flowers that bloom as tiny puffy balls against a background of delicate silver-gray leaflets. Some species grow to a 50-foot ornamental tree. It grows fast and will flower beautifully just a few years after planting. This tree does, however, have one shortcoming: the clouds of yellow pollen in the spring will stick to the windows of cars and houses. It is best to plant it where this will be a minimal problem. Zone 9.

Cedar, blue Atlas *(Cedrus atlantica glauca)*. Notable for its majestic spread of frosty-blue needled branches, this is an excellent large tree for accent in an open setting. It will grow to a height of 75 feet or more and should be allotted at least 50 feet of space to set it off well. If planted in a hole considerably larger than the root ball and filled with a mixture of ⅔ soil and ⅓ peat moss, it will grow quickly—so quickly that it will require staking for the first few years. Like the white pine, this tree takes on an entirely different and more interesting character as it passes from the juvenile stage into maturity. Zone 6.

Hemlock, Canada *(Tsuga canadensis)*. A remarkably adaptable conifer that will grow to a stately 100 feet in height or can be kept sheared so that a row of them will make a compact 5-to-6-foot hedge of lush evergreen foliage. It tolerates some shade,

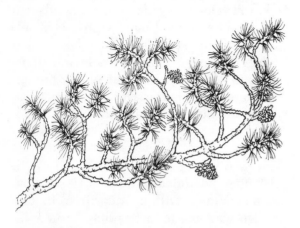

Although evergreen plants retain some of their leaves all through the year, they do drop leaves from time to time and some renew their foliage entirely.

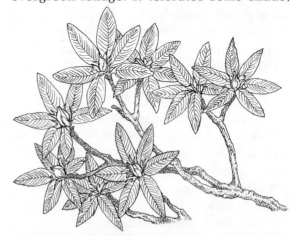

Some evergreens, like the familiar pine (at left), have needle-shaped leaves, while others, like the rhododendron (above), have broad leaves.

but the growth will not be so dense as when grown in full sun. Zone 3.

Hemlock, Carolina *(Tsuga caroliniana)*. This is the best species for Southern gardens, although it will tolerate the winters as far north as Colorado, Indiana, and New York. It grows to about 40 feet tall. Unlike the Canada hemlock, which will tolerate a slightly alkaline soil, it requires acid soil to succeed. Zone 7.

Hemlock, weeping *(Tsuga canadensis pendula)*. A horticultural "sport," this deviation from the normal upright hemlock was discovered in the Hudson Valley of New York State in the 1860s. It has been a favorite ever since for its graceful low mounding habit of growth. It is equally at home in full light or moderate shade, and in rather dry areas or low wet situations. It grows so slowly, however, that it seldom exceeds 4 feet in height and 10 feet across in its first 25 years. Zone 3.

Holly, American *(Ilex opaca)*. This native broadleaf evergreen with its bright-red berries clustered among the prickly green leaves creates a cheery picture, particularly in cold climates where there's a background of snow. Berries are borne on female trees, and only if there is a male tree nearby. This tree when mature reaches a height of 40 feet, but with judicious pruning it can be kept to an attractive 6 to 8 feet. An annual trimming will provide colorful holiday decoration and will also encourage compact growth. Although hollies are called evergreens, they do lose their leaves in late spring. New leaves appear very quickly, however. In recent years the leaf miner, a pest that makes unsightly tunnels between the layers of a leaf, has become more prevalent, and it does threaten holly trees. The miners can be kept under control. If you spray with an insecticide such as Sevin when the new leaves are about ½ inch long, and again two weeks later, the foliage will be as beautiful as it should be. Zone 5.

Holly, English *(Ilex aquifolium)*. This species is not as hardy as the American species but is preferred wherever it will grow because its leaves are glossy green, in contrast to the flat surface of the American holly. There are also varieties with variegated foliage. All of the hollies require acid soil, and a nearby male tree so the female can bear fruit. Zone 6.

Magnolia, southern *(Magnolia grandiflora)*. This stately tree, the very symbol of the South, has glossy green leaves, brown on the underside. The flowers, which bloom in midsummer, are creamy white.

It is an enormous tree, growing to a height and spread of 50 feet or more where the soil is deep and the temperature mild. Near the limit of its northern range, where winter temperatures drop to about 15° F., it makes an attractive small tree to 25 feet or so, although the leaves may occasionally drop in the fall. Zone 8.

Pine, Swiss stone *(Pinus cembra)*. A fast-growing species with clusters of long light-green needles. This tree will do best if the tips of the new growth are cut back while they can still be easily reached to promote more branching and to establish an attractive compact form. It will develop to its fullest in a sunny location. When mature it will fill a space 30 feet in diameter or more, and may grow to 100 feet. Zone 3.

7
Selecting Shrubs
for Your Garden

While trees, with their dramatic impact, help to establish a sense of scale in the landscape, it is the shrubs that most naturally create the essential framework. Shrubs are permanent plantings, and in their variety, they serve a remarkably wide range of uses. They vary in height from the prostrate juniper to the 20-foot tree lilac, but the most useful small ones are from 3 to 5 feet tall and the large ones up to about 10. Within this range of sizes is every imaginable shape, texture of foliage, color of flower, fragrance, size and color of berry, and, of course, your choice of deciduous or evergreen forms.

No matter what the conditions of soil or climate may be in your garden, there are attractive shrubs that will thrive there. In general, it is best to choose species that are suited to the conditions in your garden rather than to wage an uphill fight to grow those that are better adapted to other soils and climates. But even if a favored exotic shrub should wane, it is not too difficult to transplant it to a more favorable location.

The list that follows is highly selective and includes only those that are the most dependable and rewarding to grow in residential landscapes and gardens.

Deciduous Shrubs

Bayberry (*Myrica pensylvanica*). This native northeastern shrub has long been grown for its attractive, compact foliage and the small gray berries which literally clothe the stems in late summer. In colonial days the berries, which have a high wax content, were used for making candles. The leaves were used to lend their pungent scent to the product. The plant will thrive in light shade but develops a bushier habit in full sun. Although it will grow to 6 or 7 feet in a few years, it takes well to pruning and can easily be kept to a smaller size if required. Bayberry does best in acid soil but will also grow where the pH of the soil is neutral. Zone 2.

Beautybush (*Kolkwitzia amabilis*). The many small pink flowers on this vigorous plant make a good show in late spring. The arching branches develop into a shrub about 7 feet tall and almost as wide, and it is best used where there is plenty of space. Although it can be pruned to reduce the size, it's at its beautiful best when allowed to grow freely. Zone 6.

Butterfly bush *(Buddleia davidii)*. Few plants live up to their common names so dependably as this one. When its arching spires of purple flowers are in full bloom in late summer they are almost always surrounded by a fluttering display of butterflies, attracted by the scent of the nectar.

Named varieties with lavender, red, pink, or white flowers are now available. A full-grown shrub reaches about 6 feet tall and 7 feet across. In its northernmost range its branches are subject to winterkill. But if the plant is cut to within inches of the ground new growth will invariably surge forth in the spring. Zone 5.

B. alternifolia is a more vigorous plant, often reaching 10 feet in height. It flowers in late spring with fragrant purple spires. It grows in all but the coldest areas of Zone 5.

Ceanothus *(Ceanothus delilianus)*. Shrubs with blue flowers that have no trace of red are rather rare, and ceanothus is one of the best in this category. Although it is grown most successfully in the moderate climate along the Pacific coast, it is worth trying in mild humid climates elsewhere. The species blooms in late spring, but the many nursery-grown hybrids offer a wider range of blooming times. The most desirable of these deciduous hybrids grow to about 4 feet tall. Give it a sheltered place with good air circulation and drainage in the root area. Zone 7.

Cotoneaster, rock *(Cotoneaster horizontalis)*. One plant of this prostrate shrub will reach out to cover an area about 4 feet square, which makes it a most useful rough-textured ground cover. Its network of slender horizontal stems in an attractive chevron pattern are covered with small pink flowers in the spring. By midsummer the green berries have inconspicuously increased in size. As the cool fall season approaches the berries turn red and make an outstanding show against the deep-green leaves. The leaves then turn red before they fall—in Zones 5 and 6. In Zone 7 the plant is an evergreen.

Daphne *(Daphne mezereum)*. The heady color of the rose-purple flowers in early spring makes this a useful shrub. Plant it near the busiest doorway, where the fragrance can be enjoyed most frequently. Each of the flowers, which are borne on upright stems, becomes a red berry in the fall, and this makes this 2-to-3-foot ornamental even more worthy of consideration. It should be grown in well-drained soil of neutral pH. Zone 5.

Enkianthus, redvein *(Enkianthus campanulatus)*. Enkianthus is one of those shrubs that adapt well to pruning and can be used in a variety of garden situations. It will reach more than 15 feet in height if let alone, but can be kept as low as 4 or 5 feet and still maintain its essential character. In midspring it brings forth clusters of yellow red-veined flowers before the long, narrow, deep-green leaves appear. As fall approaches the foliage begins to turn, and it changes color almost daily, ranging from orange to deep scarlet. For the best growth, flowering, and leaf color, plant it in well-drained, slightly acid soil and water frequently. Zone 5.

SHRUBS

Firethorn *(Pyracantha coccinea lalandi).* From coast to coast this is one of the most popular of all shrubs. Most of the plants are grown in California, but they are shipped to nurseries as far afield as Massachusetts, Michigan, and Louisiana. Firethorn is usually grown against a wall or fence and can easily be trained to fit the available space. It can be kept to 4 feet in height, or will grow to more than 20. In warm climates (to Zone 7) it is evergreen. In the North, where it is deciduous, it starts the growing season with small green leaves. By late spring small white flowers run the length of every stem. As the blossoms develop into berries, the shrub becomes the blaze of color that suggested the common name. There are many named varieties selected for berry size and color—from yellow and orange through to bright red. If the birds don't get the berries before the holidays, the branches are excellent for decoration in the house, and the pruning simply encourages more growth. But handle with care; the thorns are very sharp. Zone 6.

Forsythia *(Forsythia intermedia).* The masses of yellow flowers covering the long arching stems of this familiar shrub are a welcome harbinger of spring. Each plant will grow to 6 to 8 feet in height and about the same in width. Also welcome are its resistance to pests and disease and its ability to thrive in rather poor soil. It must, however, have 4 to 5 hours of sunlight a day.

In order to grow a well-shaped shrub with the maximum display of flowers, cut at least a third of the older canes to within 6 inches of the ground after it flowers in the spring. Forsythia blooms on branches that have grown during the previous summer. Or, if you prefer, cut the branches when the buds have begun to swell and bring them in the house for a glorious show of early-season color.

Selected varieties such as 'Spectabilis', 'Lynwood Gold', and 'Beatrix Farrand' will provide more and larger flowers than the species. Zone 5.

Fothergilla *(Fothergilla monticola).* Any plant with a compact spreading habit, attractive fall color, and bright white spring flowers, plus an ability to thrive in partial shade, deserves a place on the list of most-desirable shrubs. The flowers resemble bottlebrushes held upright among the sturdy dark-green leaves. It grows 3 to 5 feet high and is attractive when planted with evergreens, which accentuate the pure white blooms. It is not particularly demanding, although it does best in soil with plenty of humus. *F. major* is a larger, more pyramidal shrub. Zone 6.

Hydrangea, oak leaf *(Hydrangea quercifolia).* Superlatives must be bestowed grudgingly lest overuse diminish their effect, but this must be considered one of the great shrubs. It grows about 5 feet tall and to 6 or 8 feet across, at a rate of about a foot a year. Its handsome leathery leaves, shaped like those of the oak tree, are dark-green during the summer and turn rosy-red and yellow in the fall. The large clusters of white flowers, held well above the foliage on stiff stems, are ideal for cutting for indoor display. Even after they dry, the flowers make effective arrangements. Hydrangea does best in full sun but will tolerate some shade. Zone 5.

Kerria *(Kerria japonica).* Bright-yellow flowers seem to be especially welcome in early spring, and the kerria with its myriad single 2-inch blossoms provides them in abundance. The thin apple-green branches and deeply toothed leaves create an overall impression of delicacy, although kerria grows to 6 feet tall or more. A location in full sun is best. The double-flowered *K. j. pleniflora* is more often seen, although the more attractive single-flowered *K. japonica* is worth seeking out. Zone 6.

Pussy willow *(Salix discolor)*. Given a sunny location and soil that is moist to moderately moist, this native of the northeastern U.S. will begin to perform within a year after propagation from a stem cutting. While it can become a small tree, it more often grows as a shrub and can easily be made to do so by cutting back the top growth for the first few years. The furry catkins that push out of the shiny buds in early spring are the major attraction. They can be dazzling when seen against the early-morning or late-afternoon sun. Don't hesitate to cut the interesting branches for display indoors. For the rest of the growing season, the up-right branches create a rather dense shrub useful for screening, until the leaves drop in the fall. Zone 3.

Strawberry bush *(Calycanthus floridus)*. This is an intriguing plant with flowers that are up to 2 inches across but are rather inconspicuous because of their dull reddish-brown color. Their fragrance, however, is another matter. The perfume lingers in the area for several weeks in midsummer while it is in flower. It grows rather quickly to a height of 4 feet or so and then, more slowly, to about 6 feet. It does best in partial to full sun in good soil, and needs considerable water in the summer months. Zone 6.

Sweet pepperbush *(Clethra alnifolia)*. It is always a pleasure to find native plants that are as rewarding to grow as the exotics. A good example is the sweet pepperbush. Its deciduous foliage is deep-green, turning a rich yellow-orange in the fall. But it is the 6-inch white flowers shaped like a bottle-brush that crown the season's growth. The flowers also have a lovely fragrance when in bloom in the early summer. This can be best enjoyed if the shrub is planted near a

The unusual finely textured white flowers of *Fothergilla major* appear in early spring. A deciduous shrub, it carries handsomely veined leaves which turn to attractive shades of red and yellow before they drop in autumn.

sitting area in the garden. While growth can reach 6 feet or more, it is easy to maintain at any size you prefer by pruning in the fall. *Clethra* will tolerate light shade or will grow vigorously in full sun if moderate moisture is maintained in the root area. Zone 5.

Tree peony *(Paeonia suffruticosa)*. The imposing flowers, up to 10 inches across, come in pink, yellow, red, or white. When they open their delicate petals in spring, this plant is sure to become a center of interest in any garden. The shrublike struc-

The impact that a bed of showy shrubs can have on a landscape is demonstrated here by these tree peonies. Even their foliage is of sufficient substance to stand out in the design of a garden.

ture has woody stems up to 5 feet high and when in leaf the plant is almost as wide. The leaves are handsome on their own.

Peonies need rich soil. When planting, set them so the buds at their base are covered with soil. For the first year or two, until the plant is established, add mulch in the fall. Peonies need a cold season and do not do well in the Deep South or Southwest. Zone 5.

Winterberry *(Ilex verticillata)*. This is a most vigorous native of the northeastern states that produces sturdy branches clothed with dark-green leaves throughout the summer and berries in early fall. When the leaves drop, following a killing frost, there stands a glorious shrub with every branch displaying bright-crimson berries, which will remain until the birds get to them in late winter. A well-positioned winterberry with ample water, full sun, and slightly acid soil will grow to about 10 feet in as many years. Pruning in winter to keep the plant compact will render decorative branches for indoor display. Zone 6.

Witch hazel *(Hamamelis mollis)*. This is a large shrub with golden-yellow flowers that open in midwinter regardless of ice, snow, or severe cold. In the warmth of the afternoon sun, its sweet fragrance is a welcome bonus. Plants 12 feet high are not unusual, but hard pruning will keep them a bit lower. Good-sized branches are attractive to bring indoors for decoration.

The variety 'Pallida' is probably the most desirable. The species *H. vernalis* blooms later, and its fragrant spiderlike flowers are an interesting copper color.

In addition to the cheerful appearance of their off-season flowers and their pleasing fragrance, the witch hazels also have a handsome angular branching pattern and foliage that adds attractive shades of yellow-orange to the autumn landscape. They all do well in slightly acid soil in damp areas in full sun or partial shade. Zone 5.

Evergreen Shrubs

Ceanothus (*Ceanothus thyrsiflorus* hybrids). This species grows to 8 feet or more. Each handsome cluster of tiny blue flowers is small in itself but they literally cover the shrub. Plant ceanothus where it will be somewhat sheltered from severe weather, but not where the air may be stagnant. Good drainage in the root area is also required. Zone 7.

Heather *(Calluna vulgaris)*. The spreading form of this low-growing shrub makes it ideal as a ground cover in sunny locations. Heather will not tolerate poorly drained soil and is therefore best on sandy or gravelly slopes. While the rose-pink flower spikes are typical of the species, there are varieties with purple, red, pink, or white blooms. The plants will grow to 2 feet in height, but take well to shearing, which should be done right after they flower. This not only reduces their height but also makes them more compact and encourages their naturally spreading habit of growth. Zone 6.

Holly *(Ilex latifolia)*. This is one of the many hollies grown as shrubs that will become a good-sized tree if the top branches are not cut back from time to time. The 6-to-8-inch shiny oblong leaves have small spines along their edges. The female trees bear clusters of red berries, but only if there is a male tree nearby. The plant tolerates light

Unlike the more familiar members of the holly genus, *Ilex*, this species, *I. latifolia*, has large oval leaves. The foliage is evergreen and forms a compact pyramidal shrub that can grow to tree size.

shade and is particularly well suited to warmer climates where hollies do not usually grow. Zone 8.

Mahonia *(Mahonia bealii)*. Mahonia bealii has 2-inch-thick upright branches that reach a height of 6 to 8 feet. It is less hardy than the Oregon grape holly, *M. aquifolium* (see p. 48), but with its larger leaves and flowers is a more dramatic plant. The flowers of both species are important in late winter, before most plants have begun to perform. Zone 7.

SHRUBS

Mountain laurel *(Kalmia latifolia)*. This is among the best-loved native American shrubs to grow in acid soil. Its handsome evergreen foliage and lovely clusters of blush-pink flowers create a pleasing effect wherever used. It will attain heights of 8 feet or more but responds well to pruning if it outgrows its allotted space. If the soil contains a high percentage of organic material such as leaf mold or peat moss, which can be worked into the soil when planted, it will perform at its very best. Mountain laurel can be grown in light shade or full sun. In the latter setting, give it a mulch to keep the roots cool. This will also encourage more prolific bloom. Zone 5.

Oregon grape holly *(Mahonia aquifolium)*. Neither a grape nor a holly, this member of the barberry family is outstanding for the vigorous growth of its large spiny leaves crowned by a cluster of bright-yellow flowers in early spring, or in late winter where the weather is not too harsh. The flowers develop into blue grapelike fruit by early summer. The foliage presents a splash of yellow and orange in the fall, but almost all of the leaves are retained throughout the winter. Zone 6.

Pieris *(Pieris japonica)*. Sometimes called andromeda, this is one of the best year-round performers. In early spring the plant is literally covered with pendant clusters of flowers that look like lily of the valley. The evergreen foliage turns from light green to deep green, often with a bronzy cast. It soon grows 4 to 5 feet tall and about 4 feet wide. Eventually it can reach 10 feet or so and in the process develop an interesting sculptural form. In the colder climates of Zone 5, the native andromeda *(P. flori-*

bunda) is more dependable, and it is also more adaptable to shady sites. The flowers are held upright, which gives it a rather stiff appearance when in bloom, but the foliage is as attractive as that of *P. japonica*. A prime requisite for both species is acid soil containing a high percentage of organic matter. *P. japonica*, Zone 6.

Viburnum, leatherleaf *(V. rhytidiophyllum)*. This strong-growing shrub has narrow 7-inch dark-green leaves that are light-gray on the undersides. The very heavy veining of the leaves gives them a leatherlike texture and accounts for the common name. Zone 6.

Other viburnum species include *V. dentatum* and *V. wrightii*, which produce at-

Pieris japonica is a broad-leafed evergreen whose leaves have a rosy glow in spring. The pendant clusters of small flowers last well through the growing season, and mature plants display beautifully striated bark.

tractive red berries in addition to the white flowers, 7 to 8 feet tall, and tend to be rather upright in form. *V. dentatum*, Zone 2; *V. wrightii*, Zone 5.

V. burkwoodi and *V. carlesi* are also large handsome shrubs with fragrant white flowers that appear in midspring. Zone 5.

A Substitute for Shrubs: Ornamental Grasses

Garden books are written by enthusiasts and therefore tend to be subjective. A few of the authors' personal opinions and preferences are sure to surface. This book is no exception, and one definite preference is for ornamental grasses.

We think that any garden can be made more attractive and interesting with the addition of one or more of these appealing plants in the right place.

They require full sun and soil with considerable organic material and good drainage. Moderate application of a balanced fertilizer in the spring is beneficial, but not essential annually. Even with minimal care these grasses will thrive for years. At the northern extent of their range, these grasses will die down in the fall and come up again in the spring.

The four grasses listed here are among the most outstanding.

Pennisetum alopecuroides is not easy to pronounce, but is worth asking for. The delicate furry flower heads on 18-inch stems stand just above the upright cluster of slender leaves to produce a striking silhouette. It is particularly effective, as are all the grasses, when placed where the afternoon sun will shine through it. Hardy through Zone 6.

Miscanthus sinensis gracillimus be-

comes an arching fountain of foliage topped by full creamy plumes rising just above it in the fall. It grows to about 5 feet tall. Hardy through Zone 6.

Miscanthus sinensis giganteus is an excellent choice where a strong dramatic accent is called for. The long swordlike leaves grow to 12 feet high by midsummer, and in the fall, when it blooms, the plumes reach as high as 15 feet. Hardy through Zone 6.

Arundo donax has segmented stems similar in structure to bamboo. But when the plant is clothed with leaves it looks like a cornstalk. At 15 feet, however, it is considerably taller than corn. Hardy through Zone 7.

Ornamental grasses, with linear stems and plumed flowers, are among the most dramatic of plants. This one, *Pennisetum alopecuroides*, is wider than it is tall and useful for garden spots requiring a low plant with elegant flowers.

❧ |8| ❧
Making and Maintaining a Lawn

Tending a lawn in suburbia and other residential areas seems as inevitable as making the mortgage payments. Lawns are everywhere—and for good reason. Dollar for dollar, a lawn is the least expensive way to create a useful, attractive, year-round surface on the land surrounding a house.

But for all its advantages—as a surface for children's play, as a lovely setting for shrubs and flowers, and as a setting for the house itself—there are some places where it is not worthwhile to try to grow a lawn.

Grass does not do well in deep shade, under trees with shallow roots, in very sandy soil, in wet soggy soil, in very acid soil, in very alkaline soil, on steep slopes where water runs off before it penetrates, or anywhere else that frequent watering is impractical.

There are grasses for warm climates and for cool climates. In the transition zone between the two, some grasses from both warm and cool climates will grow. As to what will do best in your front yard, the more local the advice the better. Outstanding lawns in the neighborhood are living examples of which grasses do well in your

immediate area. Any reputable seed dealer will also tell you which varieties are best adapted to the local climate and conditions. Descriptions of some of the most widely used grasses are included later in this chapter.

A new lawn can be started from seed, or vegetatively from sprigs or stolons, which are rooted pieces of the grass. The soil preparation is essentially the same for all methods. A lawn can also be made in a matter of hours by putting down a layer of sod on the prepared ground. The surface treatment for laying sod is somewhat less critical than that required for seeding. Sod can also be installed on slopes that make seeding difficult because of surface runoff when it rains.

Seeding a Lawn

The illustrations show the basic steps, but there are a few other things to know.

In cool climates, the best time to start a lawn is in fall or spring. In warm climates it can be done in winter as well.

When you are building a new lawn,

grading is usually required to establish the proper surface drainage. The surface should be level enough to avoid low spots that will hold water and make the ground soggy. The grade should be sloped enough so water will drain away from the house gradually.

Before the grading is started, make sure that the topsoil is pushed to one side so that it can be redistributed evenly after the contours have been established. A contractor may balk at such refinements, but if you are left with only subsoil on the surface it will be impossible to grow a good lawn. Should this be the case (as it often is in new housing developments) it will pay to cover the area with a layer of topsoil or such things as spent mushroom soil, well-rotted sawdust, cocoa shells, buckwheat hulls, bagasse, peat moss, or compost, depending on availability. Four to 6 inches of topsoil or its equivalent is required for a good seedbed.

If you can afford the time and can live with the unsightliness, it is best to let the graded ground sit long enough for a couple of quick crops of weeds to appear, then turn them under before they go to seed. The more weed seed that you allow to dissipate itself before you put in the grass seed, the easier lawn maintenance will be.

Feeding, Before and After

If fertilizer is added to the soil before seeding, as is recommended, further feeding will not be required for six weeks or so after the grass is up.

Cool-season grasses grow the most in spring and fall and should be fed early in those growing seasons. They are semi-dormant in the heat of summer, and fertilization during this time is largely wasted.

The warm-season grasses, such as Bermuda, zoysia, and St. Augustine, grow

After grading the area to be planted with grass, till it to a depth of 4 to 6 inches. The easiest method is to use a rotary tiller, which can be rented, but if you are equal to the task it can be done with a spade.

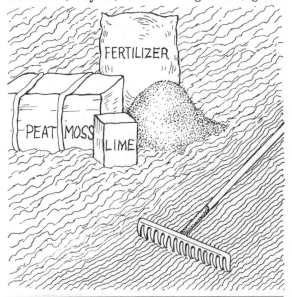

After tilling, spread and then rake in the materials that are required to improve the texture, fertility, and pH of the soil. Raking will also serve to break up clods and remove sticks, stones, and other debris.

the most during the summer months, which is when they should be fed.

The best lawn fertilizers are high in nitrogen, the element that does the most to promote leafy growth. A 10-6-4 formulation is standard. All three of the basic elements—nitrogen, phosphorus, and potassium—are needed. The annual requirement for cool-season grasses is at least 3 pounds of actual nitrogen per 1,000 square feet of lawn, which is to say an area 20 by 50 feet.

The Proper pH

Lawn grasses are significantly affected by the acid-alkaline balance of the soil in which they grow. A neutral soil, of course, has a factor of 7 on the pH scale. Soils with a lower number are acid, those with higher numbers alkaline.

The quickest way to determine the pH is with a soil kit, available from catalogs or in garden-supply stores. You can also take a soil sample and send it to your county cooperative extension agent and get a complete analysis of the soil, including the pH factor. The "county agents," as they are often called, can be most helpful in solving many garden problems. These knowledgeable horticultural specialists have their headquarters in the county seat.

Look in the phone book, or ask the operator for the cooperative extension agent or county agricultural agent. They have different titles in different counties.

Lawn grasses do best in soil with a pH of 6.5 (slightly acid) to 7.5 (slightly alkaline), and often a neutral soil is ideal.

Lime added to reduce the acidity of soil tends to leach out with continued watering. An annual check of the pH will probably

For uniform distribution of seed, use a mechanical spreader instead of spreading it by hand. The machine can be adjusted for the rate of distribution that is recommended on the package of the seed you are using.

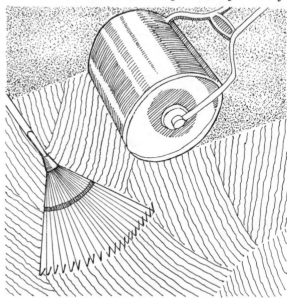

Use the back of a bamboo rake to cover the seed lightly with soil, then roll the area with a lightweight roller to press the soil and seed firmly together. Good contact is necessary for the seed to germinate.

reveal the need for a new application every three or four years.

Watering an Established Lawn

The general rule, as for most plants, is to water thoroughly and not too often. It is not necessary to water a lawn until it begins to show the first signs of dryness. The best indication of this is when footprints obviously persist after someone walks across the lawn. When the water in the blades of grass has diminished, they do not spring right up when they have been stepped on. But when the blades are turgid (filled with moisture), they soon stand upright and footprints will hardly show.

As soon as the grass begins to show signs of dryness, it should be watered thoroughly. This means until the soil is saturated to a depth of at least 6 inches. To determine how far down the water has penetrated, make a deep vertical slit with a trowel and feel the moisture with your finger. After a few such checks you can tell how long you will have to water in order to saturate the soil to the required 6 inches or so.

The easiest way to irrigate a lawn is with an underground watering system. There are kits available with plastic pipe and fittings that can be installed without the need for plumbing skills or special tools. Automatic timers can turn the system on and off on a preset schedule.

The magic of wetter water

Every so often there comes to light a new material or technique that simplifies the making or maintenance of a lawn.

One of the most useful of recent discoveries is the value of a wetting agent for

The newly planted seed must be kept constantly moist in order to sprout. Water gently to avoid washing the seed away, and cover the area lightly with straw to retain moisture.

A new lawn should be mowed when the grass is about 2 inches high. For subsequent mowings the grass should be kept at about 2 to 2½ inches high in hot weather and about 1 to 1½ inches high in the cool season.

lawn watering. A wetting agent reduces the surface tension of the molecules of water. This, in effect, makes the water wetter so it penetrates the ground more freely. The liquid is applied with a siphon device attached to the end of a hose.

Because the treated water penetrates quickly, there is little if any wasteful run-off. The water also tends to go more deeply into the root area. This quick, deep penetration also reduces the chances of waterlogging, a condition that contributes significantly to a variety of lawn diseases. There are various brand names, but the magic phrase is "wetting agent."

When and How to Mow

Ask anyone with an excellent lawn how frequently it is mowed and the answer might well be, "Just a little more often than I'd like." That's the way it is with grass—it has to be cut constantly during the growing season. The less top growth removed at any one time, the less shock to the plant's system.

There is, however, a compensating factor. If relatively little growth is removed at a time and the clippings do not completely cover the lawn, they can be left on the ground, which is easier than picking them up. As the clippings decompose they return a little nutrient to the soil. But if so much top growth is cut off that it blankets the lawn and is allowed to stay, it can smother and impair the growth of the grass and contribute to the development of disease.

The warm-climate grasses, such as zoysia and St. Augustine, should be kept at about 1 inch. Bermuda grass does best if kept below ¾ inch.

Cool-climate grasses, such as bluegrass

and the fescues, can be successfully grown at a height of 1½ to 2½ inches. The roots do better with more top growth, since the favored grasses can then shade out some of the weeds. Cut shorter in cool weather, and longer when it is warm.

Always use a sharp mower. A dull blade can fray the tips of the grass, causing them to turn brown.

What to Do About Weeds

The best advice, and the hardest to follow, is to grow a really healthy lawn. If the grass is rooted in good soil and is well fed and well watered it will create a dense sod in which weeds cannot easily get started.

But if weeds do invade the lawn, there are herbicides that will handle them if applied thoroughly according to directions at the proper time of year.

The best-known villain in the world of cool-climate lawns is crabgrass. This is an annual that grows from seeds produced the year before. The seeds continue to develop and produce new plants from late spring until early frost. The seeds need sun in order to germinate and consequently do not develop so freely if the grass is kept at a height of 1½ to 2 inches.

Crabgrass can be treated with herbicides before, during, or after its season of growth. The time of application is critical, especially for the pre-emergent controls such as Dacthal, which should be applied when apple trees are in blossom. Check with your local lawn-seed dealer, who will have the most effective controls for your area. Follow the instructions to the letter.

There are other chemical controls for specific broadleafed lawn weeds. It is best to use herbicides in granular form instead of sprays and apply them with a mechanical spreader. Sprays can drift on the wind and damage nearby trees and shrubs.

We recommend that a lawn be fertilized immediately after applying a weedkiller to help the good grass fill in where the weeds were.

Coping with Insects and Disease

The insects that are most likely to infect your lawn are the grubs of various beetles such as June beetles, chinch bugs, cutworms, and webworms.

Your local garden-supply store will doubtless recommend controls for these pests. In general, chlordane is effective against the grubs; Sevin, diazinon, and ethion can be used against chinch bugs; and diazinon is used for the control of cutworms and webworms. Japanese beetle grubs can be effectively controlled by treating the lawn with a liquid containing milky spore disease, which is fatal to this pest. This biological control is available from commercial laboratories such as the Fairfax Biological Control Laboratory, Clinton Corners, N.Y. 12514.

As for diseases, it's worth mentioning again that the best medicine is a good maintenance program. A lawn that is well fed, properly watered and mowed, and rooted in reasonably porous (well-drained) soil, with a pH near neutral, is the least likely to develop any diseases.

Among the most prevalent diseases are the following, all of which are caused by fungus and which in most cases can be controlled with the fungicides such as Benlate or Zineb.

Brown patch can be recognized by the irregular areas of brown with a darkened edge. The spots may vary in size from 1 inch to a few feet in diameter. It is sometimes caused by too heavy an application of nitrogen fertilizer.

Dollarspot can be recognized by the straw-colored spots the size of a silver dollar. As it spreads, however, it can become one large and very unsightly area. It tends to appear when nights are cool and the days humid.

Leafspot is evidenced by reddish-brown to purple spots, almost exclusively on Kentucky bluegrass. The Merion variety, however, is less susceptible. The specific fungicides must be applied about once a week for several weeks. Sometimes it can be stopped by letting the grass grow to about 2 inches high and also by feeding well with a fertilizer that does not contain too much nitrogen. A material with equal parts of nitrogen, phosphorus, and potassium (such as a 10-10-10) would be appropriate.

Snow mold turns lawns to a straw color. It can develop from late fall to early spring in northern climates where the moisture from melting snow sets up the ideal conditions for growth of the mold. The best prevention is good surface drainage, which will keep the wet conditions from prevailing for long. A fungicide can also be applied in winter to lawns that had the disease the previous year.

Slime molds are unattractive masses of viscous black, gray, or yellow material that may develop in wet weather. The best control is to sweep them away with a stiff broom. A fungicide may also be applied to prevent further damage. *Note:* Fungicides are poisonous to people as well as to fungus and should be kept locked up away from children. Use these materials only as a last resort, and then with extreme care

LAWNS

in strict accordance with directions on the package.

Selecting the Best Grass for Your Lawn

While your local lawn-seed dealers can tell you which varieties are most successful in your area, it is worthwhile to know a little about the general characteristics of the most popular kinds.

In cool climates north of Zone 7, the grasses most often used are Kentucky blue, fescue, perennial rye, and Colonial bent. In warmer climates, the most popular kinds are Bermuda, zoysia, centipedegrass, and St. Augustinegrass.

Choose the best possible grass for the situation. One consideration is the purpose of the lawn. For lawns that may get considerable wear and tear, or where an even surface and fine texture are not important, the so-called play or utility grasses will do. On the other hand, if your goal is to have the best-looking lawn you possibly can, there are other grasses, usually with a finer texture, that will make a better show.

Bermuda grass *(Cynodon dactylon)*. This is perhaps the most common of the warm-climate grasses. It spreads both by underground rootstalks and aboveground runners. It must have full sun, neutral to alkaline soil, and frequent feeding with a high-nitrogen fertilizer. It requires close clipping to develop a dense turf. There are many named varieties, and they are all established vegetatively by planting sprigs. Only the coarse-textured and quite tender common Bermuda is seeded. 'Tiflawn' is a popular variety, as are 'Everglades No. 1',

'Ormond', and 'Sunturf'. Those with the finest texture include 'Rifgreen', 'Tiffine', and 'Bayshore'. The hardiest Bermuda grasses are 'U-3' and 'Tufcote'.

Centipedegrass *(Eremochloa ephiruroides)*. This fast-growing grass with short creeping stems makes a good sturdy cover in areas where there is no danger of freezing. It requires relatively little mowing and gets by with less water and fertilizer than other grasses for Southern lawns. It is not recommended for coastal gardens where there might be salt spray. Although seed is sometimes available it is usually started vegetatively.

Colonial bentgrass *(Agrostis tenuis)*. This takes close mowing and is a favorite grass for putting greens. It makes a fine green carpet and does well in partial shade, but it requires frequent mowing, feeding, and watering. It is also susceptible to more diseases than the other cool-climate grasses. The best-known strains are 'Highland' (the hardiest of the bentgrasses), 'Astoria', and 'New Zealand Browntop'.

Kentucky bluegrass *(Poa pratensis)*. This is excellent for lawns because it spreads by underground rootstalks and forms a good firm sod. It is reasonably drought-resistant and does best in well-drained soil that is neutral to slightly alkaline. There are a number of selected varieties. 'Merion' is probably the best known. Other popular kinds are 'Baron', 'Fylking', 'Newport', 'Nugget', 'Park', 'Pennstar', and 'Windsor'.

Perennial rye *(Lolium perenne)* and **annual rye** *(L. multiflorum)*. Perennial rye alone, or combined with the annual, is often used

LAWNS

in lawn-seed mixtures to provide a grass that sprouts quickly and helps cover the ground and hold the soil in place until the other grasses develop. If much more than 5% of the rye is used, the texture of the lawn will be uneven. Among the most popular rye grasses are 'Norlea', 'Pelo', 'Pennfine', and 'Manhattan'.

Red fescue *(Festuca rubra).* This grass also spreads by underground rootstocks. It does better in slightly shady places than the bluegrasses, and also tolerates acid soil. Improved strains include 'Illahee', 'Pennlawn', and 'Rainier'.

St. Augustinegrass *(Stenotaphrum secundatum).* Another good grass for warm climates, St. Augustinegrass has the valuable characteristic of surviving in shady situations. It will also withstand saltwater spray. It does, however, require more moisture and more fertilizer than other warm-climate grasses, particularly in sandy soils. It is started only with sprigs or plugs.

Zoysia *(Zoysia japonica).* Sometimes called Japanese lawngrass, this species has runners and shallow rootstocks that make a turf so dense that few weeds can get started. The species has a rough texture, but the selected variety 'Meyer Zoysia' is not so coarse and is better for home lawns. Zoysia is resistant to wear even when clipped close. It stays green the year round in warm climates, but in cold climates it turns the color of straw with the first hard frost. It does not turn green again until warm weather in the spring. Zoysia is started from plugs or sprigs, which are inserted in the soil on 18-inch centers. It takes about two years for the zoysia to

cover the ground completely. There are no seeds available.

What to Do for an Ailing Lawn

Established lawns that have obviously lost their vigor will profit from a thorough treatment with an aerator and a follow-up with fertilizer and top dressing.

An aerator punches holes in the soil to a depth of 4 to 6 inches. This creates space for air, water, and plant food to enter the root area. In sandy soil you can use a spiker for this job. But in stiff clay soils the spikes can compact the sides and bottoms of the holes they make and defeat their purpose. On stiff soils, use a machine that removes a plug of soil. These machines, as well as spikers, can usually be rented.

When the holes are punched and the debris raked off the lawn, make a regular application of fertilizer, much of which will go into the holes. Then spread an even light covering of topsoil mixed thoroughly with peat moss, and water the lawn thoroughly. The top dressing will wash into the holes and the fertilizer will be leached down into the root area. If this is done, as it should be, in the growing season, a noticeable improvement should follow in a few weeks.

If a thick layer of thatch—an accumulation of clippings and dead leaves—is smothering the new growth on your lawn, it can be removed with a dethatching machine, which can be rented. This treatment is best done in early spring. You will probably be amazed at how much material comes to the surface. If, after raking, the lawn seems thin, add seed in the appropriate season. Use about a third the density recommended for new lawns, and give it the aftercare recommended for making a new lawn.

❧|9|❧
Getting the Most from Annuals

An annual is so called because it starts from seed, grows, produces a flower—which develops into a seed head—and dies down all in one year. In order to progress from seed to seed in this short time the plant must grow fast, and this is one characteristic that makes annuals so useful in the garden. In general, they bloom longer and produce more flowers than any other group of plants. These are the plants to use where you want quick, easy, dependable results with lowest possible cost.

Another valuable attribute is their amazing array of colors and sizes. If you have a favorite flower color, you are sure to find it among the annuals. In size, they range from miniature daisies with a ½-inch flower to sunflowers up to 20 inches across.

Annuals are native to various climates in all parts of the world, and thus there are varieties that will grow in almost any garden situation—from hot to cold, shady to sunny, and moist to dry.

In some seed catalogs you will find them listed as hardy annuals (HA), half-hardy annuals (HHA), or tender annuals (TA).

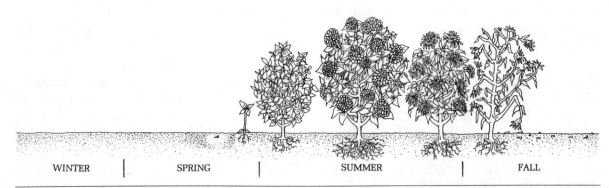

WINTER | SPRING | SUMMER | FALL

Annuals that are sown or set out as plants when the soil warms in the spring will be in full flower by midsummer. By summer's end the flower begins to fade and the seed starts to develop. In fall the plant dies down and seeds drop to the ground. The seeds will either die or come up again as plants when the soil warms in the following spring.

These terms relate to their performance in climates where there is freezing in winter.

This business of hardiness can be confusing because, obviously, *all* plants are hardy in their native situations or they could not perpetuate themselves. An annual such as a marigold is hardy in Florida but tender in Minnesota.

The tender annuals must be sown indoors in March or April and cannot be safely moved outdoors until after the usual date of last frost in your area. If you live in a frost-free climate you can plant them anytime in the spring. In the fall the tender annuals will be blackened by the first frost.

The half-hardy kinds must be started indoors but can be moved to their outdoor location when their roots are developed. This will be about three weeks earlier than the tender annuals. They can also survive a few degrees below freezing in the fall.

Those that are designated as hardy can be seeded outdoors in the fall or early spring. They will come up without protection when the soil begins to warm and will die back in the heat of summer.

Some of the half-hardy annuals and most of the hardy ones will reseed themselves year after year and come up without replanting. This can be a considerable convenience. However, if they are hybrids—crosses between two different species or varieties—they may not be identical to the parent plant. For consistent quality the hybrids must be planted anew every year.

This is as good a time as any to explain the designations "F1," "F2," etc., which you will come across when you are selecting hybrids. When two plants are selected and crossed, the resultant hybrid is called an F1 to indicate that the seed of this union is the first generation. All of the seed from this initial cross will produce plants that are quite similar to one another. If you want a plant from seed that has the most predictable characteristics—such as a particular color in a petunia, or specific flavor in a tomato—you know that if you use F1 seed, all the plants will have the characteristics for which the parents were selected and the seed produced.

The seed that is borne by the F1 hybrids is called F2, which indicates that it is of the second generation. Plants grown from this F2 seed will have some of the desired characteristics, but will not be as predictably uniform as those from F1 seed. Some plants from F2 seed may revert back to the less desirable characteristics of either of the parents used in the F1 cross.

The F1 seed is the most expensive because the only way to produce it is to make the original cross for each crop, but the price of seed is a very small part of the cost of having a garden. The best seed to buy is that which will most dependably produce the plants you want.

Because of their long period of bloom, annuals are ideal for color around a patio or terrace. The compact, low-growing kinds such as petunia, lobelia, or impatiens are good for planters and containers.

For color on a fence or trellis, try the climbers such as the scarlet runner bean, cup-and-saucer vine, or morning-glory.

The annuals in general are good for showy mass plantings. To accentuate the effect it's best to use no more than one kind in a bed—certainly no more than three.

The annuals include some of the best flowers for a cutting garden. Cosmos, zinnias, marigolds, and snapdragons are all old favorites because of their reliable growth and abundant flowers.

FLOWERS

A good-sized cutting garden also provides plants for insurance. If there is a need for quick color elsewhere in the garden, the entire plant can be dug up and transplanted to wherever you want it, even while in full bloom. First, however, water well, and do the transplanting on a cloudy day if possible. If you have some space that needs filling in between permanent plantings of shrubs, a sprinkling of hardy annual seed in the fall can solve the problem for the following season.

Some Recommended Annuals

Ageratum (*Ageratum* species). With its small neat clusters of blue powderpuff flowers on 10-inch stems, ageratum makes an excellent edging or bedding plant. In full sun it will bloom continuously all summer. Tender.

California poppy *(Eschscholtzia californica)*. The clear bright color of the large single flowers, in yellow, orange, pink, or white, makes California poppy a standout in any garden from late June until frost. It does best in full sun. Height ranges from 10 to 16 inches. Hardy.

Cosmos *(Cosmos bipinnatus)*. An excellent background plant that will reach 4 feet in height. It has a tracery of delicate leaves and a profusion of 4-inch daisylike flowers. The old-fashioned white, yellow, and orange varieties are even better than the so-called improved varieties. Flowering begins in mid-July and continues steadily until frost. Hardy.

Cup-and-saucer vine *(Cobaea scandens)*. Using vining plants such as this is often the

The yellow California poppy provides an unequaled show of shimmering color and blooms constantly for a period of several months.

only way to shield, cover, or accent an area above eye level. It grows quickly and produces a good show of 2-inch purplish-green bell-shaped flowers. In cold climates it is well worth the trouble of planting indoors during late March and putting it in the garden as soon as all danger of frost is past. Support it with a string or stick until the tendrils develop and it will soon cling as it climbs 8 to 10 feet without further help. Half-hardy.

Dahlborg daisy *(Thymophylla tenuiloba)*. This native American is one of the most useful of all the annual flowers. The 4-inch mound of feathery leaves are all but covered with 1-inch yellow daisies by early summer, and they continue blooming freely until frost. This attractive annual does best in full sun and can go for the entire summer without watering. Hardy.

Dahlia (*Dahlia* species). Although the dahlias are perennials, the dwarf varieties, with their long season of bright color, perform beautifully as annuals. The 'Coltness' and 'Unwin' hybrids are trouble-free compact plants that grow no taller than 2 feet and need no staking. They come in all colors but blue. They bloom from June until frost, or the end of summer. Although you will buy them as seed, they will produce tubers that can be lifted in the fall, stored in a cool dry place indoors (like the larger dahlias discussed in the next chapter), and planted in the garden the following spring. Tender.

Forget-me-not (*Anchusa officinalis*). There are not many good blue garden flowers; this one, with airy sprays of tiny florets, is one of the best. Although it is a perennial, it is most often grown as an annual. It grows to about 8 inches tall and is good for containers, for bedding, or as a filler in front of taller plants. The full foliage is a good rich green. The variety 'Bluebird' is the one to use. Hardy.

Impatiens (*Impatiens* species). A useful and dependable plant for bright color in shady places all summer long. The flat 1-inch flowers come in white, red, pink, and various shades in between. It grows from 1 to 2 feet tall. The freely branching plants are produced quickly from rooted cuttings or seeds. A dozen plants set out in bloom create an instant effect. Tender.

Lobelia (*Lobelia erinus*). This is the ultimate in edging plants (to make neat, low borders at the edge of planting beds) for the early and midsummer garden. The variety 'Bluestone', in particular, with its electric color, draws a line as bright as if it were done with a paintbrush. Reds and whites are also available. Each compact plant is about 6 inches across and grows 4 to 6 inches tall. In six weeks the rich green foliage will be literally hidden by masses of tiny flowers. Hardy.

Mallow (*Lavatera trimestris*). The mallow is especially suited to a background planting where you do not want a solid mass of

Another flower highly regarded for its long season of bloom and remarkable resistance to pests and disease is the annual dahlia. It usually grows to about 18 inches tall.

foliage. This hybrid of the native marsh mallow grows to 4 feet tall on stems strong enough to hold up well without staking. The upper stems are covered with pink trumpet-shaped flowers that bloom in late spring. White or rose-colored varieties are also available. Tender.

Marigold *(Tagetes signata)*. The wide variety of available forms puts this high on the list of most useful plants for bedding, cutting, or use as an accent. The low-growing bedding types produce masses of 1-inch flowers, while the taller ones, which grow 2 to 3 feet high, have flowers 3 to 4 inches across. Colors range from light yellow through orange to mahogany. They bloom from late June until late fall and do best in full sun, although they will take shade for as much as two hours a day. Some are bushy and others have single stems. Read the catalog descriptions carefully before ordering. Tender.

Morning-glory *(Ipomoea purpurea)*. This quick-growing vine is best trained on a wall or trellis that will be seen during the sunniest part of the day, since its attractive funnel-shaped flowers close as the sun goes down. 'Heavenly Blue' is perhaps the best variety, although pink, red, purple, and bicolored varieties are also available. It flowers from late June until August. Half-hardy.

Nierembergia or **Cupflower** *(Nierembergia* species). This is another perennial that does best as an annual. The variety 'Purple Robe' is one of the most useful of all plants for a solid mass of color. It makes a mound of delicate green foliage dotted with 1-inch purple cup-shaped flowers. Each plant

covers an area of about 6 inches and grows 4 to 6 inches high. The flowers will be on display for the 4th of July. Hardy.

Petunia *(Petunia hybrida)*. This dependable performer is one of the most popular of the "foolproof" plants for long-term summer bloom. It is excellent for edging and massing in beds because the stems of most varieties are prostrate and the growth seldom exceeds 8 inches in height. Some hybrids, however, grow to a foot tall and spread to 2 feet across. The funnel-shaped flowers range in color from white, pink, and red to yellow, purple, and blue, in solid colors and bicolors, and in both single- and double-petaled forms. The tiny seeds need not be covered. Simply press them into the sur-

Petunias are trouble-free annuals that are easy to care for and come in a large range of solid colors and combinations, as well as in single, double, and ruffled forms.

face of the soil, or in the seed pot if you are starting them indoors. Full sun. Tender.

Phlox *(Phlox drummondii).* A creeping plant, to 3 inches high, well suited for a border, rock garden, container, or wherever a bright mat of early springtime color is needed. Colors range from white to purple and many shades of red to pink. The tiny flowers completely cover the small leaves, and although the bloom lasts for only about three weeks the spectacular display makes it worth having. Hardy.

Pot marigold *(Calendula officinalis).* The bright-yellow or orange daisylike flowers bloom all summer long and hold up remarkably well under the heat and dryness of a southern exposure. Foliage is a refreshing rich green. As the name implies, it is excellent for pots and containers. This is a plant that deserves to be used more widely than it is. Hardy.

Salvia *(Salvia splendens).* For brilliant accents of color, planted in groups of five to ten or for a dazzling larger display, this is a hard plant to beat. Flowers are carried at the top of 18-inch stems, in shades of red, pink, salmon, or plum. Plants must be started from seed or stem cuttings in very early spring to reach sufficient maturity to plant outdoors in early summer. Flowering will span the midsummer months. Hardy.

Scarlet runner bean *(Phaseolus coccineus).* Although this is a vegetable, the vigor of the vine, the attractive purple flowers, and the mahogany-red pods make it a natural for covering a fence or trellis. Plant seed in the early spring and within five weeks the vine will be 6 feet tall. Flowers and the dark-

purple pods begin to form about two weeks later. Tender.

Snapdragon *(Antirrhinum majus).* Snaps are deservedly popular for their vigorous growth and brilliance of hue, in all colors but blue. They range in height from 6 inches (great for edging) to 2½ feet (for background plantings). Blooming from July until frost, they thrive in full sun but do best when the weather begins to cool. If you want to grow them for cutting, plant in masses and thin as needed. Continued cutting lengthens the period of bloom. Their seed will often survive the winter and new plants will come up in the fall. Hardy.

Spiderflower *(Cleome hasslerana).* Good for background plantings. Has strong stems to 2½ feet tall that stand without staking. Foliage is apple-green, which, with the airy spiderlike flower heads, adds a cheerful note from mid-June to mid-September. Spiderflower produces seed freely and often comes up on its own in the spring. 'Helen Campbell', a white-flowering hybrid, is one of the best. Hardy.

Zinnia *(Zinnia elegans).* Good for mass plantings, or for cutting. The entire plant can be lifted and moved when in full bloom to fill in where some of the perennials have begun to wane. Foliage on a strong, upright 2-foot plant is a rich green, and stems are topped with a flat flower from 1½ to 4 inches across. Give each plant a square foot of space in a place with at least 6 hours of sunlight every day. Miniature varieties with 1-inch flowers on 6-inch stems are also available in many colors. Sow seeds successively from mid-May to July for continuous bloom in summer and fall. Half-hardy.

FLOWERS

✦|10|✦
Perennials for Permanence

Perennials have a well-earned reputation for being the backbone of the flower garden. There are kinds that will perform beautifully in every season. They start in the early spring with the primroses and bleeding hearts and continue all through the season until the late-bloomers such as the chrysanthemums are cut down by frost. In mild climates a succession of perennials will provide bloom almost all year long. Their range of size, shape, color, and blooming time surpasses even that of the annuals. There are, in fact, enough choices within specific colors to provide an all-blue or all-gray or all-white planting of successive blooms with an interesting variety of height and flower form.

The word "perennial" is from the Latin *perennis*, which means "throughout the year." Trees, shrubs, and some bulbs can be considered perennials, but here we are concerned only with the herbaceous kinds. These are the plants whose top growth—stems, leaves, and flowers—dies down to the ground at the end of each growing season, while their roots persist and produce new growth in the spring for at least two years, and usually many more.

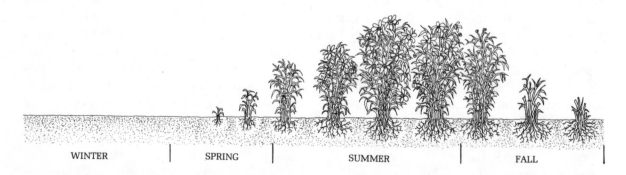

WINTER SPRING SUMMER FALL

Perennials planted when the soil warms in the spring will be in flower in early summer, midsummer, or early fall.

Although at the end of the growing season the plant will die down, the roots will stay alive over the winter.

Those that tend to spread have to be lifted and divided every few years. This requires some time and effort, but your gardening friends and neighbors can profit from the increase.

Some of the perennials, such as the delphinium, may bloom dependably for only three or four years. Others, such as phlox or campanula, can be counted on for five to ten years. A few, including day lilies and hostas, will continue to thrive for 20 years or so if planted and cared for as recommended.

There are a few varieties, as noted in the descriptions of recommended perennials, that have exceptionally beautiful leaves. This foliage can provide a full season of interest, with the flowers as an extra.

Don't be afraid to experiment with the tremendous range of planting combinations provided by the perennials. There is no such thing as an irreversible mistake. Almost any of them can be moved, even in full flower. Simply moisten the soil in advance, dig with a generous ball of earth to protect the roots, water into the new location immediately, and shade the plant from the hot sun for a few days with cheesecloth or burlap over upright stakes.

Many experienced gardeners adjust the colors in the garden or rearrange the plants as to height and color year after year. If you want to be an artist in the garden, consider the flowers as your palette.

Like annuals, perennials are classified in many mail-order catalogs as hardy, half-hardy, or tender. This classification relates to the nursery where they are grown. If you order from a source with a climate as cold or colder than your own, a hardy perennial will certainly survive. And, of course, the same is true if you buy from a local nursery.

In general, a hardy perennial will take wintertime temperatures of 10° to 20° below zero F. The half-hardy perennials require the protection of 6 to 8 inches of mulch to survive at zero, or else the roots must be dug up and moved to a cold frame or greenhouse. Tender perennials cannot be counted on to survive winter temperatures below freezing. In cold climates they must also be dug up and given winter protection indoors. The easiest method is to grow these for one season, as if they were annuals.

Because perennials are long-lived they will do best if the soil is well prepared before they are set out. Most of them need

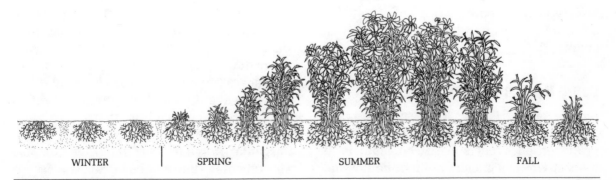

WINTER   SPRING   SUMMER   FALL

When the soil warms again in spring, the plant will renew its cycle of growth.

Most perennials will continue to grow, and repeat this process, for a period of 5 to 20 years.

good garden soil, which is to say soil with enough clay and humus to hold liquid in the root area until the plants can assimilate it, and enough sand or other gritty material to prevent water from standing long enough to suffocate the roots. (Soil conditions required by cacti, bog plants, and other special plants are discussed elsewhere.)

A complete fertilizer (containing the three essential elements—nitrogen, phosphorus, and potassium) should be thoroughly mixed into the soil before perennials are planted. Apply in amounts as suggested on the container.

All perennials grown where freezing occurs should have the root area covered with about 4 inches of mulch such as compost, hay, or dry leaves *after* the soil has frozen. This is to prevent subsequent thawing and heaving, which can damage the roots.

The superior characteristics of most flowering perennials were developed by crossing (hybridizing) plants of the same species. The only way to propagate these hybrids and guarantee that the new plants will be identical is by means of stem cuttings, root cuttings, or division.

If you plant the seed you harvest from a hybrid plant, it tends to revert to the original type and reproduce plants that are inferior to the hybrid, as is explained in chapter 9.

Some Recommended Perennials

Aster (*Aster frikarti*). This species bears lovely lavender-blue daisylike flowers in profusion on 2-foot stems. The plant is at its best where summers are not too hot and nights are comfortably cool. The best hybrid is 'Wonder of Staffa'. Hardy.

Astilbe (*Astilbe* species). One of the most valuable garden plants, astilbe can be used singly or in masses and provides interest from early summer until frost. The fernlike foliage is topped with spires of frothy flowers in pink, red, or white. In midsummer, after flowering, the handsome seed heads begin to develop and add another dimension of interest which holds even after the leaves have died down. It tolerates sun but does best in shade. There are many kinds, and they range from 6 inches to 2 feet tall. Hardy.

Baby's-breath (*Gypsophila paniculata*). The abundant tiny flowers on delicate stems create a soft veil of white that can be combined beautifully with almost any other flower in the garden. By the same token, the blooms are useful in flower arrangements. Baby's-breath grows from 2 to 3 feet high and about as broad and flowers for three to five weeks beginning in early summer. It does best in slightly alkaline soil. Hardy.

Bee balm (*Monarda didyma*). This is among those few plants that are literally foolproof. It still retains much of the toughness of its native American forebears, perhaps because it has not been too intensively hybridized. There are some newer varieties, from white to purple, but the best is still 'Cambridge Scarlet'. Its brilliance explodes in early summer and can be counted on for a month or longer if faded flowers are snipped off. It grows to about 4 feet with irregular whorls of flowers at the top of the stems. Hardy.

Bergenia (*Bergenia cordifolia*). In temperate climates the cabbagelike leaves, to about a foot high, stay green the year round. It is a useful ground cover to supplement such others as myrtle and pachysandra, which are often overused. It blooms in full sun or half shade in the spring with rosettes of small pink blossoms held on straight stems a few inches above the leaves. Hardy.

Bleeding heart *(Dicentra spectabilis)*. A dependable old-fashioned favorite that should be included in any informal spring garden. The pendant heart-shaped pink flowers, in great abundance, are carried well above the lacy foliage, which grows to about a foot tall. It will flower in the shade, and the clumps increase in size from year to year. Hardy.

Bluebell *(Anchusa azurea)*. (See also **Virginia bluebell**.) Notable for its generous display of small gentian-blue florets on multiple branching stems in early summer. Grows to about 3 feet tall. The two best varieties are 'Dropmore' and 'Royal Blue'. It's a worthwhile plant, even though it may disappear after flowering for a year or two. Hardy.

Blue false indigo *(Baptisia australis)*. This makes a dramatic showpiece in any garden with its intense blue flowers on a plant to 4½ feet tall and 3 feet across. As soon as the seed pods appear, cut them off and new flowers will develop. This indigo is one of the few perennials that does not need dividing. Just let it expand and enjoy it. Hardy.

Chrysanthemum *(Chrysanthemum species)*. Few garden plants are so universally—and deservedly—admired. Chrysanthemums are good for bedding or background planting as well as for cutting. They can also be dug and brought indoors as pot plants. Some

grow as a mound 8 inches high, literally covered with 2-inch pompom flowers; some are bushy 2-foot plants; and some grow into single stems 2½ feet tall and have blooms 6 inches across. Chrysanthemums are essentially fall-blooming, but this varies somewhat with the variety. To maintain quality of bloom, the plants should be divided every three years. For more about this excellent plant, see chapter 13. Hardy.

Cimicifuga or **Bugbane** *(Cimicifuga simplex)*. A useful plant because it is remarkably trouble-free, tolerates shade, and bears its flowers in late summer when color is most welcome. White lacy plumes emerge a foot above the leaves in late September. Although the foliage grows to 3 feet tall, the plant does not seem heavy in character. *C. racemosa* grows up to 7 feet tall and blooms in late summer. Hardy.

Coral-bells *(Heuchera sanguinea)*. Trouble-free and attractive, both for the neat foot-high mound of rich green leaves and the abundant sprays of tiny pink bell-shaped flowers on slim foot-high stems. A pure-white variety and shades of salmon through red are also available. Does well in sun or shade. Hardy.

Coreopsis *(Coreopsis lanceolata)*. Has showy daisylike flowers in single colors or bicolors combining shades of yellow, orange, or mahogany. In sunny situations it blooms from late summer to midfall and is essentially trouble-free. It grows about 3 feet tall. Hardy.

Day lily *(Hemerocallis species)*. Although each of the showy trumpet-shaped flowers lasts only a day (hence the name), new buds

FLOWERS

The brilliant white flowers of cimicifuga can brighten a cool shady place when it blooms during the last three weeks of autumn.

continue to form as the old flowers drop off and each plant provides a continuous display of color for about three weeks. With a selection of early, midseason, and late-blooming varieties you can have day lilies in flower for three months in the summer. They are available in hundreds of varieties in shades of yellow, orange, bronze, red, and pink. The best and most dependable is 'Hyperion', a heavy bloomer with large bright-yellow flowers in midsummer. For a mass effect, set plants about 2 feet apart and in about two years they will spread and fill in completely. Thrives in full sun or light shade and tolerates slightly moist soil.

Flowers are held well above the 2-foot clump of handsome straplike foliage. Hardy.

Delphinium (*Delphinium* species). With its 4-to-5-foot spires of pure-blue, deep-purple, or clear-white florets, this handsome plant deserves its reputation as an aristocrat of the garden. It must be emphasized, however, that delphiniums are easy to grow only if their requirements can be met. They need a slightly alkaline soil, excellent drainage in the root area, and a good flow of air between and around the plants. Given these conditions, the newer hybrids will bloom beautifully during June and July. Hardy.

Flax *(Linum perenne)*. Among the easiest and most accommodating perennials to grow. The small blue flowers on slender 12-inch stems give it an attractive airy appearance from midspring until the end of summer. Although this sun-loving plant will spread, it will not need dividing. Hardy.

Geranium (*Pelargonium* species). Although dependable, colorful, and easy to grow in summer where there is full sun, geraniums are tender and will not survive winter frost. To make them last beyond the summer, bring them indoors; or, better yet, keep only one or two plants indoors from which to make rooted cuttings to set out in the spring. The zonal varieties (so called because of the clearly defined zones of colors on their leaves) are available in white, pink, red, or salmon. Foliage is a rich soft green during the summer-long blooming period. Good for bedding and accent wherever bright color is needed. The ivy-leafed geraniums are particularly useful in containers because of the cascading effect of their long leafy stems. Tender.

Globe thistle *(Echinops ritro)*. With its abundant gray-green foliage, to 3 feet tall, and 3-inch globe-shaped flowers of metallic blue, this is a good plant for accent. It is a strong grower and requires no staking. Hardy.

Hibiscus *(Hibiscus* species). A half-dozen of these spectacular plants will create a dramatic show in any garden. The sparsely branched 4-foot stems are topped with flat 12-inch trumpet-shaped flowers in pastel colors. The varieties 'Cotton Candy', 'Strawberry Blonde', and 'Ruby Dot' are among the best. Set out in clumps of three, with plants 2 to 3 feet apart. Half-hardy.

Leopard's-bane *(Doronicum* species). Bright-yellow 3-inch daisylike flowers on 2-foot stems can do wonders to brighten the garden in midspring. The flowers are preceded by the heart-shaped apple-green foliage, which disappears without a trace by midsummer until it reappears the following spring. The venerable variety 'Madame Mason' is still the best. Hardy.

Liatris *(Liatris pycnostachya)*. The unique form and texture make this a useful accent plant. The 4-foot spikelike stems are clothed tightly with narrow leaves to within a foot of the top, which displays a torch of rosy-purple flowers in August and September. The shocking color can be softened by using white-flowering plants adjacent to it. Hardy.

Oriental poppy *(Papaver orientale)*. There are a few perennials that can be considered

This planting owes its success as much to the form and texture of the plants as to the color and shape of their flowers. The yellow hybrid gazania in the foreground is an annual. In the background is the white biennial *Salvia sclarea*, 'Vatican Variety', and at the right is the perennial blue bellflower *Campanula glomerata*. These plants are all readily available, and similarly contrasting plantings of annuals, biennials, and perennials can be created with other plants described under these classifications.

indispensable, and this is one of them. It provides a color accent of extraordinary power. Whether you use the soft pastel pinks or the fiery reds, the effect is spectacular in May and early June. The 3-foot stems are topped with cup-shaped flowers with paper-thin, textured petals and intricate interior design. Space the plantlets a foot apart to avoid crowding. Hardy.

Phlox *(Phlox paniculata)*. This is another indispensable. When we think of a "perennial border" we usually visualize the soft 3-foot mounds of pink, white, or red phlox in summer and early fall. Plants that revert to unattractive magenta colors can be removed when still in flower. To assure the

Two June-blooming exotics. In front, from South Africa, is the tender perennial *Dimorphotheca aurantiaca* 'Salmon Beauty', and in the rear the pink annual *Oenothera laciniata*.

maximum period of bloom, pick the faded flowers to prevent the seeds from developing. For a full display of the flowers and dark-green foliage, plant in groups of five or more and set the plants 18 inches apart. They also require good ventilation and should be lifted and divided as they get crowded. Hardy.

Physostegia *(Physostegia virginiana)*. Count this one among the plants that are remarkably easy to grow. It does well in mediocre soil and will bloom in partial shade. Flowering continues from July to September and the 4-foot stems hold the purple spires of bloom above most of the other perennials. Hardy.

Primrose *(Primula polyantha)*. In early spring this will be the first perennial to bring color to the bare brown earth of the flower bed or border or under shrubs. Colors range from pale yellow through mahogany red and deep purple, and even include shades of blue. The stems hold clusters of 1½-inch flowers just above the 8-inch straplike leaves of rich green. Where drainage is not good, use the Japanese primrose *(P. japonica)*, which is a few inches taller and has flowers in the purple, red, and pink range. These are called candelabras because the flowers are carried in rings around the upright stem. Hardy.

Rudbeckia *(Rudbeckia fulgida)*. As a hybrid of our native black-eyed Susan, this is a hardy and dependable plant. Flowers are produced in abundance in midsummer, and until they appear the rich green leaves give a good solid effect, starting in the spring. The variety 'Goldsturm' is one of the best. It has deep-yellow rays and the center cone is almost black. For greater intensity of color, try 'Robert Bloom' with its deep-red petals and orange cone. For a solid mass of color, set plants about 18 inches apart. It seldom grows more than 2½ feet tall. Hardy.

Siberian bugloss *(Brunnera macrophylla)*. An unusually adaptable plant which does equally well in sun or shade and will also tolerate some moisture at the root. Dark-green leaves in clusters to about a foot high and a foot across provide a good full cover, and in late spring there is the bonus of small dark-blue forget-me-not flowers. Hardy.

Thermopsis *(Thermopsis caroliniana)*. A showy plant that grows to 4 feet tall with spikes of bright-yellow flowers held well above the foliage. It does best in full sun and even in a dry location will provide a prolific display of color in midsummer. To prevent crowding, set the plants about 3 feet apart. Hardy.

Virginia bluebell *(Mertensia virginica)*. This woodland plant looks best in a slightly shaded informal setting such as the edge of a woodland or shrub border. The abundant foliage is about a foot high and grows in a broad tight cluster. The clear-blue funnel-shaped flowers open from red-purple buds and hang in graceful clusters on stems slightly taller than the foliage. After flowering, in May, the plant gradually dies down and disappears by the end of June. Hardy.

Windflower *(Anemone japonica)*. Add this one to your list of dependable flowering plants for fall. It produces 3-to-4-inch broad-petaled flowers of delicate pink, soft rose,

The variety of distinctive flower forms that perennials can provide in summer is illustrated here; in the foreground is the white form of *Echinacea purpurea*, in the middle is yellow day lily, and in the rear is the contrasting gray-blue of sea holly *(Eryngium maritimum)*.

or white depending upon the variety. Growing to about 2 feet tall, it can be used in front of taller perennials to hide the lower foliage, which tends to become unsightly. Hardy.

Yarrow *(Achillea filipendulina)*. Notable for its long period of bloom, from early June until late August. Its upright 3-foot stems make it excellent at the back of a perennial planting. Flowers are carried in flat clusters at the top of the stem. The variety 'Coronation Gold' will add a dependable splash of color wherever used. Set the plants about 2 feet apart. Hardy.

FLOWERS

✗ |11| ✗
Using Biennials to Best Advantage

Biennials, as the name implies, take two years to complete their cycle from seed to flower and back to seed.

You might well say, as some gardeners do, "Why bother?" Why should anyone give garden space to a plant that produces nothing but foliage for the first year? Not only does it take up space, it requires planning ahead for an extra year. Why not just stick with the easy and dependable annuals and perennials?

The garden value of the biennial is twofold, and is more than enough to keep them in good standing in the seed catalogs. Their season of bloom is advantageous, especially to gardeners in cool climates where there tend to be gaps in flowering. Most biennials start to bloom in early spring when they are needed to bridge the gap between the early-spring-flowering bulbs and the early-summer-flowering perennials. Interplanted with the former, the biennials will flower until the latter come into bloom. In addition to this, they happen to include such winsome beauties as pansies, English daisies, sweet William, and wallflowers.

In some climates, where the summers are too hot or too damp, some perennials do not persist for more than a season or two, as though they were biennials. Some of these are included on the list of recommended biennials.

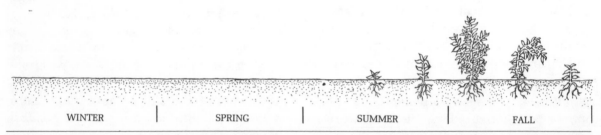

WINTER | SPRING | SUMMER | FALL

Biennials sown in midsummer will develop roots and produce a plant and possibly flowers before becoming dormant in the winter. This, however, is not the season for which they are planted. The following spring the plant begins to

You can avoid giving biennials valuable garden space when they are not in bloom by planting them in a "holding area" and moving the plants, roots and all, to their permanent place in the fall. They will then bloom in place the following year.

In cold climates it is a good idea to put down a light mulch of dry leaves or straw after the ground is frozen. This prevents thawing and heaving, which can damage the roots. Be careful, however, with those plants that develop a rosette of basal foliage in winter such as the English daisy and foxglove. The mulch can mat down on the foliage and rot the leaves. A few branched twigs around the rosette will keep the mulch off the leaves and provide air circulation.

Because biennials are in active growth in all but the coldest part of the winter, they in particular should have a proper mulch and good drainage.

All of the following genera are hardy through Zone 5.

Some Recommended Biennials

Canterbury bell *(Campanula medium)*. A grouping of five to a dozen of these clear-colored beauties will do wonders to bring new interest to a planting of waning perennials. Flowers are white, blue, lavender, or pink, and each 3-to-4-foot spire covers itself with bell-shaped blossoms in early summer. *C. calycanthema* is a foot taller, and each flower cup has a sort of saucer under it.

English daisy *(Bellis perennis)*. Wherever a low-growing small flowering plant is needed for midspring, this is an outstanding candidate. The perfect multipetaled daisies, about an inch across, are carried on 3-to-4-inch stems. The seeds invariably self-sow, assuring successive years of good display. Colors are white, pink, and red.

Evening primrose *(Oenothera hookeri)*. The yellow flowers combine well with most other garden hues. The blooming period extends over the early summer months, and because the fragrance is most pronounced in the evening a planting is most appropriate near a terrace, porch, or other sitting area. A few plants will go a long way. A well-branched 2-foot plant will cover an area 2 feet across. They should have full sun, but are otherwise undemanding.

Forget-me-not *(Myosotis alpestris)*. At the risk of crowding too many plants on the list, this one must be added. Beautiful sprays of blue flowers, either alone or

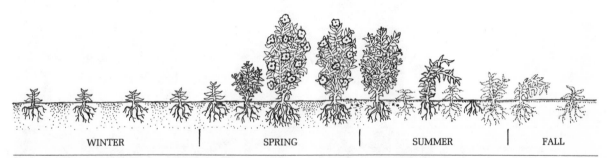

WINTER | SPRING | SUMMER | FALL

grow and will be in full flower shortly thereafter. Then, at the end of the flowering season, seed will drop to the soil, and new plants may develop to begin a new biennial cycle.

coupled with primroses, are a veritable definition of spring. Seed sprinkled in a slightly moist bed in mid to late summer will flower the following May. An early-spring sowing of this productive plant will flower six weeks later in June.

Foxglove *(Digitalis purpurea).* Lovely pastel colors are now available in the various hybrids, and they can be an asset to any garden. The top 18 inches of the 3-to-4-foot spikes are neatly arranged with overlapping pendulous bell-like florets in June and July. Flowering begins in mid-May and continues for three weeks or more. The basal foliage is a rosette of tough apple-green leaves. Foxglove does well in partial shade as well as sun and will tolerate somewhat damp soil. This useful characteristic is shared by few other biennials.

Hollyhock *(Althaea rosea).* The tall spires with their dusty-colored flat trumpets of flowers that look like crepe paper wired on the stems add a welcome old-fashioned accent. The 5-foot stalks can stand without support, and the entire show unfolds in July and continues for the rest of the summer. The hollyhock is technically a perennial, but is grown with greater success as a biennial.

Lupine *(Lupinus polyphyllus).* This is a stately 3-to-5-foot plant with 12-inch terminal spikes of massed pealike flowers and attractive deeply cut fingerlike leaves. The excellent Russell hybrids are available in blue, red, and yellow and soft shades in between. Lupine does well in almost any well-drained situation as a background border plant at the edge of woods, or back

Canterbury bells, silhouetted here against the sweep of a lawn, are excellent tall accent flowers in a border. Consider using them in combination with the low-growing perennial bell-flower *(Campanula carpatica).*

This big bed of colorful pansies will bloom from early spring until the weather gets hot in midsummer. The more flowers picked, the longer the plants will bloom.

a little way from a stream bank. This is another perennial that is best grown as a biennial.

Pansy *(Viola tricolor)*. Few plants are as dependable as this old favorite. It grows about 6 inches high and will create a solid low bed of color if you space the plants 6 to 8 inches apart. Pick off the flowers as they fade so they cannot set seed and they will continue to bloom for two months or until the weather gets too hot for them. They prefer sun, but will also thrive in light shade.

Sweet William *(Dianthus barbatus)*. This is a most cooperative spring-flowering perennial that is usually grown as a biennial. However, if all conditions are right it will persist for several years. Its needs are not so specific that they cannot be achieved in

a reasonably well-drained sunny location of moderate fertility. Sweet William comes in brilliant shades of red and pink as well as softer tones. Its abundant 10-inch stems, each topped with a flat miniature carnationlike flower, make it a natural for outlining a border. A deservedly popular variety is 'Newport Pink'.

Wallflower *(Cheiranthus cheiri)*. This 2-foot spring flowering plant is an ideal companion for a bed of tulips. Wallflowers require a cool, well-ventilated situation for successful flowering. When the temperature gets to 80° F. or above, they do not do well. Given adequate water and full sun, the flower stems are covered with small flat florets of pure color. The clear yellows, bright reds, and soft pinks refute the idea that some floral hues tend to clash.

The bulbs here, together with their typical flowers, are: 1) hyacinth; 2) snowflake; 3) snowdrop; 4) crocus; 5) freesia; 6) grape hyacinth; 7) daffodil; 8) lily; 9) amaryllis; 10) autumn crocus.

✕|12|✕
Bulbs, Corms, Tubers, and Rhizomes

If the only words you recognize in this title are "bulbs" and "tubers," don't be alarmed. "Rhizomes" and "corms" can hardly be considered familiar household terms. Although each category is technically different, they are similar enough so that garden catalogs usually carry them all under the heading of "bulbs." This is probably because they all have fleshy underground parts that store energy derived from the leaves and produce new flowers at the beginning of each growing season. There are some differences worth knowing about, but first let's consider the importance of this group of plants to the garden.

Not only are they among the easiest of all flowering plants to grow, they offer an amazing pageant of color from spring to fall. Starting in early spring—in cold climates, even before the snow has melted—you can enjoy the graceful little snowdrops and snowflakes with their nodding white flowers, the vibrant blue clusters of the scilla, and the multicolored carpet of the crocus.

With the warmth of the early spring come the deep blue of grape hyacinths, white carpets of lily of the valley, the bright golden hues of the daffodils, the rich colors and heady fragrance of the true hyacinths, and, to end the spring display, the tulips with their wide range of glowing colors.

Early summer brings the familiar iris, the alliums with their remarkable round flower clusters, the stately lilies, and the tuberous-rooted dahlias, with their many sizes, shapes, and hues. This colorful show ends in the fall with the curious colchicum, a bulb whose foliage has already waxed and waned. The crocuslike flower in white, or shades of lavender and blue, springs directly from the ground with no sign of foliage.

The fleshy underground parts of the rhizomes, corms, tubers, and bulbs contain the complete flower in embryonic form, along with sufficient stored energy to bring it into bloom. The annual cycle is triggered, after a period of dormancy, when the underground temperature hovers close to or below freezing for at least two months. The leaves and flowers then begin to push up through the ground (except for the colchicum, which, as mentioned, operates on a different schedule). The flowers make their

Bulbs are identified by their overlapping layers of thin tissue. The onion is the most familiar example. Tulips, hyacinths, and lilies are true bulbs. Shown here is a daffodil.

Corms, unlike the true bulbs, are composed of a solid fleshy material on the inside and a paperlike exterior tissue structure covered in a striated net. This corm is a crocus.

showy appearance and the seed heads begin to develop, if the flowers are not removed. The leaves persist and react with sunlight to develop energy, which is returned to the underground parts and stored for the next annual cycle of growth. This energy can be conserved by removing the flowers after they bloom to prevent the development of seeds. Most of these plants develop roots that further help to replenish the growing power of bulbs. With cold weather comes dormancy again, and the end of the cycle.

Here are the differences:

The true bulbs, such as tulips and daffodils, have layers of fleshy tissue around the growth bud in the center, like an onion.

Corms, such as the crocus, are not constructed in layers but have a mass of solid tissue with roots developing from the flat base.

Tubers are also composed of solid tissue, but the new growth comes from eyes on the surface, like the potato.

Rhizomes are similar to tubers except that they grow horizontally and often, as in the case of the iris, partially above ground.

All of these are ready to grow when they are planted, even if put in upside down or sideways. But they will develop more quickly and produce sturdier plants if you set them out with the growth points facing up.

All the bulbs, corms, tubers, and rhizomes do best in a sunny location. Keep in mind, however, that the earliest spring bulbs can often be used in a woodland set-

Ground level

Plant bulbs and corms at a depth about three times their top-to-bottom dimension. Tubers should be planted at a depth equal to twice their thickness, and rhizomes just below the surface of the soil.

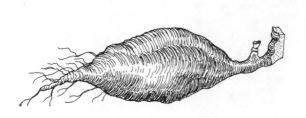

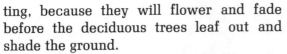

Tubers are essentially a thickened root with a solid interior. Eyes on the outside are the points from which new plants develop. A potato is a tuber. Illustrated here is a dahlia.

Rhizomes are thickened underground stems that grow horizontally. Buds on their top surface become the plant, and roots develop below. Shown here is an iris rhizome.

ting, because they will flower and fade before the deciduous trees leaf out and shade the ground.

Most plants with fleshy underground parts are susceptible to rotting if they stand in soggy soil. The surface of the planting area should slope enough so that water will not collect, and the soil itself should be light and open in texture so that water can drain through it. Notable exceptions are the lily of the valley and siberian iris, which do best in shady places and moist soil. For more on soil texture, see chapter 3.

Plantings for Early Spring

The bulbs of earliest spring bring the first welcome color to gardens in cold climates. There are four early spring beauties that lend themselves to mass plantings for impressive drifts of color. They can, of course, be used in a smaller space, but for optimum effect set out at least 100 of the same kind. Plant them in the fall 4 to 6 inches apart, and over the years by division and self-seeding they will fill in to make a solid carpet. These stars of early spring, in

their usual order of appearance, are:

Glory-of-the-snow (*Chionodoxa luciliae*) is an 8-inch plant that has star-shaped sky-blue flowers with a white center. **Snowdrop** (*Galanthus nivalis*) is a graceful plant to 1 foot high with nodding green-edged white flowers. **Snowflake** (*Leucojum vernum*) has green-tipped white flowers standing well above the foliage. **Siberian squill** (*Scilla siberica*) produces tight clusters of perfect little blossoms of vibrant blue about 6 inches high.

Somewhat later the crocuses appear in close-cropped carpets of color. They too are best suited to mass planting. They come in a wide range of solid and variegated colors.

Anemone (*Anemone blanda*) is a 6-inch delicately leafed plant with daisylike flowers of bright lavender. The variety *A.b. atrocoerulea* has flowers of a more pleasing clear blue. Anemones do best in rather moist, rich soil.

Grape hyacinth (*Muscari armeniacum*), as the name indicates, has clusters of deep-blue flowers that resemble small inverted

The deep violet-blue color and richly textured upright form of the flowers of the grape hyacinth *(Muscari armeniacum)* make an attractive companion plant for these low-growing early yellow tulips.

bunches of grapes. It grows 6 to 8 inches high and, like all the other early-spring flowers discussed above, it spreads naturally to make an attractive informal display.

Plantings for Later Spring

This is the season for such beauties as the lily of the valley, daffodils, tulips, and hyacinths.

Lily of the valley *(Convallaria majalis)* is a fragrant flower that belongs in a shady place where the soil is not dry. If left alone, the planting will spread to make a carpet of bright-green foliage with fragrant white nodding flowers that bloom in midspring about the middle of the daffodil season.

Set the tiny bulbs, called pips, 6 inches apart and cover them with about ½ inch of soil. Growth will be more rapid if you add a light covering of compost in the spring.

Daffodils *(Narcissus* species) are among the most useful, dependable, and rewarding of all bulbs. They range in size from the charming little *N. watieri* to the dramatic golden trumpets of 'King Alfred' on a 24-inch stem.

Daffodils come in white, orange, or pink as well as the glorious shades of yellow for which they are renowned. The two main parts of the flower, the trumpet and the skirtlike perianth that surrounds it, may be the same or different colors. In some cases the edge of the trumpet is highlighted with another hue. Some daffodils, classified as doubles, have many petals and look more like a small peony than a typical daffodil. A planting of daffodils will grow beautifully for many years if the foliage is allowed to complete its cycle of growth. As mentioned before, the flowers should be picked before they go to seed, but the foliage must remain until it has turned brown and fully served its purpose of returning energy to the bulb.

This means that if the bulbs are planted in a grassy area, the grass should not be cut until the bulb foliage has matured, so choose the planting site accordingly. Plant in October in cold climates; in December in the South.

Tulips (*Tulipa* species) are available in a bewildering variety of sizes and shapes and a marvelous range of rich color. They have five basic flower forms: parrot, lily-flowered, double-flowered, cottage, and Darwin (shown in frontispiece, facing title page). The species tulips that are among the earliest to appear are just that: a species of

A clump of daffodils, like this planting of *Narcissus poeticus*, can provide a welcome touch of color in early spring before the leaves appear on trees.

A large planting of bearded iris can include any or all of the myriad hues in which these plants are available.

the genus *Tulipa*. The plants, but not necessarily the flowers, are smaller than the hybrids. Hybrids, of course, are the result of man-made crosses or hybridization, and they include the largest and showiest kinds.

The most attractive varieties include:

Double early: In cold climates these bloom in late April: 'Mr. Van der Hoef', 'Orange Nassau', 'Vuurbaak'. Those below bloom in May.

Lily-flowered: 'Picotee', 'Queen of Sheba', 'White Triumphator'.

Parrot: 'Fantasy', 'Texas Gold', 'Red Parrot', 'Faraday'.

Darwin: 'Queen of Bartigons', 'Golden Niphetos', 'Zwanenburg', 'The Bishop'.

Cottage: 'Malcro', 'Blushing Bride', 'Mirella'.

Give tulips the same care as the daffodils. Tulips are at their best the first spring after planting, although they may persist, with diminishing vigor, for the next year or two.

Hyacinth *(Hyacinthus orientalis)* has tightly packed flowers on upright stems to 6 inches tall, somewhat stiff and severe in aspect. But the hyacinth's clear colors of white, yellow, blue, red, or pink and its delightful fragrance make it one of springtime's pleasures. At their best in formal planting beds or in containers, hyacinths will flower for four or five successive seasons. They bloom at the same time as the midseason tulips and, because they are shorter, are often used as a foreground planting.

A third of a cup of a complete fertilizer (5-10-5) watered in at the base of each plant after they have bloomed will promote growth the following year.

Iris (*Iris* species). The ever-popular bearded iris is a familiar favorite for good reason. Large and dependable, it makes a dramatic showing in late spring and early summer year after year with limited need for upkeep. This iris is available in solid or mixed colors, and new and more flamboyant varieties are being developed every year.

Irises should be planted in the fall. Cover the rhizomes with no more than an inch of soil. In cold climates, after the ground has frozen solid add 3 to 4 inches of mulch to prevent heaving and thawing. This should be done for the first year at least to give the root mass a chance to get established.

An iris planting should be lifted and divided as illustrated at the end of this chapter. This should be done when the amount of bloom begins to diminish, usually every three or four years.

This is the best time to eradicate pests and disease. Look carefully at each rhizome for soft spots and for the pencil holes that indicate the presence of the iris borer. Cut off and destroy all but the obviously firm and healthy growth.

Lifting and dividing is normally done after the flowers have bloomed. But if the foliage is yellowed or shows other signs of trouble, the affected plants should be removed immediately and destroyed.

Iris cristata has a star-shaped flower of bright blue that blooms in May. It literally shines in the otherwise dull shade at the edge of a tree or shrub border. At its best, in soil rich in organic material, it grows to about 4 inches high. This size is well suited

BULBS

The appeal of some irises, like this *Iris giganticaerulea*, is dependent more upon the elegance of their form and flower than their brilliance of color.

to rock gardens or groupings of other plants of similar size. Set the rhizomes out in the fall, in sun or shade.

When to Plant Spring Bloomers

In cold climates the best time to plant is just after the first killing frost and well before the ground begins to freeze.

In climates where there is no frost, the spring-flowering bulbs cannot go into the necessary dormant state. They will develop too fast and complete their cycle of growth without producing satisfactory flowers. Thus, in warm climates, bulbs require special treatment. Most dealers precool the bulbs by refrigeration to allow for the necessary slowdown in the cycle of growth. You can do this yourself, as is explained below.

Precooling bulbs for warm climates

The dormancy that is particularly necessary for tulips, daffodils, and hyacinths can be simulated in a refrigerator at about 40° F. The vegetable crisper is an ideal place. Do not let the bulbs freeze. Store them for six to eight weeks before their planting time in mid-November through December. Leave the bulbs in the ventilated paper sacks they come in.

The precooled bulbs planted in midwinter for spring bloom will not survive beyond the first year. So, in effect, in warm climates these bulbs can only be grown successfully as annuals.

Plantings for Early Summer to Early Fall

Most of the following plants will grow outdoors the year round in Southern gardens and complete their annual cycle of growth without the need for cold-weather dormancy. In climates where it freezes in winter, some require special handling, as is noted.

Alliums (*Allium* species) come into flower about the same time as the roses. *Allium giganticum*, on strong straight slender stems to 5 feet tall, topped with a remarkable 5-inch round flower like a burst of bright purple fireworks, is the most dramatic of all. Picked and hung head-down in a warm dry place, it will dry beautifully and can be used for display all winter long.

There are shorter species too, and they all have striking round flower heads. Even a small planting will make a handsome showing and will persist for several years.

A. karataviense grows to about 1 foot tall. It has broad straplike basal leaves and a rounded lavender flower head about 3 inches across. Even more dramatic is *A. albopilosum*, which grows to 3 feet tall and has a lilac-colored flower that reaches 6 to 8 inches across.

Plant alliums in the spring, in a place where they will get full sun. Set them at a depth of not more than twice the depth of the bulb itself.

Lilies (*Lilium* species) offer a remarkably useful variety of sizes, colors, and bloom times as well as two distinctive kinds of flowers. They range in height from 2 to 6 feet, in color from white and blush-pink to blood red and shades of orange, yellow, purple, and green. The flower clusters are either upright trumpet shapes or downward-facing heads with recurved petals. The early varieties start blooming in June, the midseason types flower in July and August, and the late ones will bloom in the North until the first heavy frost. Here, for example, are a few that will ensure successive bloom: For June and July, 'Regal' *(Lilium regale)*; for August and September, 'Goldband' *(L. auratum)*; and from September until frost, 'Oregon Giant' *(L. speciosum magnificum)*.

Lilies require rich well-drained soil, deeply worked to at least 12 inches. The bulbs dry out and deteriorate more quickly than most other bulbs. They should be purchased from a reliable source, preferably directly from a grower to reduce the time between digging, shipping, and planting in your garden.

Some lilies develop support roots at the lower part of the stems as well as at the base of the bulb. To facilitate this characteristic, plant the bulbs fully three times their depth. Water thoroughly after planting and mark each bulb with a stake so the area will not be disturbed until growth starts in the spring.

In cold climates, add a winter mulch of hay, evergreen boughs, or salt hay to prevent thawing and subsequent heaving of the bulbs. Remove the mulch in the spring when new growth starts and apply fertilizer high in phosphate and potash, such as a 2-8-10 or 0-10-10. This helps produce the strong stems needed to support the large flower clusters.

Calla lily *(Zantedeschia aethiopica)* is favored in the frost-free gardens of the South, where the pure-white trumpet-shaped flowers are useful for bright early-summer accents in shady places. Plant them in moist soil from early to mid-winter.

In cold climates the calla lily can take full sun and with its lush foliage is especially handsome in containers, where it does, however, need frequent watering. Plant the bulbs indoors in midwinter, about 3 inches deep. Put the containers outside when all danger of frost has passed. After flowering, continue watering, and move them indoors before frost strikes in the fall. For winter care, follow the instructions for dahlias later in this chapter.

Canna lilies *(Canna species)*. The old-fashioned cannas, with their bold masses of tropical-looking bronze or green foliage and showy upright flower heads, are making a comeback. Best known for the brilliant red flowers in midsummer and their impressive size, to 5 or 6 feet, they are now available in soft tones of peach and apricot on 3-to-4-foot plants that are more adaptable to home gardens.

In the North the rhizomes can be started indoors in flats of peat moss in late winter and put out in the garden after the last frost. Plant them about 4 inches deep. In the fall they can be dug, ripened, and stored in the same way as dahlias. Rhizomes should be separated before starting into growth again. Cut them so there are a few "eyes" or buds on each one.

In the South they are also planted in midwinter, and a well-tended bed will thrive for many years. This is a vigorous plant that does best in rich soil with fertilizer added in the spring and kept well watered all through the growing season.

Belladonna lily *(Amaryllis belladonna)* is available with red, white, or lavender blooms. The trumpet-shaped flowers of this attractive garden subject stand just above the 18-inch straplike leaves of rich green.

BULBS

This is a favorite in California, where it blooms in late summer. *A. equestris* is more frequently used in the Southeast, although it too is sometimes grown in the West. The latter has flowers of soft pink and blooms in midsummer. It is the more vigorous of the two; if it is left undisturbed it will increase annually and make a beautiful solid display.

In Zones 8, 9, and 10 this bulb can be left in place for five years or more. In the colder climates (Zones 5, 6, and 7), it must be lifted in the fall and stored in a cool frost-free place and kept covered with slightly moistened peat moss.

Lily of the Nile *(Agapanthus africanus)* has 3-foot stems of blue florets rising in the summer among the straplike leaves. It is strikingly handsome whether in garden beds (in the South) or in containers (in colder climates). In frost-free climates where it can safely be planted in the garden, it will persist year after year and increase its seasonal show. In cold climates, plant the bulbs indoors in February in large pots or tubs. Set the bulbs close to the surface with the necks exposed. When there's no further danger of frost, move them outside in their containers. By June they will be in

This hybrid typifies the sculptural beauty of the buds and flowers of the lilies. Lilies last well when used as cut flowers, and have an almost overwhelming fragrance.

flower. Whether grown in beds or containers they must be watered regularly until the leaves begin to die back in the fall. Then let them rest (lift and store indoors in the North) until they begin their next cycle of growth. Even if the planting seems crowded, they will still do well.

Gladiolus (*Gladiolus* species) has regal 3-foot stems completely covered with large colorful overlapping florets, making it an especially attractive flower for cutting, and today's hybrids offer a great variety of colors both solid and in combinations. Glads grow best in a rich soil with good drainage. They have a relatively short season of bloom.

To extend the season, make successive plantings at ten-day intervals starting after the danger of frost has passed in midspring. You can count on having flowers three months after each planting. Set the corms about 6 inches deep and 6 inches apart. In the South where winter temperature is no problem, plant at ten-day intervals starting in early February and continuing until early summer.

Colchicum (*Colchicum autumnale*) is an interesting, autumn-flowering, crocuslike plant that puts on an attractive display in the season of chrysanthemums and dahlias. Ranging in color from white to rosy lilac, the flowers are larger than the crocus and spring right from the ground without leaves, the coarse foliage having grown in the spring and died down by midsummer. Hugging the ground as they do, these little plants can be used in the foreground to good effect to divert attention from the fading foliage of earlier annuals and perennials. Colchicum tolerates some shade and can also be used at the front of a shrub border. Plant in early fall.

Soil, Drainage, Fertilizer, and Alkalinity

All of the plants mentioned in this chapter, except for the few specifically recommended for moist places, will do best in alkaline soil with good drainage, well tilled and fairly rich in nutrient.

Unless your soil has a pH of 7 or above, the addition of ground limestone to increase the alkalinity (and thus reduce the acidity) will benefit a planting of bulbs. For more on this, see chapter 3.

Fertilizer too, preferably a 5-10-10, should be added at a rate of about 4 pounds per 100 square feet. For an area planting, work it into the ground with a spade or power tiller. To save work, do this when you add the limestone.

If you are planting in individual holes, add ¼ cup fertilizer to each hole and mix it in with the soil.

Working the soil in this way also improves the tilth and lets more air into the soil, which is all to the good.

Lifting, Storing, and Dividing

There are three reasons for digging up your bulbs, tubers, corms, or rhizomes: in cold climates the tender ones must be taken up for protective winter storage; when a planting gets too crowded (or disease is evident) you may want to lift and discard some and then replant; and if you want to increase the number of plants, you can lift and divide them. Whichever reason or reasons apply, the methods are simple enough if you understand a few basic principles.

BULBS

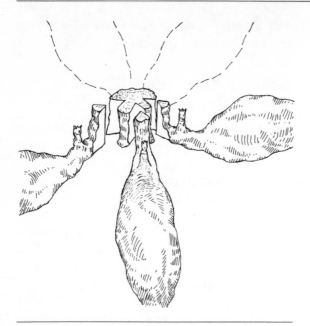

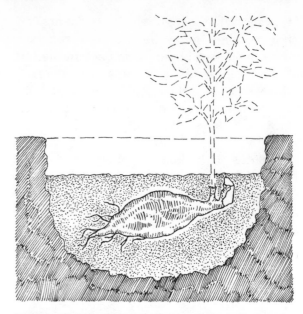

When the foliage has died down in the fall, clumps of dahlia tubers can be divided. Cut the clump apart so that each tuber includes an obvious node or growing point.

In the spring, plant tubers horizontally with their growing points barely covered. As the plant develops, gradually fill to the level of the surrounding surface.

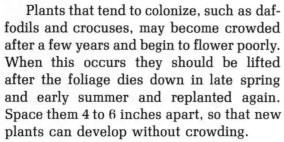

Plants that tend to colonize, such as daffodils and crocuses, may become crowded after a few years and begin to flower poorly. When this occurs they should be lifted after the foliage dies down in late spring and early summer and replanted again. Space them 4 to 6 inches apart, so that new plants can develop without crowding.

For winter storage, cut the stems at ground level when the leaves die down in the fall and carefully dig up the underground parts. Let them dry in the sun until the clinging soil can be crumbled away. Dust with powdered sulfur or some other fungicide and store in boxes filled with lightly moistened packing material to keep from drying out. Make sure to keep them separate from one another. Peat moss, sand, excelsior, or crumpled newspaper can be used for packing. Too much moisture can cause rot. On the other hand, if the packing

material becomes dry to the touch, add water until it is as moist as a well-squeezed sponge. Otherwise the plant tissue may lose its healthy plump appearance. The best storage temperature is in the range of 40° to 50° F., with a relative humidity of 50% to 60%. These conditions may well prevail in a cool corner of a heated garage or basement. Inspect about once a month. Keep an eye out for mold. If it appears, treat the bulbs by dusting them with a fungicide.

If you are dividing, first dig up the underground parts and dry them as suggested above. Separate the underground parts and cut away and destroy all diseased or damaged parts.

Division to gain rooting stock for new plants is done in one of three ways. Some plants, such as narcissus, tulips, allium, lilies, calla, and agapanthus, increase by means of offsets.

The irises, dahlias, and begonias are divided by cutting the underground sections apart as illustrated.

Gladiolus and crocus increase by developing new corms on top of the old ones. The

new corms also occasionally produce smaller pea-size cormels around the perimeter. These can be detached and planted. They will mature to flowering size the following year.

When irises of the bearded or crested type have overcrowded or outgrown their allotted space they can be lifted with a spading fork or shovel. This should be done only a few weeks after the last flower has faded.

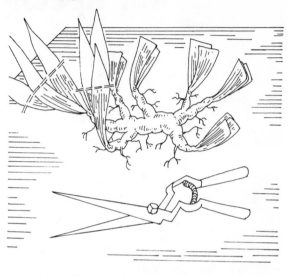

After lifting, cut back the leaves to a length of 2 to 3 inches in order to prevent rot from forming. Use scissors-action pruning shears, as the anvil-type shears tend to bruise as they cut.

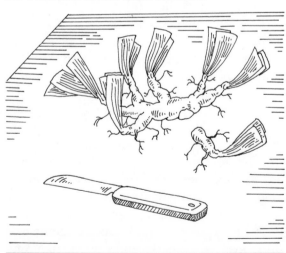

Use a clean, sharp knife to cut clumps of rhizomes into sections and to remove any diseased parts. Make sure that each section is about 3 inches long and has at least one fan of leaves. Dust all cuts with a fungicide.

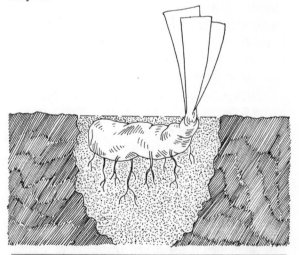

As soon as they are separated, plant each of the rhizomes just below the surface of the soil. The soil should have a generous quantity of humus to hold moisture and nutrient, but it should also be well drained.

❧ |13| ❧
Special Plants
for Special Situations

There are some garden plants that have such specific uses or such definite characteristics that they cannot merely be included in one of the more general chapters in this book. To understand their potential and requirements, you need more information than the paragraph or two that does suffice for many plants.

Among the plants discussed in this chapter are some that will be part of the basic structure of your garden and others that will be featured as highlights. All are worthy of particular consideration.

The ground covers are among the most adaptable and useful plants that you are likely to grow. Before choosing what ground cover to use, however, make sure you learn which ones are well adapted to the environment. Ground covers, like lawns, are more permanent than most other shrubby plants. Except for large trees, most plants can be moved if they are in the wrong place. But the mass plantings in which ground covers are most often used are difficult to move.

Almost any plant can be used as a hedge or screen, but included here are those of manageable size that lend themselves best to trimming or pruning. The recommended vines include only the kinds that are most useful, attractive, and dependable—the criteria used throughout the book.

Roses, of course, deserve a section of their own; they are among the most popular of all garden flowers. There are some specific requirements for their proper culture, although they are not as different from other plants as you might think.

Rhododendrons and azaleas are also among the showiest of garden plants. Although they require a particular kind of soil, they can be grown more widely than is generally realized.

The section on chrysanthemums tells how to get the most out of these plants, which, perhaps more than any other, can be the virtual backbone of the fall season. They are at their best when most other flowers have passed their peak.

The succulents, while not indispensable in the garden, are unique in character and they deserve consideration when planning accents and small points of interest.

Water plants are also in a class by themselves. There are a limited number of gardens in which they can be grown without creating the special conditions that they must have. But some of the plants that grow only in water are so colorful and interesting in their habit of growth that it is worthwhile to provide the necessary environment for at least a few of them.

Ground Covers

In most gardens there are places where compact low-growing plants can be used to good effect. In some situations, such as on a steep slope, on uneven or rocky ground, or in deep shade where grass is difficult or impossible to grow, ground covers may offer the only way to carpet an area with plants.

In other places, such as a rock garden or the front of a shrub border, they are often used because no other plants are so appropriate or pleasing to the eye. And from a practical point of view, the low-growing plants with tenacious root systems are used to prevent runoff and erosion.

The choice of attractive plants that can be used as ground covers is so wide that we have chosen for the following list only those that are the most dependable. Those that tend to fall victim to insect attack or disease are not included, regardless of their beauty.

Although they are considered low-maintenance plantings, ground covers may require considerable hand weeding between the plants until they fill in completely.

Bugleweed (*Ajuga reptans* 'Metallica Crispa'). This variety of *A. reptans* is not quite so invasive as the more common form of the species, and the foliage has a pleasing and unusual purple color. A real ground-hugger, bugleweed fills in rapidly and makes a good cover under tall shrubs, and will also thrive in full sun. The 4-inch purple flower spikes appear in midspring when lilacs are in bloom. Used as an underplanting, they echo the purple of the blossoms overhead. During the summer, new runners develop, and each year the bed increases in density. Keep any planting of bugleweed away from lawns. It can spread and become difficult to weed out. It is evergreen except in the coldest climates. Zone 4.

Foamflower (*Tiarella cordifolia*). This is a useful native plant from the Alleghany region. It is deciduous but develops rapidly in spring, and before the end of spring the short stems burst into white sparklerlike bloom. The seeds are soon scattered, and new seedlings will be well established before summer is over. A damp location in light shade is ideal, and it combines beautifully with ferns. The entire plant, flower and all, is only 6 or 7 inches high and about the same width. If you start with 25 plants, you will have 100 or more a year later. Zone 4.

Heather (*Calluna vulgaris*). This is a more adaptable garden plant than its limited use would suggest. Although it does require acid soil, there are many parts of the country where the soil is naturally acid. Heathers also need good drainage and full sun, but if these requirements are met, they thrive, flower, and spread, even in soil of minimal fertility. Some varieties have a shrublike form but many others have a creeping habit of growth and make excellent low ground covers. Those with green foliage are best known, but there are yellow or red varieties that add a special brightness the year round. Evergreen. Zone 4.

SPECIAL PLANTS

Hosta or **plantain lily** (*Hosta* species). This is a useful perennial that will thrive and cover the ground where few other plants will grow. It can compete successfully with tree roots and will grow in moist soil and in full shade. It can also take full sun. There are many species and a wide range of foliage colors from a variegated ivory and green to apple-green and frosty blue. Some, such as *H. lancifolia*, are delicate in character, while many others have bold broad leaves. *H. plantaginea*, with leaves to 2½ feet long, is a good one to plant near a sitting area, the better to enjoy its wonderfully fragrant white flowers in late summer. *H. sieboldiana* also has broad leaves to 2 feet tall. Flowers are white, lavender, or blue and are carried on upright stems above the clustered foliage. Zone 5.

Ivy, English (*Hedera helix*). The name is familiar, perhaps too familiar, and may conjure up the image of dull-green beds in neglected public places. There are, however, many interesting forms, such as the variety 'Shamrock' with handsome glossy leaves, 'Manda's Crested' with leaves that have ruffled edges, and 'Needlepoint' with tiny star-shaped leaves. These all make interesting and attractive low-growing covers. Zone 5.

In warm climates (Zone 7), *H. canariensis* with 6-inch leaves and *H. colchica* or Corsican ivy (Zone 6) with enormous dark-green leaves to 10 inches long perform admirably. In cold climates (Zone 5) *H. h. baltica* is an excellent choice.

Ivies will take sun or partial shade and, if given good drainage, are not demanding. If sheared back every year or so, they will branch out and become more compact. All are evergreen.

Juniper (*Juniperus* species). When seen on its native seashore in Japan, juniper literally smothers the sand dunes in spite of the shallow topsoil, harsh winds, and salt spray. Little wonder, then, that these plants are widely used in conditions where few others will survive.

J. procumbens, with iridescent steel-blue foliage that arches upward as high as 2 feet, is best for large areas through Zone 5. On the other hand, *J. horizontalis* hugs the ground and is adaptable to smaller areas. The varieties 'Wiltonii' and 'Bar Harbor' lie close to the ground and are among the very best of the coniferous evergreen ground covers. Zone 2.

A familiar use of low-growing ground covers is in a massed planting. This plant is sweet woodruff, which grows in both sun or shade, as under a tree.

Lily turf *(Liriope spicata)*. The small green straplike evergreen leaves are about 6 inches tall. There is also a variegated type with yellow and green leaves of about the same size. Both are attractive the year round, and in spring the spikes of purple florets add a welcome dividend. Zone 4.

Pachysandra *(Pachysandra terminalis)*. This most popular of all ground covers has won its place fairly. It is a dependable, easy-to-plant, fast-spreading evergreen that grows to about a foot high. It should not be used in sunny locations where other plants will do much better. In the shade it does beautifully if watered thoroughly during dry spells and fed every two years or so with a soluble fertilizer. Set the plants about 6 inches apart in well-drained soil and within two or three years they will make a solid carpet of deep green. Zone 4.

Periwinkle *(Vinca minor)*. This evergreen grows well in most parts of the country. However, it cannot take the extreme heat of Arizona, the California desert, and Florida, on the one hand; or, on the other, the cold of the northernmost tier of states, except for the Pacific Northwest. Keep it contained lest it become a pest. To create a dense mat, the best thing is to apply a complete fertilizer and cut the mat back as required.

The blue flowers in spring are attractive and are even more so on the variety 'Bowles'. The white-flower form 'Miss Jekyl's White' is attractive, but the familiar blue adds a special quality to the spring garden at the edge of a woods, tumbling down a bank or carpeting an area where daffodils will arise with their strong, contrasting accents of color. Zone 4.

St.-John's-wort *(Hypericum calycinum)*. This 1-foot shrub spreads rapidly on underground stems, and plants spaced at 2-foot intervals will fill in to make a solid cover in two or three years. Unlike many ground covers, this one offers a good display of flower color. From mid to late summer, the 3-inch yellow blossoms spread a delightful carpet of sunshine. It blooms in sun or shade and does best in soil with good drainage, although it is trouble-free in almost any garden situation. Evergreen. Zone 6.

Sweet woodruff *(Asperula odorata)*. The lush growth of the foliage and its uniform height of about 6 inches make this decidu-

Here a ground cover is grown in small planting pockets—but this plant and any of the others we describe can also be used on flat surfaces or slight rises.

ous perennial a favored ground cover for seasonal use. The small fragrant white flowers rise a few inches above the foliage in May. It is the tender new foliage of this plant that is traditionally used in Germany to infuse May wine with its delicate distinctive taste. Zone 4.

Hedges

There are two schools of thought about hedges. Both can be expressed in the same garden—but not, however, in the same hedge. The horticultural purist maintains that plants should not be clipped to create predetermined shapes. On the other hand, many landscape designers believe that plants should be used to serve the needs of man, and if this includes clipping a row of plants into a rectangular shape with square corners, so be it.

Thus it is that we see severely clipped formal hedges, informal hedges that are lightly pruned to an irregular outline, and natural hedges that are simply a row of closely spaced plants. They all have a role to play in the garden, and candidates for each kind are included in the following list of time-tested hedge plants.

Hedges can be used to conceal, to entice, or to serve as a frame around a thing of beauty. Sizes range widely, from a 6-inch hedge of santolina around an herb border, to a holly-lined path leading to a piece of sculpture, to a 12-foot hemlock hedge.

Acacia (Acacia longifolia). This evergreen, a favorite in the warmest climates of California, makes a hedge 10 to 15 feet tall. If young plants are set 4 to 5 feet apart, the row will fill out within three or four years. While acacia will tolerate poor soil and will even survive in salt air, it will perform more satisfactorily if grown in good garden soil and given an occasional light feeding. Use 1 pound of 10-10-10 fertilizer for every 10 feet of hedge. In late winter, the bright-yellow flowers on spikes about 3 inches long literally light up the plant. Hardy through Zone 10.

Barberry, Japanese (Berberis thunbergii). There are places in many gardens where a barrier is appropriate to keep traffic off a lawn or along a property line to prevent trespassing. There are few more effective plants for this purpose than the barberries. Closely knit branches armed with stiff, sharp thorns make a hedge of this plant impenetrable by man or dog. The small oval bronze-colored leaves, which drop in the fall, are a good background for the long-lasting bright-red berries. Barberry is far from formal in character, and requires no

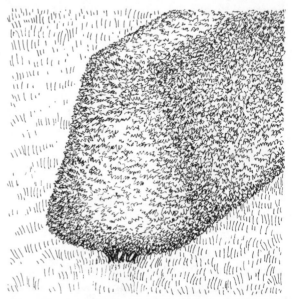

Hedges should be pruned to make their tops narrower than their bottoms, so that the top will not shade out the bottom and create a bare, leggy look.

more than a light clipping once a year to keep it looking good. Hardy through Zone 5.

Beech, European *(Fagus sylvatica).* A row of young beech trees set 5 feet apart, and then pruned when they reach the height and width you want, makes a handsome deciduous hedge. Zone 5.

Boxwood, English *(Buxus sempervirens).* This has become one of the most popular of all hedging plants. Noted for its fine-textured foliage and flowing form when left unclipped, it is so attractive that many gardeners plant it even where it is only marginally hardy. If it is grown north of Zone 7, it needs special winter protection such as an anti-desiccant spray or a protective framework covered with burlap.

The dwarf form *B. s. suffruticosa* is equally attractive and is hardy through Zone 7. *B. koriensis,* although stiffer in form, also has lovely foliage and is hardy enough to survive the winters in Zone 6.

Hemlock *(Tsuga canadensis).* This long-lived forest tree grows to 60 feet tall, but it can also be pruned as a 4-foot hedge without losing the character of its soft-textured evergreen foliage.

No other plant comes to mind that offers such a useful range of sizes for a hedge. It does best in cool climates through Zone 4. However, in the warm areas of Zones 7 and 8, *T. caroliniana* is the preferred species. Where the weather is hot and dry, hemlocks are susceptible to red spider. You can discourage this pest by spraying water into the hedge on hot days.

Set the plants 5 to 6 feet apart and prune them as they grow. If heavy pruning is required—for example, to reduce the size of

an established hedge—it should be done in late fall or winter. To encourage fast growth, particularly when the plants are young, apply a complete fertilizer to the top of the root area, rake it lightly, and water it in. Put on about 2 pounds of a 10-10-10 fertilizer per 25 feet of hedge.

Lantana *(Lantana camara).* This showy plant makes a remarkably decorative hedge for the Southern garden. The flat whorls of yellow-to-orange flowers almost cover the foliage, and it literally blooms the year round. Flower production is encouraged by light trimming, which is also helpful in shaping what otherwise becomes a loose lanky shrub. As a hedge it is best when kept to a height of 2 to 4 feet. It is dependably hardy only in Zone 10.

Oleander *(Nerium oleander).* This is a plant with recognized drawbacks, but it is still popular because of its attractive foliage and large, colorful flowers. The plant is susceptible to scale and mealy bug, and these pests must be controlled in order to assure successful growth. This is not difficult; simply spray with a miscible oil in the spring for scale and apply malathion, according to the directions on the label, for the mealy bug. Once these pests are eliminated, you will have a lovely plant with long, leathery evergreen leaves and flower clusters at the end of each stem.

Oleanders are available with either white, pink, or red flowers. The blooming period extends over two or three months in winter to make a most attractive hedge. Oleanders will reach heights of 10 to 15 feet. They are easily pruned, however, to keep them as low as 4 to 6 feet. Hardy to the southern part of Zone 7.

SPECIAL PLANTS

Privet *(Ligustrum vulgare)*. In many parts of the country, this is probably the best known of all deciduous hedge plants. There is good reason for its popularity. It has attractive light-green foliage, is inexpensive, grows fast, and takes well to pruning to any shape, and when in leaf it will provide complete concealment from 3 to 12 feet in height. It is essentially pest-free and hardy in all zones.

Yaupon holly *(Ilex vomitoria)*. The compact habit of growth and the abundance of red berries that persist all winter long make this a favorite hedge plant. An annual pruning encourages the development of new shoots. It becomes dense enough to discourage intruders and ultimately reaches a height of 10 to 15 feet. It is ideal to use for screening or enclosure. *I. v. nana* is a dwarf form that makes a beautiful 3-foot hedge. Hardy from Zone 10 to the southern part of Zone 7.

Vines

Vining plants can be used to soften or conceal an architectural feature, or to accentuate and dramatize it. They are ideal for screening out an unwanted view, and they can even meet the ultimate landscaping challenge of beautifying a chain-link fence.

Some vines, such as silver-lace vine *(Polygonum aubertii)*, are rampant growers and should be used only where large areas are to be covered. If planted in limited space they have to be continually cut back to keep them in place. The wisteria is another that requires a large area, and it also develops woody growth so strong that it can lift the roof of a porch right off its supports.

Some vines attach themselves with twining stems. These will grow on open fences or trellises. Other climbing vines attach themselves to a flat surface with clinging pads or aerial rootlets. Another category includes those plants with long stems that must be attached to a support with string or plastic-covered wire.

The versatility and beauty that vines can bring to a garden puts them near the top of our list of indispensable plants.

Actinidia *(Actinidia kolomikta)*. Trained on a south-facing wall, this vine will grow to 15 feet high and produce an outstanding display of its interesting tricolored foliage in shades of green, pink, and off-white. The female plant produces small green fruit in

The closely spaced flowers of this clematis can cover an entire mature plant when in bloom. Notice the unusual starlike arrangement of the stamens.

early fall, if a male plant is nearby to provide fertilization. But even without berries, this deciduous vine is an excellent plant. For larger and edible fruit, high-climbing *A. arguta* is superior. Actinidia is not widely available, but is well worth seeking out. Hardy to Zone 4.

Allamanda *(Allamanda cathartica)*. The butter-yellow trumpet-shaped flowers, set off by the shiny green foliage, effectively brighten many a wall in Southern gardens. Allamanda is an evergreen that flourishes the year round and blooms for months at a time. It does best growing vertically rather than horizontally overhead. The vining stems will not damage the walls of a house. They can even be taken off their supports and laid down to allow for periodic painting of walls or window trim. Evergreen except during cool spells. Hardy to Zone 10.

Clematis *(Clematis montana rubens)*. Having grown this species for 30 years without giving it more than a few hours of attention in return for its annual explosion of flowers, we rank it high on this list of favorite vines. It can be grown on almost any support where it will get at least a half-day of sunshine. If planted where it can be allowed to grow freely, it will take on a soft billowy form. But if necessary, in limited space, it can be pruned as hard as required to keep it in bounds. Clematis is deciduous, and in spring the new foliage will be covered with rose-to-red flowers up to 3 inches across.

C. *montana* has white flowers. *C. lanuginosa candida* is also white with larger flowers but does not respond well to pruning. All the clematises have seed pods that look like powderpuffs and are a feature in themselves. There are many hybrid clematises, both early- and late-flowering, that are available in shades of red, blue, and pink. The early ones bloom in late spring, the later ones in early summer. Hardy to Zone 5.

Dutchman's-pipe *(Aristolochia durior)*. This fast-growing, undemanding, twining deciduous vine has become a traditional favorite for shading the large wraparound porches of old houses in the Northeast. The gray-green heart-shaped leaves are as large as 8 inches across, and the lush growth all but obscures the interesting flowers. They are, however, worth looking for. They are purple-brown, about 3 inches long, and shaped just like the pipes smoked by the sturdy burghers in the paintings of the old Dutch masters. To keep the vine within bounds, prune after the leaves fall. It twines tightly to its support and must be cut away if painting is required. Hardy to Zone 5.

Firethorn *(Pyracantha coccinea lalandii)*. There are a number of firethorns, but this variety is the strongest-growing and produces an outstanding crop of orange-red berries. There are also other varieties with larger berries that are more red than orange. The attractive small white flowers cover the thorny stems in late spring and are followed by the berries that will stay on until taken by the birds.

Firethorn is an evergreen with a clambering habit of growth and can be easily trained on a stone wall, along a fence, or on the wall of a house. It is widely used on chimneys and other brick walls.

If allowed to grow freely, it will reach a height of 15 feet, but it can easily be kept to smaller size, and can be pruned as an informal espalier. Be careful when pruning; the

SPECIAL PLANTS

thorns are prolific and needle-sharp.

Firethorn needs sun to produce flowers and berries and is, therefore, not at its best on a north-facing wall, although it will grow there. Hardy to Zone 6.

Grape (*Vitis* species). These revered plants of the genus *Vitis* and the word "vine" are virtually synonymous. If you have ever sat under a grape arbor in the heat of summer and enjoyed the cooling shade, the wonderful aroma, and perhaps a taste of the fresh-picked fruit, you know why it has attained the status of a classic.

If you want at least some fruit, grapes must be grown in full sun and some pruning is required. You can learn which varieties are best for your climate and what each requires by checking with the agricultural extension service agent in your county seat. If you want grapes of reasonable quality and quantity, you will have to follow a demanding regimen of pruning and spraying; as many as six applications of spray may be necessary.

Hydrangea, climbing (*Hydrangea petiolaris*). Among the most useful of all vines, the climbing hydrangea supports itself with aerial rootlets and will do well in any exposure, even upon a north-facing wall. A large mature specimen may develop heavy stems that may require tying to hold them on a vertical surface. This is not a difficult chore, but, if you prefer, these hanging branches can be cut off. The flat white flowers appear in early summer. The apple-green leaves are heart-shaped and drop in the fall. Hardy to Zone 6.

Jasmine, winter (*Jasminum nudiflorum*). While this is essentially a clambering plant that usually spreads on the ground, if tied up and pruned it can be grown on a vertical support. If allowed to grow freely it will spread to 10 feet or more. The bright-yellow flowers that bloom from midwinter to early spring appear before the small sparse foliage. The plant thrives in almost any kind of soil, and the flowers will bloom in sun or shade. Hardy to Zone 6.

Silver-lace vine (*Polygonum aubertii*). When in full bloom in the summer, this lovely deciduous vine becomes a white cloud of minute flowers that totally obscure the foliage. A vigorous climber, it can be trained on supporting wires to make an excellent living fence in the summertime. If necessary, it can be cut back vigorously in winter to keep it in bounds. It has the added advantage of being virtually impervious to insects and disease. Hardy to Zone 5.

Wisteria (*Wisteria sinensis*). Perhaps the most familiar of the flowering vines, wisteria is also one of the most vigorous. If it is grown on the wall of a shingle house, it can literally pull the wall apart within a few years. It can even crush a hollow wooden porch column. Thus, it should be grown on a specially made framework. Iron pipe, which is easy to work with and almost indestructible, is the most practical support.

The long pendant racemes of white, lavender, or purple bloom for two weeks in the spring and are among the most magnificent flowers of any plant.

To keep the vine under control, prune the new rampant growth back to about 8 inches from main stems during the summer. After the leaves have dropped in the fall, shorten those same stems still more, leaving only two or three buds. This will en-

Roses are usually grown in a bed of their own, but they can also be effectively combined with other flowers, particularly those that match their growing season with the early-summer and early-fall range of the rose.

courage the formation of flower buds and help to produce more glorious blooms the following spring. Keep in mind that full sun is essential for a good show of flowers. In spite of this need, wisteria does not do well in areas of extreme heat. Hardy to Zone 6. Farther north, in Zone 5, *W. floribunda* will bloom a little more dependably, although the flowers are smaller.

Roses

When a flower reaches such a state of veneration that song, poems, and festivals are created in its name, public gardens are devoted to it, and societies are dedicated to its study, there are bound to be strong opinions on the subject. So it is with the rose.

In their understandable enthusiasm for the beauty of the flower, rose growers are apt to become so deeply involved with the plant that they sincerely believe it to be unique and not responsive to the same culture as other genera.

Roses, however, share with most other plants the need for an appropriate growing medium for the roots, air movement around the foliage, sufficient nutrients and moisture to maintain steady development during the growing season, and constant surveillance for insects and disease. The same can be said for growing potatoes, geraniums, or fir trees.

Roses do require pruning and a few other special attentions. Although not complicated, the principles of their care must be clearly understood in order to produce the glorious flowers that make this plant such a worthwhile garden subject.

Planting roses

Roses sold with their roots in containers can be planted whenever the soil can be dug. Bare-root roses, of course, are available only in the dormant season, from late fall until early spring. In climates where the ground freezes, it is safest to plant in the spring after all danger of frost is past. In warm climates they can be planted in either spring or fall. Fall planting is preferred, because it allows more time for the roots to develop before the flowering season.

Roses grow best in full sun, but in warm climates they do quite well with as little as 6 hours of sunlight. They are adaptable to a variety of soils, but basically the soil must be sufficiently water-retentive to hold moisture in the root area while the plant takes it up and, at the same time, the drainage must be good enough to allow the entry of air to supply the oxygen necessary for root growth. If the soil is too sandy and the water runs right through, you have to irrigate more often than is practical. If it contains too much clay, the water does not penetrate easily; and when the ground is soaked, it takes too long to dry out enough to let in the air. If there is any question about drainage, it should be tested. Dig a hole a foot deep in the area where you intend to plant and fill it with water. If it takes more than an hour to empty, the drainage should be improved. For details on this process see chapter 3.

The best pH for roses is neutral (7.0) to slightly acid (6.5).

Plant roses as soon as possible after you get them. If they are in containers, put them in a shaded place until they can be planted and make sure that the root ball doesn't dry out. Remove containers before planting. If they are bare-root plants, put the roots in a bucket of water as soon as you get them and keep them there until the planting holes are ready.

Plan to set roses about 2 feet apart in cool climates, and 3 feet apart in Zones 8 and 9, where it is warmer and the plants are likely to grow larger.

Dig the planting hole about 18 inches deep and 18 inches wide. Mix a shovelful of peat moss or compost with the soil that has been removed, and do the same with the soil in the bottom of the hole. Mix a handful of bone meal into the root area to provide additional phosphorus, which stimulates root growth.

Before putting the plant in place, make a mound of soil in the center of the hole of sufficient height to position the union of the roots and stem just above the level of the soil when the roots have been watered in and the soil firmed down.

If, after soaking the root area, the plant sinks down so the bud union is below the level of the soil, lift the plant and put more soil under the roots. This is important. Hybrid roses are grafted to the rootstock of a hardy species, and if the bud union is buried, the growth of the rootstock with its inferior foliage and flowers may develop and crowd out the hybrid that was selected for its superior form and flowers. The union is an obviously swollen area at the base of the stem. If spindly growth develops from the wood below the union, these are suckers that should be cut off.

A plant sustains some loss of feeder roots when it is transplanted. To bring the roots and top growth into better balance, cut back each cane to about one-third of its length when you set out the plant.

As recommended for other shrubs, it pays to make a basin around the plant just beyond the drip line of the foliage. This will keep the water in the root area.

A 2-to-4-inch mulch in the basin will reduce evaporation and inhibit the growth of weeds. A good mulch is one that readily lets air and water through, will stay in place without blowing away, and is reasonably attractive. A few regional favorites are salt hay, wood chips, bagasse, cocoa hulls, and oak leaves. Don't put the mulch against the base of the plant. Allow an inch or so of space around it for air circulation.

Watering

Water deeply. This means that you should put on enough so you know that the moisture reaches to the full depth of the root area. How long this takes, at a given rate of flow from the hose, depends on the structure of the soil. See chapter 5 for more on this.

Once the root area is thoroughly soaked, do not water again until the top inch or two of soil is dry.

Roses are strong growers and will take up more water in a given time than many other shrubs of the same size.

In hot dry areas, where the foliage will dry before nightfall, you can water the plants from above with a sprinkler. In humid climates it is better to irrigate by soaking the ground and keeping the leaves dry. Wet leaves at night can invite disease. But even in humid climates, the foliage can be hosed off early in the morning on hot days when it will dry before evening. This should be done as needed to wash soot and grime off the foliage.

Where water is alkaline, continued ap-plication can raise the pH of the soil. Check the soil every year or two, and if the pH gets much above neutral, add a light mulch of peat moss, or apply a cupful of acid fertilizer per plant to tip the balance down to the acid side.

Feeding

For an explanation of fertilizers in general and how they work, see chapter 5. Included here are some aspects of feeding that apply specifically to roses.

Most garden centers carry "rose food" that usually has a nitrogen, phosphorus, and potassium content such as 5-10-5.

Don't feed new roses before they recover from the shock of planting and the root system is well established. This may take two or three months of active growth.

The best time to feed established plants is early in the spring so that the nutrient will be in the root area when the new growth begins.

Water thoroughly a day before putting on dry fertilizer, and water it in when it is applied.

Where freezing is not a problem, it is best to feed the plants after they have finished flowering instead of before. In climates where there is freezing this is inadvisable, because the fertilizer can force tender new growth susceptible to winter damage.

Apply dry fertilizer in the amounts recommended on the package or a little less. Roses are particularly sensitive to overfeeding.

Liquid fertilizer sprayed on the foliage acts almost immediately, and is a useful supplement to the dry material. Again, follow instructions on the package.

For best results apply the spray thor-

SPECIAL PLANTS

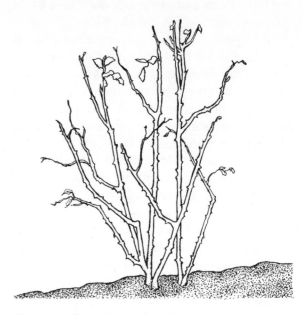

Flowers and foliage will drop from roses at the end of the growing season, leaving long arching branches.

The plant should look like this after the long and weak stems have been pruned.

oughly every two or three weeks, from the time the buds begin to swell until the bush first comes into full flower.

If the spray runs off the foliage, add a quarter of a teaspoon of soap flakes to a gallon of the fertilizer solution. This will help it stick.

Don't apply liquid fertilizer if the temperature is above 90° F., as it can dehydrate the leaves.

Pruning

Roses flower on new wood, and the main purpose of pruning is to encourage the development of this wood each year.

Roses are also pruned to control the outline of the bush, to keep it open on the inside to let in air and light, and to remove weak and dead canes.

Pruning is done as soon as the plant is dormant in late fall. In warm climates, the end-of-season pruning consists of cutting back the wood of the current year by about one-third. This is usually done in late winter just as the buds begin to swell.

Cutting flowers to use in the house is a form of pruning, and long stems should be taken only from vigorous plants. When faded flowers are cut, you should also remove inward-facing shoots to help keep the plant open.

Controlling pests and diseases

A weekly spray of an all-purpose control mixture, as recommended in chapter 18, will keep insects and disease at a minimum. But if specific problems do appear, the following controls may be called for.

Black spot. After the spots appear, the leaves usually turn yellow and fall off. To prevent this problem, use alternate sprayings of Benlate and Phaltan every 10 to 15

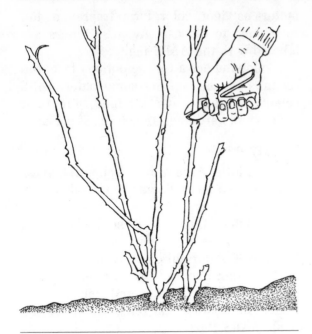

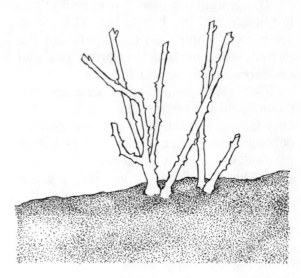

Now you prune to eliminate weak and crossing branches, and to establish a sturdy structure for future growth.

The final pruning—in the fall or early the following spring. Flowers will be borne on the new wood.

days starting in spring and continuing through the growing season.

Mildew. This may appear in humid weather. It can be controlled by spraying with Benlate or another specific control.

Insects. There are granular as well as liquid foliar systemic controls that are easy to use. Systemics have the advantage of affecting only insects that attack the plant. If mites are detected, spray with a miticide such as Kelthane.

Types of roses

The hybrid teas are the most popular of all roses. Their long-stemmed flowers, usually produced one to a stem, are noted for their shapely upright form. The plants, too, are upright and rather slender in outline.

Floribunda roses have smaller flowers than the hybrid teas but they are borne in clusters and practically cover the bush with

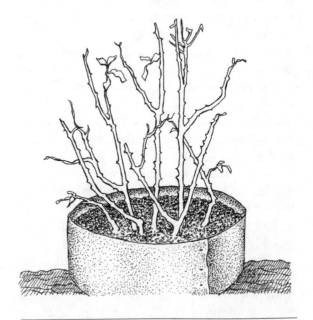

In very cold climates the buds and canes can be killed by freezing. A 6-inch tarpaper collar filled with soil or peat moss will insulate the plant and ensure the survival of sound wood and viable buds for the following season.

bloom. The plants are shorter and fuller in form than the hybrid teas.

The grandiflora rose is a hybrid of the floribunda and the hybrid tea. The plants are usually larger than the latter, and the flowers are larger than the floribundas' and are carried in showy clusters.

The "old-fashioned" rose species offer a number of interesting choices. Among the best known are the gallica (Rosa gallica), cabbage rose (R. centifolia), damask rose (R. damascena), and China rose (R. chinensis). The multiflora is another popular species.

There are some low-growing roses that can be used for ground covers, and, of course, there are climbers that can be trained on a fence or trellis.

Some roses are grafted on a 3-to-4-foot single upright trunk. These tree roses can be used as dramatic accents. At the opposite end of the spectrum are miniature roses no more than 1 foot high.

As for named varieties, suffice it to say that there are hundreds of them, and they represent almost every color imaginable. A specialist's catalog, or a visit to a large nursery, will provide many more choices than you can possibly find room for in your garden.

When sold bare-root, roses come in grades 1, 1½, and 2. The grades relate to the number and size of the canes. It is best to buy grade 1, because these will most quickly become the strongest plants.

You should get whatever kind and color of rose you want, but a guide that many gardeners consider useful is the All-America Rose Selections. Each year a number of varieties are tested under carefully controlled conditions in gardens all across the United States. Plants are scored for such factors as vigor, color, form, fragrance, and resistance to disease. Award winners are labeled with the AARS tag.

Following are a few selections from the recent past, as well as some older AARS selections that have attained, for their beauty and hardiness, the status of classics.

HYBRID TEAS

'Charlotte Armstrong'. Deep-pink buds develop into large flowers on a tall bushy plant. AARS 1941.

'Christian Dior'. Deep-red buds turn a lighter color as they open and then hold a true red. Tall upright plant. AARS 1962.

'Chrysler Imperial'. Dark-crimson flowers with velvety texture and delicate perfume. One of the best reds. Medium-sized bush. AARS 1953.

'Crimson Glory'. Large dark-crimson flowers, heavily perfumed. Strong low plant.

'Double Delight'. Cream and red. Unlike most bicolor roses, this one changes continuously. Creamy-white buds develop bright-red edges, and the petals turn red as the rose fades. Flowers on strong stems are 5 to 6 inches across with a spicy fragrance. AARS 1977.

'Forty Niner'. Attractive red-yellow buds open to become interesting bicolored flowers. The predominant color, on the outside of the buds, is yellow. Plant is medium height. AARS 1949.

'Garden Party'. Ivory color with pink along the petal edges which becomes darker as the buds open. Erect flowers on stems of medium height. AARS 1960.

'Helen Traubel'. Very full salmon-colored flowers with thin stems are borne prolifically on a tall, vigorous bush. AARS 1952.

'John F. Kennedy'. White flowers sometimes have a green cast. Tall upright stems. At its best in Zone 7 and south.

'Kings Ransom'. Deep-yellow color does not fade as the buds open to become large full flowers. Medium height. AARS 1962.

'Lowell Thomas'. Yellow. A longtime favorite as the date of its award indicates. Medium-sized bush. AARS 1944.

'Matterhorn'. The buds are yellow, but as they open they turn to an ivory color. The plant is so tall and vigorous that it is best used as a hedge or in the background of a large flower border. AARS 1966.

'McGredy's Yellow'. Light-yellow. Developed for the cool weather of England and Ireland, it does best in Zones 5 and 6. The bronze-colored foliage and red thorns on erect stems are distinctive. Medium-sized bush.

'Mrs. Sam McGredy'. Copper-and-salmon bicolor. A striking tall bush with foliage that turns from a bronze hue to strong green. Buds show copper and salmon tones as they begin to turn, then reveal pale-apricot shades on the inside as the petals reflex.

'Oklahoma'. Dark-red. Buds, almost black in color, open as large full flowers that retain a deep velvet-red. A tall plant with outstanding fragrance.

'Peace'. Yellow-pink. Yellow buds tinged with pink do not distinguish themselves until almost fully open. But as the flowers develop their soft shades of yellow to pink they reveal why this is one of the most popular of all roses. A strong vigorous bush of medium height. AARS 1946.

'Pink Peace'. Rose-pink. A large-flowered fragrant rose borne on tall vigorous canes. The deep-pink color is held until the flower fades at maturity.

'Sterling Silver'. Lavender. The surface

Here are the characteristics that set the flowers of the hybrid teas apart from other roses, particularly the long shapely bud, undulating petals, and graceful open flower. This one is 'Color Magic', an AARS winner for 1978 in varied tones of pink.

texture of the petals creates a silvery-lavender effect unlike the color of any other rose. Medium height.

'Sutter's Gold'. Yellow-orange. As the long buds open, they reveal a showy combination of these colors. A tall plant with remarkably strong fragrance.

'Swarthmore'. Bright-pink. Starting with a deeper color, the long buds become pale pink as they open. Flowers hold up well, especially in cool weather. A prolific bloomer on a tall bush.

'Tiffany'. Pink. The beautifully formed fragrant flowers are borne on an upright bush. Susceptible to fungus, it should have a well-ventilated location. Does best in Zone 7 or south. AARS 1955.

SPECIAL PLANTS

The individual flowers of the grandifloras are not so large as those of the hybrid teas, but they cluster on the stem and tend to cover the plant more fully.

'Tropicana'. The bright orange-scarlet flowers of this distinctive bicolor are considered by some to be garish. Flowers are often borne in clusters on tall stems.

FLORIBUNDAS

'Angel Face'. Deep-lavender flowers with ruffled petals have a rich fragrance. It is low-growing, which makes it useful for foreground planting. AARS 1969.

'Betty Prior'. Flowers are a deep bright pink on the outside of the petals and a soft silvery pink on the inside. A very prolific bloomer, this tall (4 to 5 feet) floribunda has been a popular variety for many years.

'Fashion'. Buds in clusters open to become 3-inch coral flowers. The delicate color makes it excellent for cutting. A low bush with a spreading habit of growth. AARS 1950.

'First Edition'. Newest of the coral-colored prizewinners. Clusters of 2½-inch flowers literally cover the plant all through the flowering season. In the fall, the coral color becomes more intense. Has a low compact habit of growth. AARS 1977.

'Gene Boerner'. Has a warm pink color and sweet fragrance. Free-flowering on a rather tall bush. An outstanding rose named for one of this country's great rose hybridizers. AARS 1969.

'Ivory Fashion'. Ivory. The flowers, to 4 inches across, open so fully that the yellow stamens become part of their beauty. Good for cutting; keeps well indoors. Medium height.

'Sarabande'. Buds open quickly and unfold fully, revealing a brilliant red flower with a center of showy yellow stamens. Prolific bloomer on a tall bush. AARS 1960.

'Saratoga'. White. Large heavily petaled flowers have a pleasant fragrance. Plant is tall for a floribunda. AARS 1964.

GRANDIFLORAS

'Comanche'. Large flowers of brilliant red are carried on branches clothed with bronze-green foliage. Medium height with a spreading habit of growth. AARS 1969.

'John S. Armstrong'. Dark red. Most roses this color tend to turn purple or blue as they age. This one retains its purity of color all through the blooming season. Well-formed medium-sized flowers are borne on a tall bush. AARS 1962.

'Queen Elizabeth'. Produces quantities of large clear-pink flowers that stay on the bush in good condition for a long time. A tall plant with strong canes. AARS 1955.

'Sundowner'. Flowers of glowing orange are suffused with salmon as they open fully. The tall plant provides long stems for cutting, and the spicy fragrance is outstanding. Foliage is moss-green with tints of copper color. AARS 1979.

SHRUB ROSES

'Austrian Copper'. A rose of great beauty dating back to the 16th century. The small single flowers are bicolored with orange on the top of the petals and gold on the bottom. Blooms in spring on a 6-foot bush with attractive small leaves.

'Harrison's Yellow'. This thorny 6-foot yellow rose blooms profusely with hundreds of small double flowers set off against delicately cut foliage. Like many of the shrub varieties it originated in the early 1800s.

'Prairie Fire'. Has clusters of bright-red double flowers on a vigorous plant to about 6 feet tall. Introduced in 1960, it is relatively new for a shrub rose.

'Sparrieshoop'. Clusters of delicate single pink flowers bloom continuously for most of the summer and fall. This is a useful shrub rose that can also be grown as a climber.

CLIMBING ROSES

'Blaze'. This scarlet climber is a well-established favorite because of its vigorous habit and superabundance of rich-red flower clusters. It often blooms two or three times during the season.

'Paul's Scarlet'. The name tells most of the story, except that it is a vigorous and dependable plant. It grows to 10 feet tall and the clarity of its brilliant red color is usually retained to the very end of its period of bloom.

Hybrid tea-rose climbers. Many hybrid tea roses are available as climbers as well as in bush form. The following, which are some of the best, have already been de-scribed as tea roses: 'Charlotte Armstrong', 'Chrysler Imperial', 'Crimson Glory', 'Mrs. Sam McGredy', 'Peace', 'Tiffany', and 'Tropicana'.

Rhododendrons and Azaleas

Among the thousands of genera of plants in cultivation, there are a few that have established themselves as aristocrats of the garden world. There are no clear-cut criteria, but the distinction seems to depend considerably upon such qualities as good looks, noble bearing, and dependable performance under appropriate conditions. Price is a factor too. The aristocrats are seldom inexpensive.

Not every gardener will agree that a particular plant deserves to be called an aristocrat. But one thing is certain: once the title is bestowed, it is hereditary. Some of the established members of this select company are the weeping hemlock, English boxwood, tree peony, and tuberous begonia.

The rhododendrons, and some of the azaleas, have also earned their rightful place in this distinguished company. Their inclusion is mostly attributed to their stately structure, attractive foliage, and elegant flowers. The total impact of a well-grown rhododendron of a choice, named variety in full bloom must be experienced to be believed. There is nothing in the garden at that season of midspring that can compare to it.

Their foliage alone is so neat and attractive that these evergreens would be well worth growing even if they did not flower.

Botanically, the rhododendrons and azaleas are all classified as the genus *Rhododendron*. But in garden use and in the

Many species of rhododendron are virtually treelike in their native habitat. Given the proper growing conditions, they can become the dominant feature in a garden.

nursery trade, they are clearly separate. Most of the large azaleas are deciduous and most of the small ones evergreen. The flowers of the azaleas are funnel-shaped, and those of the rhododendron are more bowl-shaped or bell-like.

The sizes within the genus *Rhododendron* range from creeping shrubs less than a foot high to immense trees with leaves more than a foot long. And in the nursery trade there are hundreds of varieties and species to choose from.

They all require a well-drained acid soil with a pH of 5 to 6.5, and a high percentage of humus. (For more on the acid-alkaline balance, see chapter 3.) A mixture of half loam and half peat moss will provide the aeration and the water retention necessary for the fibrous root system. The roots are

close to the surface. Don't use a hoe around the base of rhododendrons or azaleas. If weeds appear, pull them by hand.

These plants all do best in light shade, but they do need some sun in order to set flowers. Too much sun, however, will burn the leaves. The sunnier the site, the deeper the mulch should be to conserve moisture and keep the soil in the root area cool. The best mulch is a compost of oak leaves. But peat moss mixed with compost is also good.

Rhododendrons respond particularly well to high humidity and should not only be watered deeply but hosed down two or three times a week with a fine spray.

After the spring flowers have faded, it is a good idea to pick them off the plant. The energy that would normally go into the setting of seed is thus diverted back into the plant and will help produce more and larger flowers the following year.

Rhododendrons and azaleas are not particularly heavy feeders. They will do nicely if fed every year or two with cottonseed meal or a proprietary fertilizer made specifically for acid-loving plants.

Because their acid-soil requirements are so specific, be sure to test the soil where you plan to set them out. Even where the soil is generally acid, there can be variations. Sometimes when a house is built, the excess plaster and cement are buried in a trench along the outside walls. This builds up an alkaline soil condition in which rhododendrons will not grow. The usual symptom of alkaline soil is a yellowing of the leaves.

Recommended rhododendrons

The rhododendrons adaptable to the widest range of climates in this country are those that are native here. *Rhododendron maxi-*

mum, *R. catawbiense*, and *R. carolinianum* are native to the Southeast and will survive as far north as Zone 4. These latter two have attractive lavender flowers. *R. c. album*, a native of North Carolina, has white flowers that show up well in shady places.

The most impressive rhododendrons are the hybrids. They have been bred and cross-bred for generations to improve the purity of the flower color, the substance of the petals, the size of the flowers, and the strength of the truss that supports the flowers.

The hybrids are often less hardy than the native American species, and they do best where the climate is relatively mild and where there is considerable rainfall and high humidity.

They are at their best in the Pacific Northwest. They also do very well on the eastern shore of Maryland, along the Appalachian highlands, and in such relatively mild areas as the environs of Long Island Sound.

This is not to say that the hardier hybrids cannot be grown in other regions. Check with an established local nurseryman. He will know which species and varieties will do well in your climate. When you begin shopping in the nurseries and looking at the catalogs of rhododendron specialists, you will discover the wide range of choices you have in size, form, and color.

Following are a few of the most readily available varieties. They are listed according to the hardiness of the plants. In general, plants can withstand 10° to 15° F. more cold than the buds. If the buds are killed you lose only the next year's bloom. The plant will survive and flower in subsequent years.

PLANTS HARDY THROUGH ZONE 5 (TO –20° F.)

Red: 'America', 'Nova Zembla'.

Pink: 'Roseum Pink', 'Katherine Dalton' (the last is hardy to –25° F., and this puts it safely in the milder regions of Zone 4).

White: 'Album Elegans', 'Catawbiense Album'.

Mauve: 'Catawbiense Boursault', 'Catawbiense Grandiflorum', 'Roseum Elegans'. Purple-blue: 'Purpureum Elegans'.

Purple: 'P. J. Mezitt', a smaller plant than the others on this list, but handsome, floriferous, and hardy through Zone 4, to 30° below zero; a more compact plant of about the same color and almost as hardy is 'Purple Imp'.

PLANTS HARDY THROUGH ZONE 6 (TO –10° F.)

Red: 'Dr. Rutgers', 'Professor Bettex', 'Vivacious'.

Pink: 'Scintillation', 'John Wister', 'English Roseum'.

White: 'Gomer Waterer', 'Mrs. J. G. Millais', 'Catawbiense Album', 'Boule de Neige'.

Lavender: 'Blue Peter', 'A. Bedford'.

Purple: 'Purple Splendor'.

Yellow: 'Goldworth Yellow'.

Recommended azaleas

There can be some variation in flower color and size from plant to plant. It is a good idea to see the plants in bloom before you buy. This is particularly true of the azaleas.

Among the evergreen azaleas, most of which are under 5 feet tall, you will see the following popular types.

The Gable hybrids are the hardiest of the evergreens. Almost any of these can be grown where the temperature does not go below –15° F., such as the warmer parts of

Zone 5. Some of these such as the salmon-colored 'Louise Gable' and the 'Rosebud', a double-flowered pink, will survive at 25° below zero.

The Kurumes are the next hardiest. They are reasonably safe at 0° F., which would be in the colder parts of Zone 7. They bloom heavily and their foliage is more dense than that of the Gables. The hardiest is the red 'Hino Crimson', which will survive as much as 20° more cold than the other Kurumes.

The Macranthas are fully clothed with leaves, and make a beautiful (though expensive) ground cover.

Glenn Dales, slightly less hardy, are the largest of the evergreens.

The Southern Indians with their glowing warm colors are the famous azaleas of the South. Their northern limit is in areas of Zone 8 where the thermometer seldom goes below 20° F.

The Indicas, tenderest of the evergreen types in the nursery trade, are slightly less hardy than the Southern Indians. A single specimen has flowers enough to make an impressive container plant.

The deciduous varieties are the hardiest azaleas and count among their number some of the most beautiful for flower color. Look for such groups as Ghent, Mollis, Knapp Hill, and Exbury. Here you will find an impressive range of colors, from biscuit tones to yellow and orange, none of which are found in the evergreen species.

There are a few in a class by themselves for beauty and landscape value. *Azalea* (actually *Rhododendron*) *schlippenbachii* is a venerable garden aristocrat with delicate pink flowers that appear in early spring well before the foliage. *A. calendulaceum* or flame azalea is a dramatic Southeastern native worth seeking out. *A. nudiflorum* is noted for its pink flowers. *A. occidentale*, a native of the West Coast, has fragrant pink-to-yellow flowers. *A. vaseyi*, the pink shell azalea, is an excellent native of the East Coast that will do well from Zone 5 to Zone 8. This range may be surprising, but it is characteristic of rhododendrons that the ones that can take the most cold can also take the most heat.

Chrysanthemums

Any plant that can bring a fall garden of waning annuals and fading earlier perennials back to the brilliant color of midsummer is certainly worthy of our consideration.

Chrysanthemums (*Chrysanthemum* species) have this attribute and more. They are easy to propagate, bloom dependably, and are susceptible to only a few insects and diseases.

They also have the added appeal of having flower forms and colors in such variety that almost any personal preference can be accommodated.

They perform not only beautifully, but efficiently as well. There are few other plants that will grow from a 4-to-5-inch rooted stem cutting to such a fine showing of colorful flowers in just one season, with so little time and effort.

Start in early spring when you can beg, borrow, or otherwise acquire a few chrysanthemum stem cuttings. The cuttings are taken from a clump that bloomed the previous year soon after the stems have emerged from the soil.

Make the cuttings 4 to 6 inches long, strip the leaves from the lower 2 inches, and shove the bare stem into a pot of coarse sand. As many as 20 cuttings will fit in a

6-inch pot, and if the sand is kept moist the cuttings will have their own roots in two weeks.

When the roots are 2 inches long, the cuttings can be planted in their permanent place in the garden. About a week after planting, remove the growing tip just above the top pair of leaves by pinching out with the fingers. This will cause two new stems to develop. When each of these new stems is about 3 inches long, pinch out their tips in the same way. Within a week there will be still more stems, each multiplying by two. Continue pinching weekly until about the first of July. After each pinching, water

For all their exotic appearance, these spider mums can be grown outdoors with no more attention than is required for any of the other chrysanthemums. They make long-lasting cut flowers.

the plant thoroughly, using a complete soluble fertilizer at the rate recommended on the container.

As the nights get longer, which they do after June 22, the buds will begin to develop. With the arrival of fall a wonderful display of color will be yours, and it will persist until hard frost.

The available colors include yellow, red, orange, pink, rust, and white. If you multiply the colors by the variety of forms, which include pompons, ray flowers, incurved petals, and long spidery petals (to name a few), you will soon realize the variations. There are 15 different flower forms officially designated by the National Chrysanthemum Society.

The easiest to handle are the so-called hardy bush types. Most of these have single pompon, or spoon, flowers.

Over the past 25 years of chrysanthemum hybridization the time of bloom has been made predictable to a remarkable degree. The plants are divided into response groups and will bloom dependably in a given number of weeks (from 6 to 14) after the buds have set.

Those that flower in the late fall (the 12- and 14-week response groups) are of little garden value in Northern states, but are favored in frost-free climates where they can be used to extend late-season bloom.

By using lights and shading devices to control day length, commercial growers produce mums of all kinds on a predetermined schedule the year round.

If you have a greenhouse you might be interested in learning more about this, and can do so by writing to the National Chrysanthemum Society, 394 Central Avenue, Mountainside, N.J. 07092.

If you have a place for chrysanthemums

SPECIAL PLANTS

on your property, it is a good idea to raise them all together in a sunny out-of-the-way spot. Then, when they are ready to flower, you can transplant them into the garden.

They are easy to move. Water them well the day before moving. Dig them carefully and move them in the early evening. Water them as soon as they are replanted and provide shade for a day or two with sheets of dampened newspaper. If it is possible to do the job when the weather is cool and moist, the extra shading will not be needed.

Chrysanthemums may occasionally get a fungus, evidenced by the drying up of the lower leaves. This disease, called fusarium wilt, is caused by the spores of a dustlike fungus on the soil. Clouds of these spores are raised from the surface by splashing water. To avoid this problem, use soil soakers or some other means of watering that will wet the soil without splashing.

At the first sign of damaged leaves it would also be helpful to apply a fungicide (as recommended in chapter 18) at ten-day intervals.

Succulents

Succulents are plants that have the ability to store water in their thick fleshy tissue. There are succulent species in many genera, such as the geranium genus, that we do not think of in this category. Other plants that are widely grown, such as sedum, eche-

Here in Arizona is a lesson for gardeners everywhere. Rather than bringing in exotics that would be difficult or impossible to grow successfully, native cacti and succulents, perfectly suited to the desert environment, are used.

veria, portulaca, and crassula, are more readily recognized as succulents.

The most efficient water-savers of all succulents are the cacti in their many forms. They are native to hot dry climates, and their leaves have become spines that give off very little water by transpiration. In their native environment, where food is usually scarce, the spines also help protect the plants from birds and animals.

Although they developed in the desert, the cacti of the genus *Opuntia* are hardy as far north as Canada. In gardens to the south, in Georgia, Florida, Louisiana, Texas, New Mexico, and California, the temperature range is close to that of most of the areas where cacti are native, and most of them will do very well in the open garden. All succulents, including cactus, are favorite house plants.

Cacti are native to sunny sandy places and therefore need all the sunlight possible and excellent drainage for the roots. The soil should contain from 30% to 50% coarse sand. Water sparingly during the dormant season in winter, and when the growing season starts in spring water once a week. When growth starts, apply liquid fertilizer at half the strength recommended on the container. One application should suffice.

Recommended cacti

The following are some of the most popular kinds of cactus for outdoor gardens in the Southwest. In colder climates, perhaps the best-known cactus is *Opuntia compressa*, a spreading-to-upright form with flowers of soft yellow, and *O. polyacantha*, which is also low-growing but occasionally makes a low mound. Its flowers are bright-yellow flushed with red. All the opuntias have thick, flat, round green pads with scattered needlelike spines. The jointed pads face in different directions and give the plant an unusual jumbled appearance.

Cereus *(Cereus gonacanthus)*. This can become a 10-foot tree, but fortunately the branches are easily lopped off to keep it to any size you want. It starts branching at ground level and produces trunks a foot thick with five or six ribs. The flowers are red with a white throat, and, typical of the cacti, they are stemless and seem to pop right out of the plant in the most unpredictable places. As the flowers mature, they develop into wonderfully sweet fruits.

Echinocactus *(Echinocactus grusonii)*. When full-grown, this cactus becomes a broad cylinder about 3 feet wide and seldom over 4 feet tall. It covers itself with large golden-yellow spines. This tough armor all but conceals the rows of vertical ribs with their bright-green color. On sunny days in March the small yellow flowers pop through the surface on top of the barrel.

Orchid cactus *(Epiphyllum ackermannii)*. This rangy plant, with flattened stems up to 6 feet long, has bright-red funnel-shaped flowers that bloom for several weeks in late winter in Southwestern gardens. Unlike most cactus, this genus has no spines. It is an epiphyte, or air plant, that absorbs nutrients from the atmosphere and also takes up disintegrating organic matter caught in its branches. It will, therefore, grow in soil of low fertility.

Recommended succulents

Euphorbia *(Euphorbia species)*. Some species such as the popular Christmas poinsettia, *E. pulcherrima*, are good garden plants in warm climates. *E. marginata* is grown as an annual for its attractive white bracts. *E. wulfenii* is useful in mild climates as a perennial for its lovely yellow flower clusters on leafy 18-inch stems.

Hen and chickens *(Sempervivum tectorum).* This succulent is popular and frequently used in rock gardens because of its flat spreading habit of growth. The central rosette of succulent leaves (the hen) is surrounded by ever-increasing numbers of smaller plants (the chicks). The plant seldom exceeds 4 inches in height and 6 inches in diameter.

Portulaca *(Portulaca grandiflora).* Here's an annual easily sown from seed that will flourish in the bright sun and is especially suited to a hot dry terrace. The crepe-textured flowers, in a multitude of wonderfully clear colors, literally cover the leaves and the fleshy prostrate stems.

Sedum *(Sedum* species). Several evergreen varieties are grown for their creeping foliage and the added appeal of the many small yellow flowers in midsummer. *S. acre* and *S. sarmentosum* are good in rock gardens, on walls, or wherever a low carpet of color might be useful. *S. dasyphyllum* has gray-green foliage enhanced by pink flowers in midsummer.

Water Plants

One of the great pleasures of gardening is to see plants thrive because they are so obviously growing in a place for which they are perfectly suited. Among the easiest to be sure about in this regard are the plants that grow in and around the water.

Bog plants need boggy situations, and water plants need water. These are reassuringly clear-cut requirements, and the kinds of plants that thrive in these different conditions are so listed.

Many of them are so beautiful that it is worthwhile to introduce water into a garden in order to grow them. And, of course, if you have a pond, pool, or boggy place (where the soil is continually wet) on your property, you will want to grow a few water plants. Some of the best for a variety of situations are listed here.

Plants that grow in the water

Some plants float and need not be rooted in the ground. Just put them in water and they will grow. In cold climates these are usually grown as annuals, and in warm areas they grow wild and have literally blocked rivers and canals. They are not hard to control when grown in pools or small ponds. When too many accumulate in one place they can be scooped up and put on the compost pile.

Azolla caroliniana has attractive moss-like dark-green leaves. It spreads very fast. Water chestnut *(Trapa natans)* has hollow stems that keep the small triangular leaves on the surface. Water hyacinth *(Eichhornia crassipes)* has rounded leaves and lavender flowers with yellow centers. This one has become such a troublesome pest in the warm waters of the South that it cannot be legally shipped across state lines. But it is an attractive plant and easy to control in contained areas.

Marsh plants

The marsh plants, of which there are many, grow in soil that is 4 to 6 inches below the surface of the water. They can be planted at this depth at the edge of a pond, or grown in a deeper pool in pots submerged at this depth. Put a layer of coarse sand on top of the pots to hold the soil in place and to keep fish, if any, from roiling it up.

Ludwigia has flat round leaves that are coppery green on top and bright red below. Parrot's-feather, or water milfoil *(Myriophyllum proserpinacoides)*, features light-green foliage in whorls that stand above the water. Primrose creeper *(Jussiaea repens)* displays small primroselike flowers among green leaves on thin flexible stems.

Oxygenators

Oxygenators are a necessity where there are fish in still water. The plants take up carbon dioxide and release oxygen. The fish use the oxygen and release carbon dioxide. *Cabomba*, the popular aquarium plant with its fan-shaped bright-green leaves, is also well adapted to outdoor use. *Sagittaria* has dark-green pointed leaves that may rise above the surface in shallow water. It also often has small white flowers. Eelgrass *(Vallisneria spiralis)*, as the name implies, has long narrow leaves that move with the current. It is less likely to spread than the other oxygenators. When the small white flower appears, as it may, it will be on the surface of the water.

Hardy lilies

Water lilies and lotus have the advantage of producing flowers of exquisite form in a variety of sizes and a marvelous range of colors in the daytime, or at night, with remarkably little effort on the part of the gardener.

While planting them is rather more of a chore than planting flowers in the open ground, they require no cultivation, watering, weeding, or thinning, and little if any pest control. They do need feeding, but this is easy to do.

The hardy lilies are the species with flowers at water level that open in the morning and close in the afternoon. If the roots are not frozen, they will come up year after year.

There are many varieties in a wide range of sizes and colors. The most attractive plantings do not completely cover all the available water, but leave open areas to reflect the sky, reveal the goldfish, and show the riffle of wind on the surface.

One of the large vigorous hardy kinds will cover an area about 5 feet in diameter. The smallest standard varieties cover about a 2-foot circle, and the pygmy types are even smaller.

In order to bloom well, the lilies and the

The lotus *(Nelumbo nucifera)* has impressive foliage, and huge flowers and pods. A water lily floats at the lower right.

lotus require sunshine all day long. They need rich clayey loam and lots of fertilizer. Do not use peat or compost in the soil. Organic materials decompose under water and create noxious gases.

The easy way to plant is in boxes. The inside measurements should be at least 12 inches deep and 18 to 24 inches square. The best woods for containers are those that are resistant to rot, such as cedar or cypress. The boxes should be set deep enough to allow for 12 to 16 inches of water above the roots.

In cold climates, plant when all danger of frost is past. Where frost is not a problem, you can plant in February. Fill the pool well in advance of planting, so the water reaches its normal temperature. It is best to soak the soil-filled box for a few days before planting.

Plant the roots with the growing points facing upward and protruding just above the surface of the soil. Cover the soil with a layer of sand to keep it firmly in place. The growing points are easily damaged. Handle the roots with care.

The roots will survive the winter if they do not freeze. If only the surface of the pool freezes over, the roots will be safe underwater.

If there is danger of the water freezing solid, drain the pool and fill it with leaves or straw held in place with wire or plastic netting. The container, with roots intact, can also be stored in any frost-free location. The soil, however, must not be allowed to dry out.

In natural ponds, the hardy lilies can be planted on the bottom. There are varieties, so designated in the catalogs, that can be planted as deep as 10 feet underwater. You can plant these in a half-bushel peach basket, weighed down with heavy rock and lowered to the bottom. The roots will find their way into the soil.

A few choice varieties from which to choose:

White: 'Candida', upright; 'Dawn', rounded, fragrant; 'Gonnere', double flowers; 'Virginalis', large clear white.

Yellow: 'Chromatella', canary yellow, mottled foliage; 'Sunrise', clear yellow, textured petals.

Pink: 'Amabiles', color changes shades as it flowers; 'Lustrous', silvery rose-pink; 'Margarite La Place', rose-pink to soft lilac; 'Mme. J. Chifflot', glowing color, large flower; 'Pink Sensation', clear color, fragrant.

Red: 'Attraction', garnet to dark-red, stamens tipped yellow, large flower; 'Gloriosa', early, fragrant; 'Sultan', deep-red, blooms freely.

Changeables: 'Aurora', changes yellow to orange to dark red from day to day; 'Comanche', rose-pink to bronze, tolerates some shade; 'Sioux', changes from yellow-bronze to copper-orange.

Tropical lilies

These will not grow unprotected the year round in areas where there are hard frosts. They are considered hardy wherever oranges will grow outdoors. They too are available in many colors, including purple and blue, which the hardy lilies do not have. Both the leaves and the flowers are larger.

The tropicals include day-bloomers, like the hardies, and night-bloomers that open in the early evening and hold until about noon the next day. Many of each kind are remarkably fragrant. The flowers on sturdy stems are held well above the water.

Because they are larger plants, they need about half again more soil than the hardy kinds. The water temperature should be at least 70° F. Submerge the containers of soil for a few days before planting to saturate the soil. As soon as you get the roots, simply press them into the soil. Leave the crown of the plant uncovered. To hold them in place, cover the soil with sand and put a heavy flat rock over the roots, but not on the central bud.

Start the plants with about 4 inches of water over the soil. Use bricks or concrete blocks to adjust the height of the containers. After a few weeks, lower it so there is about 6 to 8 inches of water above the surface.

The relatively shallow planting is recommended because the water is warmer near the surface. In the fall, when the plants turn brown, remove all the top growth and store in a cool place for replanting the following spring.

Tropical lily varieties include:

White: 'Alice Tricker', a strong grower; 'Mrs. George H. Pring', very large, pure white, fragrant; 'Ted Uber', yellow stamens. One of the showiest night-blooming tropical lilies is 'Sir Galahad', which has large pure-white flowers that stand well above the water.

Yellow: 'Aviator Pring', rich color, large flowers, heavy bloomer; 'St. Louis', large flower, star-shaped, mottled foliage; 'Yellow Dazzler', open flower, heavy bloomer.

Pink: 'Cleveland', rose-pink, mottled leaves; 'General Pershing', orchid-pink, fragrant double flowers; 'Pink Pearl', pale-pink, keeps well after cutting.

Changeables: 'Afterglow', pink to rose; 'Golden West', pink to yellow; 'Talisman', suffused with yellow to pink.

Among the miniature varieties that can be grown in small space, there is 'White Laydekeri', 'Yellow Pygmy', 'Jeanne Pring'

(pink), 'Aurora' (changeable), and 'Royal Purple'. The last is a day-blooming tropical. The former are hardy kinds that also open in the daytime.

The lotus

The foliage of lotus *(Nelumbo nucifera)* is the size and somewhat the shape of a small parasol and stands above the water. The fragrant flower, as broad as a dinner plate, blooms well above the foliage. The display is unforgettable and it is an easy plant to grow. Flowers are white, pink, yellow, or red and some are double.

The lotus will grow for years where there is no frost, or where the growing points can be protected from freezing temperatures.

It is best to plant in a round container so the long, vigorous roots can keep growing; the corners of a square box would stop them. Use a container 18 to 24 inches in diameter. Fill it with heavy clay soil, and add two cups of 10-10-10 fertilizer to the bottom 2 inches. Plant as recommended for water lilies. Be sure to leave ½ inch or more of the growing tip well above the soil. Cover the soil with sand and plant the container in the sunniest possible place with 4 to 6 inches of water above the soil level.

The plants may not flower until the second year. When they start, they flower for six months or so. Protect the growing points from frost with a mulch of hay and they will grow for years.

In the catalogs you will find lotus smaller than standard that are recommended for growing in a container on a deck or terrace.

Lilies and lotus are resistant to pests and disease. The most common predators are aphids. Wash them off the leaves when you see them. If this doesn't work, submerge the leaves for a few hours and drown the bugs.

SPECIAL PLANTS

14
The Vegetable Garden

There is only one way to truly savor the crispness of a radish, the sweetness of peas in the pod, or the meaty richness of sun-warmed vine-ripened tomatoes. That way is to grow your own. The potential of these vegetables, and a score of others, cannot be realized when they are picked before they are ripe, then shipped to market where they may sit for days before they get into your refrigerator and to the table. For most vegetables, freshness is the essence of flavor, and the product you find in the market has suffered irreparable damage by the time you get to eat it.

There is also the matter of the specific kinds of produce you find in the market. There are, for example, 100 or more varieties of tomato. The commercial grower, quite understandably, plants only those that are best for shipping—that have been, indeed, "improved" by hybridization for just this purpose. Flavor is not the first criterion, and the commercial product does little justice to the noble "love apple." The same is true of many other vegetables and fruits. Some of the best-tasting varieties are available only as seed or small plants, to be

grown and harvested in your garden. Those are the kinds that are recommended here.

Don't be put off by the size and seeming complexity of the 25-by-60-foot plot-plan shown here. You need only select those vegetables in which you are interested and for which you have space. The suggested number of plants of each kind will, in general, suffice for a family of four, although the harvest will vary from year to year depending on the weather and the gardener's attention. You can adjust the number if your family is smaller or larger. The varieties recommended on the following pages are selected for flavor, relative ease of culture, and production in limited space. If these kinds are not available in your local seed store or nursery, seeds can be ordered from mail-order catalogues.

Planting and Cultivation

When to plant depends on where you live. If you live where frost is no problem, you can start your vegetable garden tomorrow evening. If you live where the climate is freezing cold, you must be more careful.

Tomatoes

Tomatoes

Chinese cabbage

Onions

Snowpeas

New Zealand spinach   Celeriac

Peppers

Snap beans

Spinach

Carrots

Beets

Lettuce   Beets

Lettuce   Carrots

Parsley   Chives   Dill   Shallots

Eggplant

Cauliflower

Broccoli

Cabbage

Leeks   Salsify

Peas

Cucumbers

Asparagus

Asparagus

VEGETABLES

Many vegetable plants are tender and cannot survive aboveground if frost strikes in the spring. To forestall this potential problem you must know the "average date of last frost," as the weather bureau puts it.

If you are setting out plants from a garden center or plants that you have grown indoors from seed, wait until you are sure it is safe to do so. If you are planting seed directly in the garden it should not be put in so early that the seedlings will come up before all danger of frost is past. If you are willing to settle for a later harvest, you can reduce the chances of getting caught by waiting a week or so after the average date.

There are a few vegetables, including peas, parsley, dill, spinach, and lettuce, that can withstand a few degrees of frost and so can be planted to come up before that critical date, giving you the earliest possible sampling from your garden.

No matter what your climate or where you live, if you have a place with at least four hours of sun a day, you can grow vegetables of your own.

Starting plants indoors

In climates where there may be frost in early spring, you must start seeds of some vegetables in a protected place (where the temperature is 60° to 70° F.) and then transplant the seedlings into the garden when all danger of frost has passed and the soil has begun to warm up. If this precaution is required, it is so noted in the plant descriptions later in this chapter.

The average date of last frost is the key to determining when to sow seed indoors. Starting with the seed packet, look for the number of days required for germination. Make no assumptions; the times vary considerably. To this number, add 18 more days to allow for the seedling to develop to transplantable size. The total is the number of days before the last frost date to start seed indoors. If, when the so-called last frost date rolls around, you have a few more seedlings than will be needed, you can plant the extra ones in the garden, and should it turn out to be a warm spring you will have an earlier crop with those plants. If frost strikes them down, you will still have the number you need waiting inside to be planted a few days later when there is no more danger of frost.

Seeding indoors is basically simple. Fill a shallow flowerpot or wooden flat with garden soil that has been sieved to remove all rocks, sticks, and lumps. Or, if you prefer, use a commercially prepared potting mix. The container must have a drainage hole in the bottom and then a layer of gravel or broken pots so that excess water can drain off.

Scatter the seeds lightly over the surface and cover them with a layer of the potting soil no deeper than three times the thickness of the seed. Keep the surface moist at all times. If the germinating seeds or the developing plants are allowed to dry out, they will die. In the earliest stages, the container can be covered with a sheet of newspaper to retain moisture. When the seedlings break through the soil, remove the paper and put the container by a sunny window. Water the seedlings daily.

When the second pair of leaves appear, the seedlings can be transplanted into individual peat pots or spaced 2 inches apart in a wooden flat. When the garden soil begins to warm in the spring, scoop up the little plants, without disturbing the roots, and set them out as explained in the next sections of this chapter.

Most garden centers and mail-order houses have a variety of seed-starting kits and containers that are easy and convenient to use.

Preparing the soil for seeds or seedlings

As soon as the ground is dry enough to work easily in the spring, the garden plot should be thoroughly turned to a depth of 10 or 12 inches. Use a spade or spading fork if you relish the exercise, or a power tiller, which can be rented. After tilling, rake the surface to remove stones, sticks, and trash.

To tell whether or not the soil is dry enough, turn up a spadeful of soil and take a handful from about 6 inches below the surface. Squeeze it firmly, open your hand, and tap the soil ball sharply with your finger. If it breaks apart, the soil is dry enough to work. If the ball holds firm, wait a week or so and test again.

Vegetables grow best in a slightly acid soil, with a pH of about 6.5. If your soil tests at a figure lower than this, you will have a better garden if you raise the pH by adding ground limestone. For more on this, see chapter 3.

Sowing seed outdoors

Referring to your planting plan, stretch heavy twine between two stakes to mark the row and draw the corner of a hoe the full length to a depth about three times the diameter of the seed to be planted. Sow seed according to directions on the packet. You can cover the seed with garden soil, but it is much better to fill the furrow with sieved leaf mold or compost. This material is richer in nutrients for the growing seedlings, and its darker color helps retain heat and hasten germination and initial growth.

In warm climates, where seed of such slow starters as lettuce, eggplant, and onions can be planted directly in the ground, drop a few radish seeds along the row every few inches. These will germinate quickly and mark the row to protect it from unwary feet or a careless hoe.

Setting out plants

To set out seedlings or larger plants, use the string for alignment and, for each plant, make a separate hole large enough to accommodate the roots without crowding. A pointed stick can be used to make holes for small plants, or a trowel for larger ones. Before filling the hole and firming down the soil around the plant by hand, pour on a cup of starter solution to help get the plant off to a good beginning. Make this solution by adding 1 pound of 5-10-5 fertilizer to 1 gallon of water and letting it stand overnight to dissolve. The next day stir it up and pour this concentrate into 4 more gallons of water. This makes 5 gallons, which is enough for about 150 plants.

Further feeding

During the summer it would be helpful to apply the same 5-10-5 fertilizer in its dry form as it comes from the bag. Use about ½ pound for each of a 25-foot row. Spread it in a band along the sides of the row about 6 inches away from the plants. Water it down to keep it from blowing away.

Watering

A sufficient supply of water is essential for all plant growth, and vegetables, because of their high water content, require more than most plants. Enough water must be applied to soak down into the root area but not so much, or so fast, that it runs off the

VEGETABLES

surface and erodes the soil. If the ground is light and sandy there is more danger of underwatering than overwatering. But if the soil is relatively heavy, with a high clay content, it is possible to overwater.

The amount of water required depends on conditions of soil and climate, but, in general, a once-a-week watering that moistens the soil to a depth of 6 inches should be enough. In sandy soil, or when hot weather and drying winds prevail, more frequent watering will be required. It is a good idea to water early enough in the day so the leaves will be dry by nightfall. Foliage that stays damp for any length of time, especially in the cool of the night, is likely to develop fungus disease. Instead of drenching the whole plant it is better to add water only to the root area. Perforated hoses or canvas soil soakers are ideal for this.

Plants should never be allowed to dry out enough to show signs of wilting. Among other things this indicates that the rate of growth has been slowed down and that quality will be adversely affected.

The not-quite-magic of mulch

Although a mulch is not the sheer magic that some enthusiasts for organic gardening make it out to be, it has much to recommend it. Simply stated, a mulch is a layer of material put on the surface of the soil. It may be peat moss, salt hay, straw, dry leaves, compost, buckwheat hulls, bagasse, plastic sheeting, or old newspapers. They all serve the same three primary purposes: they retard surface evaporation and thus retain moisture in the soil; they smother unwanted weed seedlings, thus preventing competition with the cultivated plants for food and water; and they keep the ground from compacting under heavy rain or foot

traffic, which helps let needed air into the soil.

Use whatever mulch is readily available. Compost has the added advantage of providing some plant food, but it is not a substitute for fertilizer.

A loose mulch should be 4 to 6 inches deep, spread evenly on the ground. The few weeds that may come up will be rooted in the loose material on the surface, and easy to pull.

Don't use grass clippings unless they have been piled elsewhere for a few weeks first in order to release any excessive heat. And don't use any leaves but oak, or sogginess is apt to create a breeding place for fungus diseases.

If you use a mulch of sheet plastic, it must have holes punched in it to let water through.

Keep it growing

When growth slows down, the quality of the fruit suffers. Thus the best advice for success with a vegetable garden in the fewest possible words is: "Keep it growing."

There are basically four things that impede the normal growth of an established vegetable garden. These are drought, weeds, pests and disease, and the natural process of going to seed. Cope with these and you will have optimum success with your garden.

If there should be a dry spell of a week or more, water will definitely be needed. When you water, do it thoroughly. Soak the ground to a depth of 4 to 6 inches, and dig down with a trowel to make sure that you really have done so. Apply the water to the ground, not to the foliage. Do your watering early in the day so that there will be time for the ground to dry before nightfall. Plants in a damp condition are more susceptible to fungus disease.

Weeds compete with plants for water and nutrients and have nothing to offer in return. Pull existing weeds, or hoe them out, taking care not to damage the roots of the plants. Better yet, prevent weeds from starting in the first place. The best deterrent is a 3-to-6-inch application of straw, leaves, or hay on the open ground. Such a mulch also helps to conserve moisture in the soil.

Pests are most easily controlled before the infestation gets too heavy, so keep a close eye on your plants. At the first sign of trouble, apply an appropriate control, preferably one in dust form that comes in a plastic squeeze applicator. The most dependable single ingredient in a pesticide is rotenone, and a concentration of 1% in a proprietary control is enough to make it effective. Also watch for a powdery deposit on the leaves. This indicates a fungus attack, and a fungicide should be applied immediately. Here, too, the squeeze-duster is most convenient and efficient. *When using pesticides or fungicides, always read the directions on the labels with care, and follow them to the letter.*

The above precautions may seem discouraging when you read them all at once. But not all of these woes may befall your garden, and even if they do, they will not all come at one time. Sometimes pests can be picked off by hand.

While on the subject of possible problems, here's some advice for country dwellers who may find rabbits beating them to the harvest. A 3-foot chicken-wire fence placed around the garden will keep these voracious feeders on the outside. Just make sure that the bottom strand of wire is 2 or 3 inches under the ground and completely circles the garden plot.

The Best Vegetables to Grow

Asparagus

Few indeed are the vegetables that can match the savory enticement of fresh asparagus. Properly planted and cared for, an asparagus bed will produce for ten years or more. The long-term yield and the succulence of the product make the work well worthwhile. Here's what's required for two 25-foot rows:

Put down a layer of peat moss, manure, rotted hay, or leaf mold about 6 inches deep and 1 foot wide. Dig this in, by hand or with a power tiller, to a depth of 8 or 10 inches. If none of these organic materials is available, work in 2 pounds of 5-10-15 fertilizer to a depth of 4 to 6 inches in each row. In early spring, plant one-to-three-year-old roots 4 inches deep at intervals of 18 to 24 inches. Spread the roots gently and set them with the bud pointing up. The first year the spears will be spindly, but delicious. These should be harvested only for a few weeks. The tender shoots eaten raw have a flavor much like raw peas fresh from the pod. In subsequent years the stems will be the familiar full and stocky form. Cultivate after the last harvest in summer, and again in early spring, before the new growth starts, applying ½ pound of 5-10-5 fertilizer per row and working it lightly into the surface. This continued feeding is essential to keep the bed producing.

After the spring cultivation, sprinkle the bed with agricultural-quality salt or regular table salt at the rate of ½ pound for each 25-foot row in order to prevent excessive weed growth.

The classic variety is 'Mary Washington'.

Plant two rows.

Beets

Baby beets in jars are a familiar and colorful delicacy, but the only way to have them fresh and even sweeter is to grow your own. Good soil preparation and adequate water are the keys to quality, as with all root crops. Use a spading fork to dig down 10 to 12 inches and break up all clods. In heavy soil, add leaf mold or peat moss and sand. Scatter a few cupfuls of bone meal in each row and work it in.

As soon as the soil is workable in the spring, sow seeds about 1 inch apart. When the leaves are 1 inch high, thin the row to leave one strong plant per inch. As the beets develop and the row gets crowded, pull every other one and you will have delicious baby beets. This planting can be harvested right into midsummer, and a second sowing made in late July will keep them coming until fall.

Keep the beds well watered. If they get dry and the growth slows down, they will not be tender.

The variety 'Detroit Dark Red' is an old standby, and 'Early Wonder' is good for sowing early. Beet seeds produce tight little clusters of plants which must be thinned. The specially bred variety 'Mono Germ' has the advantage of producing only one plant per seed and requires no extra thinning.

Plant 1½ rows.

Broccoli

The nice thing about growing broccoli at home, especially the variety 'Cleopatra', is the long period of harvest. Like cauliflower, it should be started from seed indoors late in the winter, and it requires about 60 days to mature if it is kept well watered all during the growing season. Well-developed side shoots will provide a continued harvest for several weeks after the main crop is cut. Keep an eye out for insects as the plants develop, and use controls as necessary (see chapter 18). Set out plants at 2-foot intervals.

Cabbage

Cabbage is of the genus *Brassica*, various species of which are called "cole," which accounts for the word "coleslaw." You can enjoy early cabbage with such varieties as 'Early Jersey' or 'Wakefield'. For later crops, try 'Savoy King' or 'Penn State Ballhead'. Sow the early kinds indoors in late winter and set the seedlings out when they are about 3 inches high. Sow the later ones directly in the garden. Start 10% more than the number of plants you want and thin them to a spacing of 18 to 20 inches.

Plant one row.

Carrots

Among the special pleasures of growing carrots are the "thinnings" pulled up to make growing space for those to come. These finger-sized beauties cooked for two to three minutes are memorably tender and sweet.

Carrots must have well-drained soil of loose texture. If the soil in your garden tends to be heavy or sticky, the ground where carrots are grown must be improved. You can do this with a mixture of equal parts sand and peat moss, or compost without sand. Put down a strip of the material about 10 inches wide and 4 inches deep and dig or rototill it in to a depth of 12 inches.

All of the root crops, such as carrots,

beets, celeriac, and such, should be planted where drainage is best. If the ground slopes, this, of course, will be the highest part.

To have a continuous harvest, sow seed in rows every two weeks from early spring until the weather gets hot in summer. Thin to leave about 1½ inches between plants.

The varieties 'Baby Finger' and 'Royal Chantenay' are small enough to serve whole and are of excellent quality. If your soil remains on the heavy side, the only carrot that stands a chance of doing well is the short and blocky 'Oxheart'.

Plant 1½ rows.

Cauliflower

As far as flavor is concerned there is little to choose between cauliflower varieties. But there is one, 'Early Purple Head', that brings a new dimension to this good old standby. As the name implies, the head is purple instead of white and, most surprising, it turns to a lovely fresh apple-green color when cooked. It is taller than the usual kind, and the stem is as tasty as the head.

Plants are best grown from seed started indoors in late winter. The seedlings can go outdoors in early spring, even before the last frost. Set them 18 inches apart in the row. Heads will be ready for cutting about 2½ months after planting outdoors. If you have grown cauliflower, you will know that the white kind requires "blanching," which is done by tying the outer leaves up to protect the head from the sun. 'Early Purple Head' does not require this treatment.

Set out 12 plants.

Celeriac (knob celery)

Most unprepossessing when dug from the ground, this knobby clump of roots is the prime ingredient in an elegant zesty dish, celery remoulade. Seeds sown indoors can be moved outside but kept in their seed containers until a row of snow peas, radishes, or some other early crop is vacant. Then set the knob celeriac at 6-to-8-inch intervals. This is a greedy plant which requires a thorough watering every day or so and a side dressing of fertilizer every two or three weeks. It is ready to dig when the root ball is about 4 inches across. The variety 'Large Smooth Prague' is less knobby than others and easier to clean.

Set out 20 plants.

Chinese cabbage

This is a most welcome late-season salad green. The crunchy yet tender leaves have a distinctive flavor, not the least like cab-

The carrots in the foreground and the beets behind them are mature and are ready for harvest in the fall. They can be left in the ground for weeks without risk of deterioration, and pulled when needed.

bage. The upright heads grow to 15 inches tall, and as with most tightly headed vegetables, the outer leaves serve to keep the inner leaves moist, crisp, tender, and free from toughening sunburn.

The favored variety for flavor is 'Michihli', although 'Wintertime' runs a close second and keeps better in storage. Sow seed in midsummer and thin to about 1 foot apart for late-September harvest.

Plant one row.

Corn

Corn loses its flavor faster than any other vegetable. Only if you have eaten corn minutes after it has been picked do you know how delicious it can be. However, it also takes up more room for its yield than any other vegetable in the garden, and requires eight hours of sun a day. Without that amount, it is not worth growing.

Corn is self-pollinating, which means that the pollen is carried by the wind from the tassel to the silk. A dense planting is more efficient for this process than a single narrow row. The minimum recommended planting area is 100 square feet. The best way to plant corn is in a 10-foot square. If this is impractical, make a 25-foot row 4 feet wide. In either case, set the seeds 10 inches apart in all directions. At one end of the planting area, set out a half-dozen extra seeds to replace any that fail to develop.

An easy approach to planting is to make a series of furrows 2 inches deep and 10 inches apart. As each 25-foot furrow is planted, distribute about four cups of 5-10-10 fertilizer before covering the seeds with soil. As soon as the plot is planted, water the area well.

Corn grows at an amazing rate. They say in Kansas that on a quiet summer night in a big field you can actually hear it grow. To keep its normal pace, it must have great quantities of water. If there is no rain for a period of five days, water the soil enough to wet it to a depth of 6 inches. This is especially important as soon as the tassels on top of the stalks begin to appear.

Pull or hoe as many weeds as you can, but be careful not to work so close to the plants as to damage the roots.

The ears are ready to pick when the silk turns brown. Strip back the husk to make sure that the kernels are plump.

Corn is a tender crop, and if frost should hit after the plants are up they might not survive.

There are many excellent varieties, and the catalogs list the number of days required from the time the seedlings appear until maturity. This time varies from about 60 days to over 90. If you start with an early variety (fewer days to maturity), you may be able to bring in two crops in one season. Some varieties to consider: 'Early Sunglow Hybrid' (62 days), 'Butter and Sugar' (78 days), 'Super Sweet Illinichief' (83 days), 'Iochief' (89 days).

Cucumbers

Cucumber vines tend to spread, and it is best to grow them on a 2- or 3-foot trellis of lath or woven wire. They can also be trained against a wall.

Seeds of the 1972 award-winning variety 'Victory' will produce 7-to-8-inch cukes with good color and crisp white meat. This one is resistant to the several blights and mildews to which other kinds are susceptible. Start seed indoors in late winter for spring planting and a summer crop.

Set out flour plants spaced about 2 feet apart in the row.

Eggplant

Until recent years the eggplant was generally disdained in American backyard gardens. It is now finding favor for its versatility in the kitchen and, perhaps, for its incomparable dark red-purple color. In ancient times the fruit was small, rounded, and white, thus the name. The changes in color, size, and shape are due to hybridizing, both in its natural state and by the hand of man.

The newest varieties, such as 'Dusky' and 'Royal Knight', are smaller and more oblong than the older round varieties. They are excellent for slicing, and half an eggplant stuffed is not too large for one serving. They are also more prolific and can be picked even when quite small, say 5 to 7 inches, which is not the case with the rounder ones. Since they are borne on a taller plant, there is no problem of their rotting on the ground. Start seed indoors, or buy plants to set out when frost no longer threatens.

Set out 12 plants at 2-foot intervals.

Leeks

This seems to be one of those vegetables that has had its day. There was a time when many varieties were offered in all seed catalogs; now there is seldom more than one listed. But as fashion and taste often come full circle, this old-timer is being rediscovered through such delicacies as braised leeks and leek-and-potato soup.

Leeks are seldom available in the marketplace but can be harvested the year round in your own garden. Sow seed in late February, indoors in cold climates, outdoors where it is warm. Where it is cold, the plants can be covered with a light mulch in the fall and the leeks can be dug out as needed until spring. When the last of these over-wintered leeks are pulled in early summer, the newly planted seedlings will be only a few weeks away from their first harvest.

'Giant Musselburgh' is the variety to grow. If it is not available, 'Broad London' probably will be.

Plant half a row about 6 inches apart.

Lettuce, 'Buttercrunch'

This lettuce is of the Bibb type that forms a loose head. You can pick just a few leaves at a time as needed, or harvest the whole head. The leaves are crisp and flavorful, especially when picked before they are fully mature. This variety, along with 'Salad Bowl' and 'Hot Weather', holds up better than most in midsummer.

Seed started indoors will take about a month to produce garden-ready plants. Plant them outdoors in early spring. Set plants about 8 inches apart in the row. In about 30 days they will be ready to pick. A second sowing can be made about a month before cool weather in the fall.

All the Bibb-type lettuces do best in slightly alkaline soil. If your garden soil is alkaline, and you plan to add gypsum to make it more acid for other vegetables, leave an untreated strip for the lettuce. On the other hand, if you are adding limestone to raise the pH to the 6.5 recommended for vegetables in general, add enough more to bring the pH up to about 7.5. You will have the best lettuce in the neighborhood. Any reasonably fertile garden soil is rich enough for lettuce. Do not fertilize during its growing season, or it will tend to have a bitter flavor.

The second planting of lettuce can be made in late summer for fall harvest. Anoth-

VEGETABLES

er dimension can be added to the salad garden with the variety 'Ruby', which has striking red foliage.

Thirty plants will be plenty.

Onions

These are Jekyll-and-Hyde performers, in that some varieties are strong and harsh while others are sweet and mild. There is no need to speculate as to which is which when such dependably mild varieties as 'White Ebenezer' and 'Southport White (or Red) Globe' are available. These are most often sold as seed. Two other excellent mild varieties, 'White Sweet Spanish' and 'Yellow Bermuda', are also sold as "sets." These are young bulbs that are set out immediately in the garden in early spring and are ready to pull and use as scallions in a couple of weeks.

The true scallions do not form a bulb, and they are grown as much for the slender green tops as for the white cylindrical part that grows underground. These are often listed as "bunching onions" in the seed catalogs. One of the best varieties is 'Beltsville Bunching'. Six or eight seedlings can be put together in one planting hole at 6-inch intervals in early spring.

Regular onions need about 5 inches of space between plants to allow the bulbs to grow without crowding. This can be attained by spacing the sets at this distance or by planting a row of seed and thinning as required. If you wait until the tops are scallion-size to thin the row you will have gained another useful vegetable. Technically these are green onions, not scallions, but when they are in the salad no one will ever know.

The tops of the onions you have left in the ground to mature will begin to yellow in late summer. When this happens, bend the tops over sharply to prevent the development of seed, which drains energy (and quality) from the bulb. When the leaves have all turned brown, pull the onions out of the ground and let them dry in the sun for a few days before bringing them in to store in a cool dry place. They will keep for many months.

Plant one row.

Peas

We must use some superlatives about the quality of peas fresh from the garden. They are sweeter, tenderer, and more colorful and delicious than any peas you can possibly get from the store. This is because the natural sugars in peas start turning to starch within a few hours after they are picked.

Sow seeds early in the spring or in the late fall for a late-spring harvest. Put them about 2 inches apart. If you have some small branches such as tree prunings, to stick in the ground for the bush to climb on, picking will be easier.

'Little Marvel' is our favorite, with 'Thomas Laxton' a close second.

Plant one row.

Peppers

To some aficionados, only the hot chili pepper truly deserves the name, but here we refer to the sweet pepper, the one used for stuffing and cooking and eating raw in a salad. 'California Wonder' is the crisp, dark-green, blocky variety that, deservedly, has been a favorite for years.

Peppers are sensitive to heat and cold. Young plants should not be set out in the garden until night temperatures are dependably above 55°. When daytime temperatures go above 90°, production will slow down markedly. But keep them watered and when the heat wave passes they will come back to normal growth. Peppers will benefit from a thick mulch that keeps the soil cool and moist.

Set out 15 plants, about a foot apart.

Potatoes

The idea that growing the common potato is worth the effort and the space it takes may come as a surprise. But when you sample a bowl of them, newly harvested and not much larger than olives, boiled, lightly salted, and drenched in butter, you will know that this is special fare indeed.

Although the potatoes you order to use as seed may look like those you can buy for less in the store, the seed potatoes have the advantage of being true to the variety you specify and are usually certified as being disease-free.

Potatoes should be planted in early spring. But in cold climates wait until there is no further danger of frost. When you are prepared to plant, cut each potato into parts so that each piece has at least two eyes or buds. These are the growth points from which the new plants will develop. Some seed houses will ship the individual eyes all ready to plant.

Make a furrow about 6 inches deep, drop the pieces into the furrow at 1-foot intervals, and cover them with an inch of soil. As the plants begin to grow, gradually fill in the planting hole until the soil is level. Then add a 4-to-6-inch layer of straw, old hay, or partly decomposed leaves or soil. This mulch will encourage the formation of more potatoes and protect those that may push up through the soil from being sunburned, which turns them green and bitter.

The appearance of white flowers is a signal that potatoes are beginning to develop on their underground stems. About three weeks later you can dig for the small ones, which are especially sweet and tender. You can continue to dig new potatoes as they grow throughout the summer, but those that you want to store for winter must be left in the ground until early autumn, when they are fully mature.

Recommended varieties are the very early 'Red Russet', early 'Superior', and mid-season 'Kennebec'.

About three 25-foot rows should be enough, with plants 1 foot apart and 2 to 3 feet of space between the rows.

Radishes

Most radishes look better than they taste. A welcome exception is the white, crisp, and mild-when-young 'Icicle Radish'. Befitting its name, it is a tapered cylindrical shape rather like a small carrot. Sow seeds in early spring to fill in the spaces between such later plants as peppers, eggplant, and Chinese cabbage. It will be ready to pull before these are tall enough to shade it out.

Salsify or oyster plant

Unlikely as it seems, this root crop does have an oysterlike flavor that is uniquely delicious. Seeds planted in spring produce white 6-inch carrotlike roots by late summer. 'Sandwich Island Mammoth', while not so large as the name suggests, is dependably good. Cultural requirements are the same as for carrots.

Plant ½ row and thin to 4 inches apart.

Shallots

Among the varied personalities of the onion family, the shallots provide the most delicate flavor. They come as clove-shaped bulblets which are planted about 4 inches apart in early spring. By fall each one will have multiplied by six or more. Set aside the amount you will want for planting next year and store them in a paper bag. The rest are yours to cook with all through the winter.

Plant about a dozen bulblets.

Snap beans

You might think of these as string beans but, happily, the newer hybrids are almost stringless. They are not snapless, however, and this is all to the good. If they snap when broken they are fresh. If they don't snap, not only has the texture deteriorated, but the flavor as well.

The quality of the variety 'Tenderpod' is excellent. This is also a bush type that does not need staking or training. Sow seed early, thin the plants to 6 inches apart, and they will grow to about 18 inches high and produce bountifully. Pick them often, while the pods are 3 to 4 inches long, to prolong the bearing season.

Plant one row.

Snowpeas

Although these crisp and colorful peas with edible pods are a staple in Chinese restaurants and produce stores, it is quite likely that you have never tasted them at their best. They should be cooked within a few hours after picking, and the only way this can be assured is to grow your own.

Early in spring, as soon as the soil can be easily worked, sow the seeds about 3 inches apart in a furrow about 2 inches deep. They will sprout when the weather warms up, and even if late frost strikes, the seedlings will undoubtedly survive. The small bushlike plants produce prolifically,

and pods should be picked when they are about 2 inches long. A second planting can be set out in late summer for a fall harvest. A support such as is recommended for peas is useful, for the same reasons.

The variety 'Super Sweetpod' lives up to its name.

Plant one row.

Spinach

This is one of the few vegetables with a season so fleeting that one might doubt its worth. But once you have picked it fresh for cooking or as a salad green, you may want to plant three different kinds and have it available all season long.

For the first crop, try 'Longstanding Bloomsdale Dark', sown in early spring. It can be picked for a few weeks before going to seed. Next, also planted in spring, is 'New Zealand Spinach'. While this is not the true article, it is flavorful and matures during the heat of summer. Then, a midsummer sowing of the late variety 'Cold Resistant Savory' will yield good greens well into the fall.

Plant one row and thin seedlings to about 8 inches apart.

Squash, acorn

This is not the big bland pumpkinlike variety that might come first to mind. It has dark-green skin and yellow meat and is just the right size for a serving for two. Just cut the squash in half, dot it with butter and brown sugar, and bake it.

This squash grows on a small bush about 3 feet across. If you can't get plants that are already started, the seeds can be sown outdoors in the middle of spring as soon as the soil is warm. As the plants come up, choose the strongest-looking ones and thin the rest to leave about 3 feet between plants.

For each plant, dig up an area about 1 foot across and 1 foot deep. To condition the soil, mix in a generous amount of peat moss, leaf mold, or compost. Before planting, also add a cup of 5-10-5 fertilizer to the soil. Water the new plants thoroughly, and continue watering them to keep the root area from drying out. They can be harvested in midsummer but have hard shells and will keep well into winter.

Squash beetles can be a problem, but they are not too difficult to control if you spot them before they get too big. See the pest identification chart in chapter 18. Dust the plants as soon as you see the bugs, and continue the treatment once a week. Use a pesticide containing 1% rotenone.

The most dependable variety of acorn squash is 'Table Queen'.

Four plants should suffice for our hypothetical family of four.

Squash, zucchini

Zucchini is another small squash well worth considering. This is a summer squash and should be used soon after picking. The plants are, however, about the same size as acorn squash, and the planting, spacing, and culture are essentially the same. This tractable plant needs no shelling or peeling, and its smooth shiny skin is easily wiped clean. Quickly stir-fried in oil or blanched in water, young tender crops of zucchini under 6 inches long are appealing additions to much seasonal fare. Zucchini is also comparatively free of insects and disease, and can be harvested in abundance all summer long.

The variety 'Aristocrat' is a good choice, for it will produce a crop of cylindrical

Here is evidence that summer squash bears successively for a long period: mature fruit, buds, and blossoms are all carried on the same plant.

fruits ideal for slicing and it is more compact and bushy than the rambling vines of some of the older varieties.

Strawberries

The flavor and fragrance of the strawberry speak eloquently for the fruit. Suffice it to say, this is a fruit worth growing if you have the space and the proper location. The proper location—and the only one—is where the plants will get full sun from morning until night. The space required for a satisfying supply of berries for a family of four is a plot about 25 by 15 feet. This plot will accommodate six 25-foot rows that are 3 feet apart. With 25 plants set 1 foot apart in each row, you will have a total of 150 plants, which is an investment of about $10.

VEGETABLES

For the first season, until the roots get well established, you will probably wish you had more plants. But when they begin to produce at their maximum rate, there will certainly be enough. Strawberries, of course, are perennials, and a well-tended patch will produce efficiently for about four years. In the fourth or fifth year it is a good idea to salvage the new plantlets and reset them in rows. Dig and discard all the older plants to maintain a vigorous planting.

The soil for strawberries should be reasonably light (not heavy clay) and slightly on the acid side. The plants are fairly heavy feeders and will do better with an annual application of fertilizer. The first should be put on before they are planted in the spring. About 1½ pounds of 5-10-5 fertilizer per 100 square feet will suffice. A 25-by-15-foot plot will thus require about 6 pounds. Spread the fertilizer evenly and dig it in. If you also have access to compost or leaf mold, spread a 2-inch layer on the soil and work it in with a spade, fork, or power tiller to a depth of 8 to 10 inches. This can be done when the fertilizer is applied.

There are strawberry varieties for cool climates and for warm. If you live where there is little or no frost to contend with, choose a warm-climate variety such as 'Earlibelle', 'Surecrop', 'Beauty', or 'Pocahontas'. The last has the largest berries. For cool climates the varieties 'Premier', 'Sparkle', 'Fletcher', and 'Catskill' are excellent. Again, the last has berries that are considerably larger than the others. The big berries are more impressive; but the smaller ones bear somewhat more abundantly and usually have a slightly better flavor.

Put out the plants in early spring after all danger of frost is past. Dig shallow holes in the well-loosened soil, spread the roots out flat, and set the plants at the recommended 2-foot intervals. Plant them to the exact depth that they were grown originally. The soil line is easy to see when you look at the plant. Press the soil firmly around the roots with your hands. After planting a row, fill a sprinkling can and water the soil around the root area of each plant. Watch for the runners that will develop and snip them off as they appear.

Blossoms emerge in about two weeks, and the first berries will be ready to pick about three to four weeks later. In late summer, when the berries are all picked, put on another application of fertilizer at the rate suggested above. This will help to ensure a better crop next year.

If you live where the winters are cold, wait until after the first few hard frosts and cover the entire strawberry bed with 2 to 3 inches of straw. This will protect the plants from the rigors of that hard season. If birds should be a problem, thin strips of aluminum foil about 8 inches long and 3 to 4 feet apart strung above the berries will help to scare them away. But if the birds persist, the only thorough protection is netting (sold for that purpose at garden stores) draped over the entire planting, over short stakes or low pieces of brush.

Swiss chard

For a vegetable that is different, yet easy to grow, the red-stemmed varieties, such as Burpee's 'Rhubarb' and 'Ruby Red', or the white 'Fordhook Giant', will provide an attractive and tasty green when the leaves are cooked.

Stem sections can be braised, steamed, or boiled. They have a mild beetlike flavor and the texture of asparagus.

One of the pleasures of growing a few

plants of Swiss chard is that about six weeks after the seeds are sown in early spring, a few of the stems can be harvested from each plant every few days, and a fresh supply will keep growing all summer until killed by a hard frost. The young stems are particularly tender.

Six plants should be enough.

Tomato

This is the fruit most likely to impel one to grow a garden. They are only at their best when picked fully ripe from the vine. In the world of tomatoes, bigger is not better except, perhaps, to impress the neighbors. The seedsmen, however, continue to bring out bigger and bigger varieties, and the goal seems to be a tomato that weighs a full pound. But the plant researchers have been busy developing varieties of medium size and high yield that are resistant to wilts and blights and, most important, have superior texture and flavor. Among the best are 'Ultra Girl', 'Rutgers', and 'Better Boy'. The last, in particular, is favored for its disease resistance. Every variety requires a certain number of days from the time it is set out until the first fruit ripens. This varies from 62 days for 'Springset' (an excellent variety) to as much as 75 days for the well-known 'Big Boy'.

The tomato is a hot-season plant. In cold climates the growing season is limited by frost. Plants started from seed indoors must not be set out in spring until all danger of frost is past, and they must be ripe before the first frost in fall. You can get the number of average frost-free days in your area from the weather bureau or from a local nursery or garden center and choose your varieties accordingly. Sun is also a factor. The more direct sunshine the better—toma-

Given a sunny location and plenty of water and fertilizer, two or three tomato plants, like this 'Sub-Arctic Maxi', can entice your family and even a few neighbors.

toes will not do well with less than six hours of full sun a day.

Before setting out the plants, loosen the soil for each one to a depth of 6 inches in a circle about 1 foot in diameter. Put the plant a little deeper in the hole than it had been growing in its pot or flat. Set the plant at a 45° angle rather than straight up. Tomatoes will root all along the stem, and this will help to develop a wider root system and a stronger plant. Although the plants will grow and produce fruit without staking, they will be less susceptible to rot and disease if they are staked up to provide good air circulation. Use one sturdy stake, a tri-

VEGETABLES

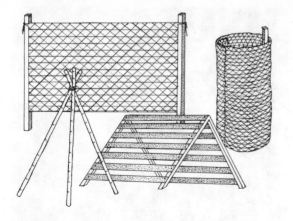

These four easy-to-build structures are useful frames for vegetables with sprawling habits such as tomatoes, melons, beans, and peas.

pod of three stakes crossed at the top, or a cylindrical wire cage about 4 feet high. Tie the strongest stems to the support with soft twine. Mulch the ground around the plants with hay or straw. This is especially important if the plants are not staked. For maximum flavor do not pick until the fruit is fully ripe on the vine.

There are a number of small colorful "cherry tomatoes" available, but some are tough-skinned. An exception is 'Sugar Lump' (sometimes called 'Gardener's Delight'), which is savory, tender, and somewhat larger than the others. Plant eight of this variety spaced at least 2 feet apart.

With the large varieties, a dozen plants should be enough. Allow about 4 feet between plants.

Useful Herbs for the Garden

Some herbs are annuals, which means that they have to be planted anew each year. Others are perennials that persist for years without replanting. One, caraway, is a biennial, which means that the seeds do not develop until the second year after planting. If plants of the herbs you want are available, it is quicker and easier to use them. However, if you can only get seeds, don't be concerned. The planting is not difficult.

Start seed in early spring. Scratch up the surface of the soil, sprinkle the area with a few seeds, cover them lightly with the soil, and firm it down. Keep the planting moist. If seeds are allowed to dry out they will not sprout and grow. As the plants develop, thin out all but the strongest ones. As you will see in the following descriptions, a few plants of most herbs go a long way. Just one well-grown plant is often enough, which is why we also suggest growing them in containers.

Except for caraway, which is a seed, and garlic, a bulb, these herbs are grown for their foliage. The tender new leaves are the most aromatic and flavorful. As tough stems and coarse older leaves develop, they can be cut back to half their length to promote the tender new growth. As the season draws to a close, and preferably before the plant starts to flower, the foliage can be picked for drying and winter use.

If chives are growing in your garden, you can enjoy them easily the year round. Dig up a healthy bunch, roots and all, set them in a flowerpot, and water them well. Put the pot in a kitchen window, and snip off the tops of the chives with scissors as needed all winter long. Water them when the surface of the soil shows signs of dryness.

How to dry herbs

On a sunny day, snip off a fistful of stems at ground level, wash them if they are dusty, and spread them in the sun to dry.

Take them indoors at night to protect them from the dew, and bring them out for a full second day in the sun. After this preconditioning they can be tied in bunches and hung upside down in a dry room with a moderate temperature of 45° to 65° F. Within a week they will be ready. For convenience, the dried leaves can be stripped from the stems and stored in moistureproof jars.

Caraway

Caraway is grown for its pungent and flavorful seeds, widely respected for their use in rye bread and cheeses. As noted earlier, it is a biennial; but if you continue to set it out annually, seeds will be available for harvest every year thereafter.

A 3-to-4-foot row of plants spaced about 6 inches apart will be fine, unless you expect to bake rye bread every day.

Chervil

The finely divided leaves, rather resembling some kinds of parsley, make this an attractive plant. The *fines herbes* called for in many French recipes include equal parts of chervil, tarragon, parsley, and chives. One or two plants of this annual will be plenty.

Florence fennel

This herb is also a good-looking plant. Also called *finocchio*—its Italian name—fennel has feathery leaves and the hearty flavor of licorice. It is often used to heighten the taste of beets, potatoes, and cooked cabbage. It is an annual, and one plant should suffice.

Garlic

This assertive little bulb needs no introduction. A tender perennial, it is treated

Herbs are easily grown in pots and can be kept near the kitchen for ready use. They must have a location that gets at least 5 hours of sun daily.

here as an annual. Plant the garlic clove, pointed end up, deep enough so that the top can be covered with 1 or 2 inches of soil. Each clove will develop into a whole garlic, an increase of about eight to one. Estimate the number you will need for the year and plant accordingly. When the top growth dies down in the fall, the bulb is ready to harvest—but not before. Let the whole bulb dry in the sun for a day or two, and then store it in a cool dry place.

Lemon balm

This plant belongs to the mint family and, as such, is a rampant grower that does best in rather moist soil. Its lemony flavor is delightful, especially when the leaves are cut into slivers and sprinkled over fish. Lemon balm is a perennial, and one plant will be enough.

Mint

In addition to the usual variety of mint—without which the julep could not survive—there is also spearmint, orange mint, and

VEGETABLES

apple mint. These are all perennials and grow with remarkable vigor, especially in moist soil. You may want to put them in containers to keep them in bounds. One or two sprigs will create a small persistent colony in a year or two.

Purple sage

Sage imparts the flavor that is so familiar in turkey stuffing. This variety has the added advantage of handsome leaves of frosted red-purple. It is a perennial, and one or two plants should be the correct number to add a colorful grace note to the kitchen garden and provide a full measure of pungent leaves for you and your neighbors.

Rosemary

This is a classic herb to match up with lamb, because of the woody, aromatic essence of the leaves and stems. It is a hardy perennial, whose shrubby stems may look bedraggled in winter, but lovely new green growth will emerge from the ground in spring. It is especially well adapted to dry sunny places. Two plants should be sufficient.

Sweet basil

The small tender leaves of this annual can be clipped for their piquancy all through the growing season. This herb, in particular, will become bushier and produce more new leaves if the top 6 inches of all the stems is pinched off periodically. One plant should be enough for your needs.

Sweet marjoram

The subtle but spicy savor of marjoram makes it one of the most frequently used of kitchen herbs. One or two plants of this annual will provide plenty of leaves from midsummer on.

Tarragon

The fragrant leaves are traditionally used to flavor vinegar and butter. In all but the coldest climates, tarragon will be perennial. Set out one or two plants, but if they should die out simply treat the herb as an annual, setting out a new plant or two in the spring.

Thyme

This herb, along with parsley and bay leaf, is a necessary ingredient in the classic *bouquet garni*. There are many varieties of thyme, each with a distinct flavor, but common thyme is still the most useful. Thyme does best in a hot dry situation. It is a perennial, and one plant should be enough.

Storing the Harvest

There are a few vegetables worth planting in obvious excess. The cucumber is one such. Any that are not eaten fresh can be pickled in numerous ways—as dill pickles, bread-and-butter pickles, and relishes. One asset of a plentiful harvest is that it really makes pickle-making worthwhile. After all, why make only six pickles at a time? An ample planting also enables you to select only those fruits that are at their peak, rather than having to settle for a small supply, regardless of condition.

If there are other vegetables left at the end of the season, one might say that these are the fruits of poor planning. So be it, but there are various crops that can provide excellent provender well into the winter without pickling, preserving, or freezing.

The easiest method of storage is to leave the vegetables in the ground or on the vine. Snap beans are the least difficult of all to store—a snap, in fact. They have a way of ripening slowly early in the season and then coming on at such a pace that you can't or don't want to keep up with them. No problem. Pick what you want—the tender young ones are best—and let the others go to seed. When the pods turn a yellow-tan color, they can be shelled, and the plump dry ivory-colored beans can be stored decoratively in glass jars and used for bean soup or in the preparation of cassoulet.

One of the frustrations of growing tomatoes in cold climates is seeing many almost-ripe fruits cut down by frost. Tomatoes, in particular, are often at their peak of production at this time. Although there is nothing to compare with the sun-ripened fruit, your own green tomatoes ripened indoors will be as good as or better than those you can get in the market at that time of year.

Pick the largest of the fully green tomatoes, and put them on a shelf in a dry place with a temperature of 50° to 60° and good ventilation. Do not let the tomatoes touch one another. If space is limited and the tomatoes must be stacked, wrap each one in tissue or newspaper. They will ripen gradually, even in the dark, and should be consumed as soon as they soften and turn red.

If you live where the winter temperature does not go below 10° F., there are some vegetables that can simply be left in the ground. These include beets, carrots, salsify, leeks, and celeriac, all of which are described earlier in this chapter. When frosty nights are imminent, and before the ground freezes, cover the rows with 4 or 5 inches of straw or salt hay. With the soil thus protected from freezing, the vegetables will be edible for five or six months and can be dug up when you want them. One note of precaution: if straw is used to insulate the soil, it is likely to blow away.

Cover it with chicken wire or plastic netting staked down to keep it in place.

In climates where winter temperatures do go below 10°, these same crops can be stored successfully in a root cellar if you happen to have one. If not, perhaps you can improvise one in a corner of an unheated garage. The temperature of this storage area must be above freezing, but not much —a range, say, of 34° to 45° is good. Dig up the plants remaining in the garden and cut off all but an inch or so of the green stem on top. Put the roots in wooden boxes and cover the underground parts with sand or peat moss that has been dampened thoroughly but not saturated. This material will insulate the vegetables and help them to retain their moisture.

There is another group of vegetables, including potatoes, onions, cauliflower, and cabbage, that require a similar temperature range of 34° to 45° but need less humidity. Store this produce on open shelves at least 2 feet off the floor.

Another good winter keeper, acorn squash, also requires a dry place but a warmer temperature, in the range of 50° to 60°. A corner in a basement will probably be fine for storing squash. A little checking with a minimum-maximum recording thermometer will reveal the places best suited for storing any vegetables that you may have.

Good ventilation is also important in all cases. Slatted shelves or racks of chicken wire are ideal for dry storage. Make sure, too, that you store only firm and sound vegetables. Bruised spots on vegetables are likely to develop rot, and the resulting fungus spores will infect the other vegetables. Remember the adage about the one rotten apple that spoiled the whole barrel.

VEGETABLES

❧ |15| ❧
Plants to Grow in the House

There is good reason for the burgeoning interest in house plants. Few pleasures are so inexpensive and easily attained, yet so immediately rewarding, as having the ever-changing form and color of growing plants as part of one's everyday life.

Indoor plants also have a beneficial effect on the quality of air in the house. They take up carbon dioxide and give off oxygen, and in heated rooms in cold climates the level of humidity (about 60%) that is best for plants is beneficial to your health and even to your furniture.

The two most important requirements in growing plants successfully are water and light. More potted plants are killed by excessive water than by any other single cause. Wait just until the surface of the soil in the container is dry before watering. Then water thoroughly, making sure that all the soil has been moistened. This is indicated when the excess drains off through the hole in the bottom of the pot. A small pot might need watering every two or three days, and a larger one once a week. Plastic pots do not require watering as often as clay pots because there is less evaporation

through the container. But regardless of the container, light frequent waterings are no substitute for thorough watering when the soil is dry.

One good way to create an efficient environment for house plants is to set them in a tray of gravel with water added to a level that almost covers the surface. This will allow the pot to drain freely, and also provides the humidity so often lacking indoors, particularly in the winter when houses are heated.

Spraying house-plant foliage with water every day, or at least once a week, will help still further to create conditions conducive to good growth. Make sure, however, that this is done early enough in the day so the leaves will dry before the temperature begins to drop at night.

The amount of light provided for house plants is often either too little or too much. Too much light evaporates the available moisture too rapidly and can cause burning of the leaves, while too little light does not provide the necessary amount for photosynthesis to produce the essential nutrients. As a rough guideline, any daylight that is comfortable for reading is within the acceptable range for plant growth. Flowering plants will need the most light; foliage plants can do with less. But even the minimum must be sufficient for comfortable reading. So position plants accordingly.

House plants usually extract all available nutrients from their potting soil within a year or two. In order to maintain a vigorous plant, the soil should be replaced every second year. The more practical approach is to provide additional nutrients, preferably in the form of an application of a soluble fertilizer every two weeks in the amount recommended on the package.

A good general potting-soil mixture for house plants can be made of equal parts of garden soil, peat moss or leaf mold, and coarse builder's sand. Excellent sterilized soil mixtures for potting can be bought in garden-supply stores or from mail-order houses. You can also make a good potting mix at home. By volume: Use 2 parts garden soil put through a coarse sieve to remove small pebbles and debris. Add 1 part peat moss and 1 part coarse builder's sand. To each 2-gallon bucket of this mixture add ½ cup 5-10-10 fertilizer and ¼ cup ground limestone. Except for the soil in a vegetable garden, where fungus diseases are often a problem, any good garden loam can be used for the soil in this potting mixture.

Plants should be potted in a container that allows 1 to 2 inches of soil under the roots and 1 inch all around on the sides. This will provide adequate growing space and serve to put the water where the roots are. In a pot that is too large for the root area, the water beyond the roots tends to fill the air spaces in the soil. This saturated soil reduces the available oxygen and slows the growth of the plant.

Examine your plants often and regularly. A monthly combination spray of an insecticide and fungicide will usually prevent any outbreaks of disease. A mixture of 1 tablespoon of malathion and ¼ teaspoon of Benomyl to 1 quart of water can be applied with a hand sprayer. This will not endanger pets, but fish tanks, baby toys, or areas where food is served should be covered to protect them from drifting spray.

If you find that certain plants seem to attract quantities of insects in spite of this preventive spray, eliminate them from your collection. There are too many agreeable plants available to justify your putting up with troublemakers. It takes a degree of resolve to discard a plant, but this is an important step toward arriving at those that are dependable and can make house-plant gardening a pleasure instead of an endless chore.

The following selection in each category includes only those plants that we feel will grow easily, bloom successfully, and present the minimum number of problems.

Foliage Plants

Low plants, to 18 inches tall

Asparagus fern (*Asparagus densiflorus*). Noted for the fluffy upright plumes of bright-green foliage.

Begonia (*Begonia rex*). A long-lasting plant available in great variety. Each variety has a distinct shape. The leaves have colorful patterns of silver, red, or green. There are also interesting two-tone varieties.

Birdnest fern (*Asplenium nidus*). Makes a loosely formed rosette of long oval pointed leaves.

To encourage bushier and more compact growth in a plant, pinch off the stem just below the topmost leaves and above a dormant bud. This process works with plants of any size.

Here is the new growth that developed after pinching. New stems may be pinched back as they grow to obtain added compactness.

Boston fern *(Nephrolepis exaltata bostoniensis)*. A fern that produces its feathery fronds from a central growing point. Put the tip of a frond in contact with soil for a week or two, and it will root and produce a new plantlet. Does best in warm locations.

Coleus *(Coleus blumei)*. Its easy culture and the scalloped leaves that are literally splashed with color make this a favorite.

Holly fern *(Cyrtomium falcatum)*. The holly-like leaves form upright 20-inch fronds. Holly fern foliage is tougher than that of most ferns. It can also survive with relatively little light.

Peperomia *(Peperomia caperata)*. This will cover an entire pot with a mound of small crinkled leaves. Small sprigs of white flowers emerge in the spring and sometimes again in the fall.

Prayer plant *(Maranta leuconeura)*. The dark-green oval leaves are symmetrically marked with darker-green spots along the midrib. New leaves unfold continuously to make a compact plant that is easily divided.

Vriesia *(Vriesia speciosa)*. A dramatic bromeliad with brown and green zebra-striped leaves emerging from a central core that actually forms a water-holding vase. As the stem grows, small brilliantly colored florets pop out from each of the colorful bracts.

Medium-sized plants, to 36 inches tall

Aglaonema *(Aglaonema roebellinii)*. The pointed oval bright-green leaves, brushed with silver markings, clothe the stem almost to the level of the soil. The foliage looks like fluffy upright plumes.

Jade plant *(Crassula argentea)*. Masses of small succulent oval leaves are carried on thick stems. A well-known plant, still popular.

Tall plants, more than 36 inches tall

Dracaena *(Dracaena marginata)*. Thin sinuous woody stems that will grow to 6 feet or more are tipped with an arching whorl of long pointed leaves about 1 inch wide. *D. fragrans massengeana* has rosettes of broad succulent leaves with yellow markings along their central vein. Tolerates low light levels.

Dumb cane *(Dieffenbachia maculata)*. Large oval green leaves boldly marked with white blotches grow out of a central stem to 5 or 6 feet tall. Can be kept lower by pruning, and can be air-layered (see chapter 17).

Fiddleleaf fig *(Ficus lyrata)*. Large pear-shaped tough-textured green leaves grow on a central woody stem. Does not do well in drafty places.

Fig tree *(Ficus benjamina)*. A tall loosely stemmed plant with dark-green oval leaves and light-gray bark. If provided with warmth, high humidity, moderate ventilation, and a medium level of light, it will continue to grow for years and reach to the ceiling.

Palm *(Howea belmoreana)*. This is the potted palm popular in the Victorian era. Drooping fronds gracefully emerge at different levels from the main stem.

Philodendron *(Philodendron melanochrysum)*. A dramatic plant with large green arrow-shaped yellow-veined leaves that point downward from a thin main stem. Dependable in warm places with considerable humidity.

Scheffelera *(Brassaia actinophylla)*. This is a tree that can be kept to house-plant size by pruning. The stems terminate with five rich-green oval leaflets carried in a fan shape. It tolerates moderate shade but needs high humidity.

Flowering Plants

Low plants, to 18 inches tall

Aechmea *(Aechmea fasciata)*. The tough gray-green pineapplelike foliage forms a rosette with a short stem bearing a striking blue and pink flower from 4 to 6 inches across. It looks like the plume on a drum major's hat.

African violet *(Saintpaulia ionantha)*. Flowers in single, double, or ruffled form, in colors of purple, pink, blue, or white, bloom almost continuously. They are set attractively in a crown of fleshy dark-green leaves with a velvety surface. Dependable, easy to grow, and deservedly popular.

Anthurium *(Anthurium scherzerianum)*. From a tangle of long large green leaves comes a wiry 18-inch stem bearing a unique flower that verges on the grotesque. It has a white curved pigtail set off against a shining shield of bright red, pink, or white about 6 inches long and 4 inches wide.

Begonia *(Begonia semperflorens)*. These dependable plants, easily grown from seed, flower continuously and so prolifically that the foliage is all but hidden. They are available in white, pink, and shades of red.

Coleus *(Coleus thyrsoideus)*. The bushy form and heart-shaped scalloped leaves are undistinguished, but the plant comes

Among the rex begonias there is an amazing variety of leaf shapes, textures, markings, and colors, and many varieties hold their flowers well above the foliage.

to vibrant life in winter when the small electric-blue flowers appear in great abundance.

Episcia (*Episcia cupreata* hybrids). Has handsome rough brown-green and metallic-splashed leaves from which lipstick-shaped flowers emerge in bright shades of red and orange. The habit of growth is low and trailing. Needs shade, even temperature, and humid atmosphere but is worth the attention it requires. The varieties 'Chocolate Soldier' and 'Silver Sheen' are particularly attractive.

Geranium (*Pelargonium domesticum*). The lush foliage of these bushy plants is a perfect foil for the tall-stemmed rounded flower clusters. There is a wide choice of species

and of varieties. The Martha Washington type is an excellent choice.

Impatiens (*Impatiens sultanii*). No wonder the British call it "Busy Lizzie." It seems to bloom all the time with its many small white, pink, red, or two-toned flat flowers amid a mass of small leaves. The succulent stems are easily rooted to make new plants.

Oxalis (*Oxalis bowerei*). The cloverlike leaves of this bulbous plant are dark-green and grow only a few inches high. In the fall, dark-pink flowers are held just above the foliage. Both the leaves and flowers close at night. Does well in a cool location.

Shrimp plant (*Beloperone guttata*). A bushy plant that blooms the year round with pinkish-brown shrimp-shaped flowers with overlapping bracts that look like scales.

Sinningia (*Sinningia pusilla*). One of the jewels of the flower world. The entire plant, flower and all, is 1 inch high and not much wider. Do not wet the flat hairy leaves. This tiny flower is a miniature version of its cousin, the gloxinia (*S. speciosa*). The gloxinia's large oval leaves cover the pot it is grown in and support a cluster of colorful upright trumpet-shaped flowers. Available in white and many shades of blue, red, and pink and some bicolors. Both the leaves and the flowers have a velvety texture. As with the sinningia, you should not wet the leaves.

Spathiphyllum (*Spathiphyllum floribundum clevelandii*). The pure white waxlike flower spathes stand out dramatically against the long dark leaves. Does best where the temperature does not get colder than 65° F.

Medium-sized plants, to 36 inches tall

Clivia *(Clivia miniata).* A mass of dark-green straplike leaves hides the emerging flower stem until the clusters of small orange trumpets open in the spring. Does best when the root mass tightly fills the pot.

Fuchsia *(Fuchsia hybrids).* A long-stemmed plant with small dark-green leaves that set off dramatic two-toned flowers with a pendant "petticoat" surrounded by small sepals of contrasting colors. Stems can be staked and trained to make an upright standard or miniature tree.

Jacobinia *(Jacobinia carnea).* Tall square stems are topped with rounded red or pink flowers that have unusual recurved florets.

Schlumbergera *(Schlumbergera bridgesii).* Succulent flat stem segments form arching branches with drooping pink flowers erupting from each tip in midwinter.

Sweet olive *(Osmanthus fragrans).* The small white flowers on short stems along the branches produce the sweetest fragrance of any plant we know. It is tolerant of cool locations and can be pruned to keep in bounds, or it can be controlled by taking stem cuttings periodically for propagation.

Climbing Plants

Some house plants have twining tendrils or aerial rootlets and will attach themselves to a support and climb on their own, as noted in the descriptions below. Others have long sinuous stems and must be tied to a support.

Many of the clambering plants are attractive when grown in hanging containers.

Some of the most useful for this purpose are listed separately.

Allamanda *(Allamanda cathartica).* This handsome clambering vine provides a display of glossy leaves and flowers for several months starting in the spring. The butter-yellow trumpet-shaped flowers have flattened petals at the open end of the bell. Rooted in a 12-inch tub and trained on a trellis, it can be easily kept under control.

Black-eyed Susan vine *(Thunbergia elata).* A small plant with 2-inch heart-shaped leaves that set off the many individual flowers. The five orange petals and dark purple centers account for the common name. It can be kept short by training it around a few stakes in a 5-inch pot.

Clerodendron *(Clerodendron thomsoniae).* The lanky stems will produce striking white flowers with red centers in the spring. To bloom, this plant must have a resting period with very little water in the winter. Do not, however, allow the root area to dry out completely.

Cobaea *(Cobaea scandens).* The 2-inch purple bell-shaped flowers accent the foliage of this vine that ordinarily climbs no more than 5 or 6 feet high. The tip of each leaf produces a twining tendril with which it holds to its support. It is easily grown from seeds.

Creeping fig *(Ficus pumila).* The evergreen 1-inch oval leaves literally cover anything they grow on. It is an excellent plant to grow on an established framework. It climbs by aerial roots along its stems and lies completely flat.

HOUSE PLANTS

Jasmine *(Jasminum polyanthus)*. A popular climber of vigorous habit with wonderfully scented white flowers in midwinter. If cut back every year after flowering, it can easily be kept in bounds.

Passionflower *(Passiflora coerulea)*. The beautifully intricate blue-and-white flowers must be seen to be believed. The vigorous growth can be cut back in the fall, since the flowers appear on new growth during the summer. The plant needs a support on which the tendrils can climb without tying.

Philodendron *(Philodendron scandens)*. The small heart-shaped leaves and their vining branches are adaptable to hanging or growing on a sturdy support. To keep the leaves as close together as possible, give it lots of light and fertilize regularly. Use a balanced house-plant fertilizer, following the directions on the package.

Plumbago *(Plumbago capensis)*. The blue phloxlike flowers of this clambering plant continue to bloom all summer long. Plumbago is particularly well suited to hot dry conditions.

Wax plant *(Hoya carnosa)*. A popular vine with beautiful clusters of small star-shaped waxen flowers arising from among the pointed oval waxlike leaves. Inspect weekly for mealy bugs, which look like tufts of cotton, at the base of leaf stems. If detected, dab them with alcohol on a cotton swab.

Hanging Plants

Hanging plants, with air on all sides of the container, dry out quickly and need watering daily.

The frequent watering tends to leach the nutrients out of the soil, so a monthly feeding with liquid fertilizer is also recommended.

Asparagus fern *(Asparagus sprengeri)*. A popular hanging plant noted for its arching plumes of fluffy bright-green foliage. Requires frequent watering.

Kangaroo vine *(Cissus antarctica)*. A vigorous climbing plant with dark-green leaves. A useful plant because it does reasonably well in limited sunlight.

Manettia *(Manettia bicolor)*. A climber with inch-long red-and-yellow firecracker-shaped flowers scattered among the slender leaf-covered stems. It is attractive grown two or three to a pot and trained on a teepee of three bamboo stakes.

Philodendron *(Philodendron scandens)*. Discussed above, as a climbing plant.

Piggyback plant *(Tolmiea menziesii)*. Individual plantlets develop in the center of the mature leaves and can be removed and easily rooted in water or soil.

Spider plant *(Chlorophytum comosum)*. Extending from a cluster of green-and-white-striped leaves are stems with insignificant white flowers that bloom and continue growing to become complete plants on their own. When roots form, the new plants can be cut off and potted.

Bulbs for Indoors

Amaryllis *(Hippeastrum aulicum)*. This popular showpiece develops a strong 18-inch stem topped with a few colorful trumpet-shaped flowers as large as 6 inches across and 6 to 8 inches long. The leaves that follow are long and straplike. It can be carried over to bear flowers in successive years.

Blood lily *(Haemanthus puniceus).* If you plant this bulb half-buried and start it slowly into growth in midwinter it will produce its brilliant red flowers in early spring. To start it into growth, move it into full light. Give it only 2 or 3 ounces of water at first and increase the amount weekly until it gets a full cup after about four weeks. At the same time, increase the heat. Move it from its storage temperature of 45° to 60° F. in the same length of time. It may not be possible to do this exactly, but come as close as you can.

Daffodil *(Narcissus pseudo-narcissus).*
These are beautiful, inexpensive, dependable bulbs. They are available in white or yellow, and some are fragrant. Start the bulbs in the fall in pots and keep them cold (from 20° to 40° F.) for about three months and then put them where the temperature is about 50°, and in a few weeks they will come into bloom. Discard them after they flower.

Guernsey lily *(Nerine sariensis).* This has salmon-colored blooms with long recurved stamens, and as with many other South African bulbs, the flower opens before the straplike leaves appear. To bring it into flower in successive years, follow the instructions at the end of this section.

Hyacinth *(Hyacinthus orientalis).* The stubby columns of florets exude more perfume per square inch than almost any other plant.

The amaryllis never fails to please, and sometimes amaze, even the most experienced gardener, with its long stem and large flower.

Available in white and various shades of blue and pink and red, it can be forced like a daffodil and is also best discarded after flowering.

Iris *(Iris reticulata* hybrids). This miniature iris blooms in midwinter. Start it in a pot in early November and let the roots develop for about three weeks, then put it in a cool frost-free place where it can rest. In January bring it to a warm light place and water well, and it will come beautifully into bloom. It will flower in successive years if rested over the following summer and fall.

To rest a plant in preparation for the next cycle of growth, put it, pot and all, in a cool place (40° to 45° F.) where there is very little light or complete darkness, and

HOUSE PLANTS

give it only enough water every week or so to keep the bulb from shriveling.

Jacobean lily *(Spreklia formosissima)*. The petals of this lively flower reach out to form a cross. The soft red color is attractively set off by the narrow straplike leaves. They bloom during the summer and can be carried over to successive years (see next column), except that they rest during the winter and start to grow in early spring.

Lily *(Lilium auratum* hybrids). There is a wide choice of spectacular hybrid lilies now available. Grow them as you would daffodils (but in larger pots), and provide sticks for support if needed. They will flower in late winter in successive years if allowed to continue growing until the foliage has turned completely brown as the current cycle of growth comes to its end. It is during this segment of the cycle (after flowering) that the bulb accumulates the necessary energy for the next season of growth.

Paper white narcissus *(Narcissus tazetta)*. This is the familiar fragrant foolproof variety that will flower in shallow water alone if the bulbs are simply held upright in a container or supported by pebbles. Don't cover the bulb with water, and don't let it dry out. It's the roots that take up the water. Discard them after flowering.

Tulip *(Tulipa gesneriana* hybrids). There are hundreds of varieties of tulips, and many are bred and specially prepared for forcing. These varieties are so indicated in the catalogs and garden stores. Put five or six bulbs, touching one another, in a shallow 6-inch pot or bulb pan. Handle them as recommended for daffodils, and don't

bother to save them for forcing the following year. The cost of a dozen or two is small, and it is fun to try new ones.

Keeping bulbs going in successive years

The preceding descriptions mention bulbs that will respond to this treatment. First let them continue to grow until after all the flowers have faded. Cut off the flowers and continue to water as in previous weeks. Then, when the leaves begin to turn brown, about three weeks after the flowers are gone, gradually reduce the amount of water applied daily. In a week or so when the foliage dies down cut it off and put the pot in a dark place with a temperature of from 40° to 50° F.

If, upon periodic examination, the bulb shows signs of shrinking, add a cup of water to the pot.

In the fall, when you want to start them into growth for flowers the following spring, scrape away some of the old soil, taking care not to damage the roots, and replace the top inch or so with a soil mixture enriched with a complete fertilizer. Use about one tablespoon of a 10-10-10 fertilizer or equivalent for a 6-inch pot.

Move the pot to a warmer place and start to water again about every other day. When the new green tips emerge from the bulbs, put the pot in full light and water daily until it blooms.

Growing Plants Under Artificial Light

There's no question that house plants will grow beautifully under artificial light; the question is what kind of light and how much.

The amount of light required for growth

of most plants, as mentioned before, is the level required to read a newspaper comfortably. The key word is "comfortably." Keep in mind that the eye adapts quickly to light levels that are less than ideal. For plants (as well as for your eyes) it is better to have the light intensity on the high side than on the low.

Plants will grow under either incandescent or fluorescent light. The fluorescents, however, have three advantages. One is that they produce a wider spectrum of light rays, including the short end of the scale that is particularly important to photosynthesis and other aspects of plant growth. They also give off less heat, which makes it possible to put them closer to the plant without danger of excessive drying. Finally, fluorescent light is cheaper. If only incandescent light is available, keep it at least 2 feet from the plant. Fluorescent light can be as close as a foot from the plant.

In order to grow well, produce flowers, and set seed, plants grown under artificial light should have at least 14 hours of illumination a day. The fixtures can easily be controlled with an electric timer.

Reflected light can be used to good advantage. Mirrors, bright metal, or white paint on surrounding surfaces will help decrease the loss of light.

In working with artificial light, it is useful to understand that its intensity varies inversely with the square of the distance from the source. This means that if you have a light 1 foot from a plant and move it to 2 feet away, the light intensity is reduced to one-fourth of what it was at 1 foot. Move to 4 feet away and the intensity is reduced to one-sixteenth of what it was when the light was a foot from the plant.

The required frequency of watering can be reduced if the pots are set on a 1-inch layer of pebbles in a shallow tray of water to a depth somewhat less than that of the gravel. This will create a moist atmosphere and keep the pots from sitting in the water, which would promote root rot.

Good ventilation (but not a drafty place) is a necessity for house plants. This is often overlooked in the creation of areas for plants under artificial light.

For optimum plant growth, the lighting fixtures must often be so close to the plants that they tend to obscure them. This is particularly true of the fixtures that have fluorescent lights hung just above the shelves that hold the plants. These fixtures can often be used in an out-of-the-way place for the rejuvenation of plants that do not get all the light they need where they are normally displayed.

A container like this one can be used when house plants must be left unattended for a week or so. Line a box with seamless plastic sheeting, fill with perlite or vermiculite, soak the material thoroughly, and insert pots.

❧ |16| ❧
Pruning

There are probably more misconceptions about pruning than about any other aspect of gardening.

You may have heard, for example, that a dogwood can bleed to death if it is pruned in the spring, or that an apple tree pruned too hard will produce a large crop of soft willowy stems called suckers. It's true that the dogwood will bleed and that the apple may have a lot of sucker growth, but the trees will not be harmed. There's more danger of doing damage by pruning too little than by pruning too much. The point is, don't be afraid to remove wood when there is good reason for doing so. The timing is not all-important.

When Liberty Hyde Bailey, the late dean of American horticulture, was asked when was the best time to prune, his answer was, "When your knife is sharp."

Pruning for Health

Pruning to improve the health of a plant can begin before it is put in the ground and can continue annually, or more often, for as long as it lives.

When setting out plants with bare roots, remove any of the larger roots that are broken. When the necessary root pruning has been done, it is almost certain that there will be more top growth than the roots can properly support. This is why it is recommended that as much as one-fourth to one-third of the top growth be removed at planting time. Don't be timid. This heavy pruning leads to vigorous new growth.

Any branches that are broken or dead should be removed. In doing so, make sure that you cut back to sound wood. You can tell if the wood is green and alive or brown and dead by making a nick in the bark with your fingernail.

Do not remove sound branches just because they may be damaged by insects or have holes in them made by birds. The insects can be eliminated with the proper controls, and when they are gone the birds will not peck holes.

Pruning for Production

Once a plant is well established, a primary purpose of further pruning is to help it to

If left unpruned many trees will develop a V-shaped crotch that is structurally weak and can split off in a heavy wind or ice storm. The crotch should be eliminated, favoring the larger trunk of the two. Here the first cut is being made.

When final pruning cuts have been made, the edges should be trimmed smooth with a sharp clean knife, so that the wound can heal evenly. Tree paint can be used on the cut, but most experts today say it is not really necessary.

produce the flowers and fruit for which it was planted.

A somewhat oversimplified, but usable, rule is to prune shrubs immediately after they flower and to prune trees in winter during their period of slowest growth.

Flowering shrubs can actually be pruned at any time of the year. But if it is

done before they flower you will obviously lose that year's display.

If the shrub only needs thinning out, the ideal time to do this is just before it comes into bloom. The prunings can be taken into the house and plunged in a container of water, and in a week or so they will burst into flower before those that were left on

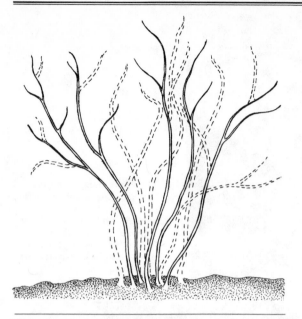

The oldest, thickest growth on an overgrown shrub should be cut out at ground level. The dotted lines show stems that can typically be removed on shrubs like forsythia, deutzia, and philadelphus.

you cut a branch of wood that is in active growth, you encourage two branches to grow in its place. This increased branching not only helps to produce more flowers and fruit, but also can provide you with attractive branches to use for decoration indoors. Holly, pyracantha, rhododendron, white pine, and mountain ash all fit into this category.

Pruning for Better Appearance

The pruning that is done for this purpose calls for considerable courage and sharp shears. Don't underestimate the importance of the latter.

Always prune young trees and shrubs with an eye toward their future shape. Select the strongest stems, eliminate crossed branches, and prevent the development of narrow crotches that might split.

Keep in mind that where you make the pruning cut can control the direction of

the shrub. Such shrubs as flowering quince and forsythia as well as branches of apple and pear trees are some that are readily forced into bloom.

Much of the pruning done in the name of production will, of course, improve the health of the plant. Removing branches to let more sun into the center of a tree for the purpose of increasing fruit production also lets in more air, which will reduce the incidence of fungus diseases.

The flowers of some shrubs turn into decorative berries that you will want to keep on the plant, while others go to unattractive seed that, in most cases, you will want to remove. If seeds are allowed to form they take energy that would otherwise go into increasing the strength of the plant.

Shrubs and trees that produce berries and fruits will be more productive if some of the branches are shortened. Each time

A small tree or shrub may take on an unattractive, unbalanced shape because of wind or other weather conditions. The pruned shape, shown here by a solid line, is clearly more pleasing.

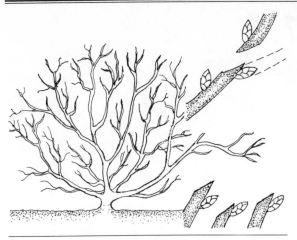

All plants should be pruned to the outside-pointing buds in order to force growth outward and let light and air into the center. The enlarged insets at lower right show how the cuts should be made. In relation to the bud, the first cut from the left is too far, the next is too close, but the third is just right.

propriate as low-growing azaleas or conifers trimmed into rigid shapes.

Rejuvenating Overgrown Plants

You can restore neglected shrubs in late spring or early summer by pruning about half of the branches back to just above the ground. Remove the oldest branches first. Then feed the plant with a 10-10-10 fertilizer and water liberally every week thereafter for the rest of the growing season.

The following spring the rest of the old branches can be removed, and by the third season you will have a vigorous shrub with all the old wood removed. Flowers will clothe the new branches almost down to ground level.

For information about the best tools to use for pruning, see chapter 19. There are some jobs that should be turned over to a professional arborist or tree surgeon. It is not safe for a novice to work from a ladder or to climb a tree to cut off branches. Don't use a chain saw unless you have had experience with this dangerous tool.

Call for professional help in cleaning out areas of rot or installing drains, guy wires, or lightning protection in a tree.

growth. If you cut to an inside bud, the new growth will face inward and create more crossing branches. But if you prune so the bud just below the cut faces to the outside, the new growth will be in that direction.

Whether a plant should be pruned to maintain its natural shape or sheared to conform to a more formal appearance is a matter of preference and landscape use. Most hedges look best when neatly trimmed. On the other hand, there is nothing so inap-

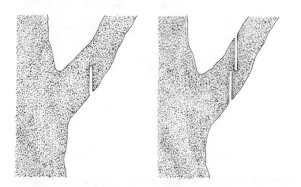

To avoid stripping bark from the trunk when removing a limb, make an undercut, then a cut from above.

After the limb has been removed, cut the stub flush with the trunk.

✻|17|✻
Propagation

An interest in this subject usually begins with the need for a few more of a particular plant—at minimum expense. But be forewarned, it is a fascinating process that can become something of an end in itself.

It can be as simple as rooting a stem of ivy in a glass of water and planting it in a pot, or as complex as growing orchids from seed. Part of the pleasure of propagating is experimenting with the variety of available techniques.

Plants are produced either sexually, by seed or spores; or asexually, by the establishment of new roots on some part of the plant or the attachment of a new plant to established roots. With the exception of propagation by spores (primarily used for ferns and mosses), all of these techniques

Make furrows for seed in a soil mixture of equal parts coarse sand and peat moss. Space large seed 1½ inches apart, or scatter fine seed in a thin line. Cover the seed with soil mixture that has been sifted through a sieve.

Keep the seeding mixture warm, shaded, and slightly moist. In one to three weeks the seeds will sprout and you can put the flat in full sun. Lift the seedlings when the roots are about 1 inch long.

are explained and illustrated on the pages that follow.

Propagation by Seed

Propagation by seed is called "sexual," because the seed is developed from within the flower by the interaction of the stamens and pistils—the reproductive organs of the plant.

The seed from a given species of any plant tends to "come true," which is to say that the plant it produces will be remarkably similar in all respects to the plant from which it came.

Take a sweet gum tree *(Liquidambar styraciflua)*, for example. The seed of this tree will produce trees that are almost, but not quite, identical to one another. The "not quite" will be considered later on.

A seed obviously has the capacity to germinate, root, and develop into a healthy plant entirely on its own; otherwise, seed-bearing plants could not survive in the wild.

Their success can be attributed primarily to the prodigious number of seeds the plants produce. To assure the continuation of a species in its natural habitat, only a tiny percentage of the seeds need to find the conditions of light, soil, humidity, and temperature required for germination.

When a gardener plants seed, he can provide the required environment and often attain nearly 100% germination. Some, but not all, seed requires little more than scattering on the garden soil, a gentle raking, tamping, and watering, and then, presto, in two or three weeks a whole new generation of zinnias, marigolds, parsley, basil, or snapdragons will emerge. Most vegetables and annual flowers are grown in this way.

Seed can also be started indoors to make seedlings that can later be planted in the garden.

Although a greenhouse or cold frame makes it easier, seeds can also be started in a shallow flower pot on a sunny window sill.

Set the rooted seedlings 2 to 3 inches apart in a market pack or similar container that is filled with equal parts of garden soil, peat moss or leaf mold, and coarse builder's sand.

When the plants begin to form branches (in cool climates, when the ground begins to warm) the rooted seedlings can be set out in the garden. Space them far enough apart so that they won't have to be moved again.

PROPAGATION

The sowing medium can be peat moss, vermiculite, perlite, or sand, or a mixture of any of these. Ready-made mixes are also available.

Moisten the mixture thoroughly the night before with water to which has been added an anti-damping-off chemical (sold in garden stores).

Sow the seed at the depth recommended on the package and syringe the surface with water. Then cover the container with a layer of newspaper. This is to keep the sun off the mixture, which must not be allowed to dry out.

When the first leaves show, remove the newspaper to expose them to the sun. Keep the mixture moist, but not wet, and provide good air circulation.

When the second set of leaves begins to form, transplant the seedlings to a potting mixture, allowing about 1½ inches between the plants.

Seed should be purchased fresh from a dependable commercial source. This will increase the likelihood of viability and produce plants that are reasonably disease-free. They will also be more likely to retain the desirable characteristics that were created by hybridization.

Plants are hybridized by taking the pollen from the anther (a part of the stamen) of one plant and putting it on the pistil of another plant, which will bear the seed. From this cross will come seed that will produce plants combining various characteristics of both parents.

A blue delphinium crossed with a white one, for example, is likely to produce some light-blue or lavender flowers. Let us say that among hundreds of crosses, a light-blue delphinium appeared that was so superior that the hybridizer gave it a variety name and made plans to sell it commercially. This means that all plants bearing this name must be nearly identical. This uniformity of seed is accomplished by carefully controlled production.

Asexual or vegetative propagation is accomplished without the interaction of the reproductive parts. As explained and illustrated here, the easiest methods are by divisions, offsets, cuttings, or layers. The techniques of dividing plants with fleshy roots are explained in chapter 12. Growing new plants on established roots is done by the more specialized processes of budding and grafting, used mostly by commercial nurserymen.

Vegetative propagation is used to reproduce a particular plant exactly. Say a specific azalea has spectacular color, or a coleus has a distinctive pattern and color on the leaves. Cuttings from these will

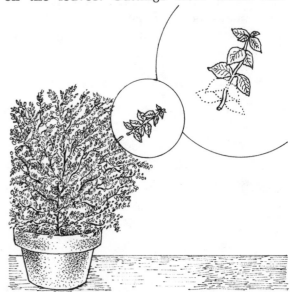

Softwood stem cuttings can be made from branching plants when their green stems have reached a point where they will break when bent. Make cuttings about 5 inches long. Remove the bottom leaves to leave 1 to 2 inches of bare stem and dust the cut end with rooting hormone.

make plants with the identical characteristics of the parent.

Now, back to the sweet gum mentioned before. If you plant 20 seedlings, they will all have the magnificent fall color for which the tree is renowned. In any given year the color of some will be richer and more intense than the others. If you select the one with the most brilliant color and make cuttings, layers, or grafts of that tree, the progeny will have the same outstanding color. Although color varies somewhat depending on the weather, this tree will always have the superior qualities for which it was selected.

Making Cuttings

Nipping off a small piece of a plant and growing an entirely new one, with roots, stems, leaves, and flowers, is a particularly

Insert the stems in a pot of perlite, vermiculite, or seeding mix. As shown here, a number can go in one shallow pot. When the roots are about 1 inch long, move them to individual pots or to the garden when the ground is warm and there is no longer any danger of frost.

Most leaf cuttings are made from plants usually considered to be house plants, particularly those with fleshy leaves such as African violets. Fill a pot with seeding mix, moisten thoroughly, and insert leaf stems to the base of the leaf. Cover the pot with a tent of clear plastic supported by wire or sticks in order to maintain humidity, and keep the cuttings in good light but not direct sun. When rooted, transplant each leaf to an individual pot.

valuable form of propagation during the times of year when seeds are not available or when you want to get a plant started as quickly as possible.

And, as explained above, growing from seed will not exactly duplicate a given plant, whereas this process of making vegetative cuttings will. Cuttings can be made of so-called softwood or hardwood cuttings. The former are most often used for herbaceous plants, whose stems die down at the end of the growing season. This kind of cutting is used for tropical plants that do not develop woody stems. Most house plants are in this category.

The branch or stem that will constitute the cutting should be selected from side growth rather than from top or terminal growth. The stage of growth is critical. The branch should break off when bent over. If it doesn't break readily, it is either too soft or too hard. The branch will be at this stage when the active growth has slowed down and the tissue has just begun to ripen or harden. The stems, however, should still be in full leaf. There is no specific date or season for this stage of growth, since each species of plant grows on its own schedule. So, depend upon the aforementioned test.

Select stems that are most typical of the plant. Those that are too vigorous will have already used most of their food supply. Stems that are more fully ripened than the average on the plant will be less able to develop the cell growth required to initiate rooting.

Rooting can be accelerated by the use of a heating cable (available at garden stores) set in the bottom portion of the rooting medium. Since the soil temperature will be consistently above 65°, it will be necessary to add water frequently to maintain the desired high level of humidity.

Hardwood cuttings

These are used mainly to propagate trees and shrubs. The cuttings, which should be 6 to 8 inches long, are made in the fall after growth has stopped and the leaves have fallen. They should be taken either before a hard freeze or during a period of thaw, not during freezing weather.

The cutting should be about the diameter of a lead pencil. Cut square across the stem about ⅛ inch below a node. Then at the recommended length above this, make a slanting cut. The slant serves to indicate the top end of the cuttings.

A dozen or more cuttings can be gathered together like a fistful of pencils and held with a rubber band. Stack them uniformly with all the tops in one direction.

Bury the bunch of cuttings either lying on their side or upside down (square-cut ends facing upward) in a box of slightly damp sand or sawdust and keep in a cold place, such as an unheated garage, root cellar, or crawl space. The temperature should be cool but not freezing. From 40° to 45° F. is ideal.

When spring comes, the bottoms of the cuttings should have developed a hard covering or callus. After this occurs, they can be planted in the garden in a trench filled with a mixture of half soil and half peat moss.

Set them about 1 inch apart with two or three leaf buds showing above the soil. The cuttings will do best in partial shade and with the soil-and-peat-moss mixture kept slightly moist.

The new plants should be well rooted and ready to transplant by the end of the summer.

To get an earlier start on hardwood cuttings, check in early spring to see if the bottoms have developed the necessary callus. If they have, they can be moved into pots or flats containing a mixture of equal parts coarse sand and peat moss. Set them, bottom down, about 1 inch apart. They should develop roots within a month, at which time they can be transplanted into the garden as explained above.

Dividing

Many plants grow as clumps rather than as either a single stem or a rosette of leaves that come as a single stem. The root area of these clump-forming plants can be divided into parts, thus rendering new plants to set out in other areas of the garden or to give to friends.

The easiest plants to propagate by division are those with a fibrous rootstock. Among the most familiar of these are day lilies, hostas, chrysanthemums, and peonies. Whether you want a supply of new plants or not, perennials should be lifted and divided when they are obviously overcrowded.

When a clump of flowers begins to thin out noticeably in the center, it is time for dividing. Thinning occurs at the center because the flowers tend to grow more readily toward the perimeter of the root area than in the center. This tendency is not so noticeable when the clump is small, but as it gets larger, there are comparatively fewer flowers in the center, and if the roots are not lifted and divided, some plantings of perennials can eventually choke themselves out.

Some shrubs, such as philadelphus, kerria, and forsythia, lend themselves readily to propagation by division. While these vigorous plants are not likely to die out from overcrowding, the appearance of a planting can often be improved by dividing.

In dividing the root mass of a plant, be it a shrub or an herbaceous perennial, make sure that each division includes healthy roots and growth buds. In separating the plants, do as little damage as possible to the roots.

It is a good idea to have the new planting area ready before dividing; the divisions can then be planted immediately, which will forestall their drying out.

Plants with fine roots can usually be divided by gently pulling them apart with the fingers.

If the roots are badly tangled, it is better to cut through them with a sharp knife than to cause undue damage by tearing them apart. See the illustration.

Most plants that grow from a clump of stems or leaves can be divided into two or more parts by simply cutting down through the root mass. Each section is complete and can be treated as a mature plant.

Some bulbs and corms produce offsets which can be removed and planted. For more about this form of division, see the "Lifting, Storing, and Dividing" section of chapter 12, page 87.

For illustrated instructions on dividing dahlias and iris, see pages 88 and 89.

Some plants develop underground suckers that can be dug up, detached, and replanted. Raspberries and lilacs are among the plants easily divided by this method. Do not, however, use suckers to propagate fruit trees or roses that are grafted on the (hardier) understock of another plant. The suckers are most likely to come from the understock and will not produce the flowers or fruit you expect.

Layering

There are many plants whose branches will root readily if they are covered with soil at one or more leaf nodes. The process is simple.

Scrape through the bark on the underside of the stem and put the stem in contact with the soil, which is kept slightly moist, until the roots form. Peat moss mixed with the soil will improve water retention.

Layering is most easily done with plants that have flexible low-growing branches, such as raspberries, forsythia, philadelphus, and beauty bush. Plants with branches too stiff to bend to the ground can be layered by covering the base with a mound of soil about 1 foot high. Scrape through the bark at the base of the stems you have chosen to root. When they have been covered for about a month, roots will form on the wounded stems in the mound of soil. Cut the stems below the new roots, cut the tops back to about 1 foot long, and plant the rooted cuttings.

Air layering

When the lower part of a tall spindly plant is too woody to develop new growth readily, air layering, as shown below, is often an efficient way to start a new plant.

When the new plant is severed from the parent plant it may be set out in the garden or potted. A little judicious tip-pruning will encourage it to fill out and develop an attractive compact habit of growth.

Some of the garden plants that are good candidates for this treatment are hollies, andromedas, and laurels. House plants such as the scheffeleras, figs, and dracaenas whose stems may have gotten too long can often be improved by this technique.

Air layering is used to shorten plants that have grown too tall or spindly. In the spot where you want the new roots to form, cut a flap a third of the way through the stem. Insert a matchstick to hold the wound open and dust the cut with rooting hormone. Wrap a handful of sphagnum moss around the cut, cover the moss with clear plastic, and tie it top and bottom. In one to three months roots will form and you can cut the stem below them and pot the new plant.

❧ |18| ❧
Controlling Pests and Diseases

When a plant is obviously not doing well, it needs attention. In fact, it is accurate to say that it is sick. As is stated in the textbooks on the subject, anything affecting a plant adversely can be considered a disease.

Some diseases are noninfectious. These diseases include severe reactions to the temperature or a lack of food or water, or a critical chemical imbalance in the soil and thus in the plant. Elsewhere in this book, in the chapters on cultivation and on different kinds of plants, we explain how to detect and avoid such noninfectious diseases.

In this chapter we are concerned with the infectious diseases—those caused by insects, fungus, and virus. Insects and disease are facts of life in a garden and should be no cause for panic. You may have to accept some unsightliness and a few losses here and there, but these can be kept to a minimum if you practice preventive maintenance.

It is a fact that healthy plants are less susceptible to the debilitating effects of insects, fungi, and viruses than plants in a weakened condition. Proper attention to the purchase of healthy plants, to soil conditioning, and to watering and fertilizing will not only produce healthier and more attractive plants but will also help keep pest and disease damage to a minimum.

When a plant does show signs of distress and you know that it has the right exposure, soil, and general care, you obviously have to look further for the source of trouble. If you keep a sharp eye on your plants and take the appropriate action as soon as trouble is spotted, you should be able to keep things well under control. And this does not mean that you must be perpetually armed with a spraygun or in a constant state of nervous watchfulness.

Diagnosis

As with any diagnosis, the process is one of elimination.

First look for insects and insect damage. Close observation is part of the pleasure of gardening. While you are looking at the changing color of new growth, the swelling of buds, and the development of flowers and seed, watch also for insects and any damage they may have done.

Look particularly on the underside of the leaves, as this is where insects are often found. In the process of looking here you will also discover that many plants have leaves with interesting and unexpected color and attractive vein patterns on their undersides.

Insect damage to leaves may be in the form of punctured or chewed places, or the leaves may be rolled up to surround the insect. Look too for small holes in twigs and stems, as these may be caused by borers.

Next, look for signs of disease. Inspect leaves and buds for the grayish-white powder of powdery mildew, for black spots, and for the small wartlike growths called rusts. Most of these problems are caused by fungus and call for the application of fungicides.

The most difficult diseases to diagnose and control are those caused by viruses. In general, they show up on leaves as areas where color has been lost. These diseases are most often spread by insects or transmitted by a diseased plant to its progeny—if it was propagated vegetatively. It is therefore best to destroy any infected plants as soon as they are discovered to be diseased, and before they can infect others.

Methods of Control

One way to reduce the likelihood of insects and disease attacking your plants is to keep the garden and surrounding area as clean as possible. This will help to eliminate hiding places for bugs and places where diseases might be nurtured. You should burn all diseased plants. Don't put them on the compost pile, where conditions are often ideal for the proliferation of disease, which can be spread along with the compost.

Biological controls

Biological controls are effectively practiced by some gardeners. These controls do, however, require commitment and persistence.

Such natural predators as ladybugs and praying mantises, as well as milky spore disease, are the most frequently used controls. The ladybug can keep aphids in bounds, the mantis preys on a variety of insects, and milky spore disease infects and kills the Japanese beetle.

Keep in mind that once you commit yourself to biological control, you cannot use chemicals without endangering the beneficial insects. There must also be enough of the specific pests in the garden to provide a continuing supply of food for the predators during the growing season.

When the aphids are gone, the ladybugs may starve out, permitting the aphids to reappear later on. The praying mantises, with their more varied diet, are less likely to starve.

The most direct (and least inviting) way to deal with some insects, such as the Japanese beetle, is to pick them off the plant before their numbers have become overwhelming, and get rid of them in a can of kerosene.

Controls for specific pests

While there are some broad-spectrum sprays and dusts that will kill most insects, the chances of control are increased if you know exactly which culprit you are dealing with. *Precaution:* Keep all pest-control materials in a safe place where children cannot get at them. Use all these materials in strict accordance with the directions on the labels.

The following brief descriptions may be of help in identifying the most common garden insects. A specific control is recommended for each.

Aphids. When they are first noticeable, they look like pieces of white lint about the size of a grain of sand. As they suck the juices from leaves and stems they turn green and grow to a length of about $\frac{1}{16}$ inch. They are commonly found on roses, chrysanthemums, and dahlias as well as many fruits and vegetables of the Brassica family (cabbage, broccoli, and such). You will see them clustered on tender new growth, on flower buds, and on the undersides of leaves.

Control: Wash them off the plant with a strong spray of water, or spray or dust with malathion.

Borers. These are the larvae of beetles, and there are several kinds that look like hairless caterpillars about $\frac{1}{4}$ inch thick and 1 inch long. They burrow into woody stems and roots of many plants. Dogwood and iris are particularly susceptible.

Control: Borers can be cut out of rhizomes such as iris. When they infest woody stems, pruning and burning are recommended. When the insect has chewed its way into the trunk of a tree such as dogwood, insert a stiff wire in the hole to kill the grub. This will prevent the beetle (the next stage in the life cycle) from laying eggs and producing a new destructive generation. Also spray with lindane to ensure the kill.

Japanese beetles. These orange and iridescent-green flying insects are about $\frac{1}{2}$ inch long and are easily seen in clusters as they chew the leaves, flowers, and stems of roses, willows, and many other plants. The numbers vary greatly from year to year depending on the weather during the late-summer breeding season. Many other

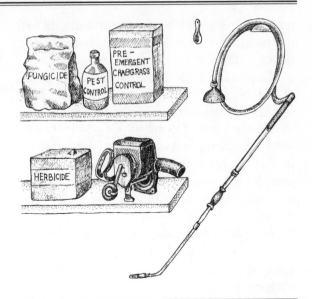

The most prevalent weeds, insects, and diseases can be treated with a few basic materials and applicators. Useful tools are a duster for dry materials, and a trombone sprayer which can shoot a stream of liquid about 30 feet high and is indispensable for spraying trees.

beetle species are nonflying, and most of these feed at night. The damage they do to the leaves is readily apparent. Beetles in their larval stage are called grubs. These fat, cream-colored, inch-long worms eat grass roots until they emerge as mature beetles.

Control: For beetles in general, spray with Sevin. For Japanese beetles in particular, you can also inoculate the lawn with the milky spore disease that will infect and kill the grubs.

Leafhoppers. These $\frac{1}{2}$-inch green insects are square at both ends. Their back ridge is raised and they hop when disturbed. They usually suck plant juices from the underside of the leaves.

Control: Spray with Sevin.

Leaf miners. These tiny larvae of very small flies eat a meandering path between the upper and lower leaf surfaces of such trees as holly and birch. Their tunnels are white at first and then turn brown as the tissue dries out.

Control: Spray with Sevin three times at ten-day intervals. Make the first application as the new leaves begin to unfold.

Mealy bugs. These sucking insects are seen mostly on house plants. Clustered on leaf axils, the flat oval ⅛-inch insects look like pieces of wax. Their eggs are enveloped in a cottonlike mass that is also easily detected.

Control: Spray with malathion. If there are only a few to deal with, remove them with a cotton swab dipped in rubbing alcohol.

Nematodes. Nematodes are almost-microscopic worms in the soil that live on roots. A sickly-looking plant is usually the first evidence of their presence. A diagnosis often requires that a sample of the roots be sent to a soil laboratory at a state agricultural college.

Control: Eradication is difficult and should be accomplished under the direction of a county agricultural extension service agent. His recommendation will probably be to use a specialized chemical such as Nemagon.

Red spider mites. This pest causes drying of plant tissue and can eventually cause leaves to drop. The mites are only about half the size of the period at the end of this sentence, and are thus difficult to detect. They are particularly bothersome on pieris, azaleas and rhododendrons, and hemlock. If you suspect an infestation, hold a piece of white paper under some of the leaves and tap them sharply. See if any black specks drop onto the paper. If they move, they are spider mites, and they can literally suck the life out of a plant.

Control: Spray with Kelthane.

Scale insects. These look less like insects than most. They are covered by a turtle-shaped, brittle, oyster-colored shell about ⅛ inch long. They congregate in large numbers on the stems of trees and shrubs over the winter and begin their debilitating activity of sucking juices from the plant in early spring.

Control: Spray with an oil emulsion before leaf growth starts in the spring. They can also be killed by swabbing with oil if they are detected later.

Slugs. These unattractive nocturnal foragers are snails without shells. They chew on leaves and buds. In the daytime they hide in dark cool places. They leave a slimy trail that helps to reveal their presence.

Control: Use a slug bait such as Slugit, Slug-kill, or Snarol. Put the bait in an empty coffee can laid on its side. This protects the bait from rain but will allow the slugs to enter and take it. Slugs seem to be attracted to beer. As an alternate control, put some in a saucer in the evening and you will likely find some dead slugs in the morning.

Tent caterpillars. An unsightly web in the crotch of tree branches is usually the first sign of this insect. The hairy caterpillar is 1½ inches long and has a red stripe bordered with white dots down the ridge of its back. All caterpillars are the destructive stage in the life cycle of moths and butterflies. The voracious caterpillars defoliate trees as their colonies spread.

Control: Spray with Sevin on sight.

Whitefly. These tiny white specks are a familiar pest on indoor plants. If you brush against the foliage, literally hundreds of the flies will rise up and dart about and then light again on the leaves and crawl to

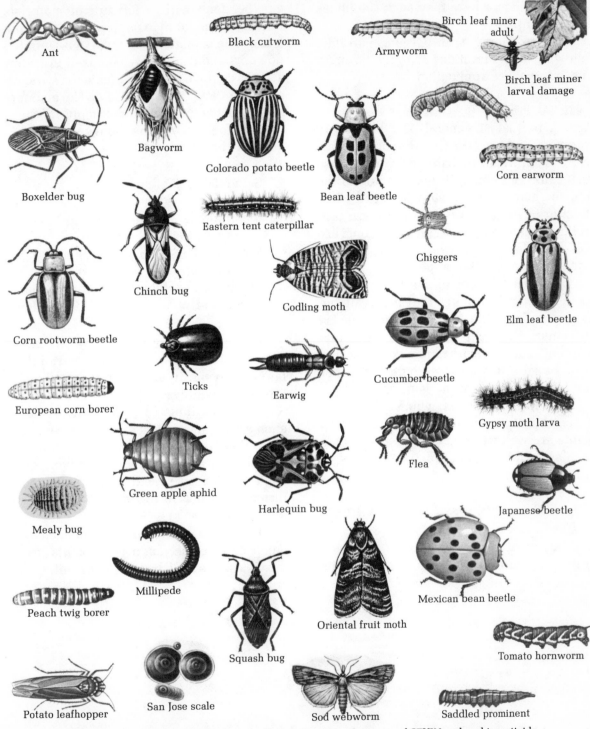

Ant

Bagworm

Black cutworm

Armyworm

Birch leaf miner adult

Birch leaf miner larval damage

Boxelder bug

Colorado potato beetle

Corn earworm

Bean leaf beetle

Chinch bug

Eastern tent caterpillar

Codling moth

Chiggers

Elm leaf beetle

Corn rootworm beetle

Ticks

Earwig

Cucumber beetle

European corn borer

Green apple aphid

Harlequin bug

Flea

Gypsy moth larva

Japanese beetle

Mealy bug

Millipede

Peach twig borer

Squash bug

Oriental fruit moth

Mexican bean beetle

Tomato hornworm

Potato leafhopper

San Jose scale

Sod webworm

Saddled prominent

Illustrations courtesy of Union Carbide Corporation, manufacturers of SEVIN carbaryl insecticide.

PESTS AND DISEASE

the undersides, where they suck the juices of the plant.

Control: Spray with Cygon, carefully following label directions as to the strength and intervals of application.

A general pest control

Among the safest general pest killers are rotenone and pyrethrum. (Rotenone, however, is injurious to fish, so avoid its use near tanks or ponds.) If these do not do the job, you may need the more powerful malathion or Sevin carbaryl. But if you are controlling pests on vegetables, do not use malathion later than two weeks before you intend to harvest the crop.

It is most efficient to use these materials in dust form, although they are available as sprays. With the handy plastic squeeze container, the dust can be applied just where it should go with minimum waste and drift. Be sure to apply it to both the upper and lower surfaces of the leaves.

For control of fungus, which may be evidenced by mildew or wilting (even when the plants are well watered), apply a fungicide such as liquid Benlate, Zineb, or other specific fungicides.

An all-purpose mixture for insect and disease control

You may want to try a preventive approach to the control of insects and disease. This can be done with a mixture of materials that are formulated to control specific problems. These materials come as wettable powders and can simply be mixed in water. The percentage figures indicate the strength at which they are usually sold. The amounts are for 1 gallon of water. Simply measure out a gallon and add the following materials and stir thoroughly.

Sevin (50%), 2 tablespoons
  (for chewing insects)
Malathion (25%), 4 tablespoons
  (for sucking insects)
Kelthane (35%), 1½ tablespoons
  (for mites)
Zineb (65%), 1 tablespoon (for fungus)
Karathane (22%), 1 teaspoon (for mildew)

If this solution is used on vegetables it should not be applied later than seven days before harvest. In any case, wash all vegetables thoroughly.

For crops that are picked almost daily, such as carrots, radishes, and lettuce, spray only those rows that will not be used immediately. Always wash the sprayer thoroughly after use, and run clear water through the nozzle to remove all traces of the chemicals.

To minimize the use of chemicals as much as possible, keep your plants growing well so they will be more resistant.

|19|
The Best of the Basic Garden Tools

The quality and character of your garden and landscape do not depend on the array of tools and equipment you have. But on the other hand, there is no point in handicapping yourself and doing things the hard way when there are tools that can definitely make the job easier.

No matter how many or how few tools you buy, it always pays to get the best possible quality. There is nothing more frustrating than blades that won't hold an edge, handles that come loose, and tools that are not well balanced and do not fit the hand comfortably.

Never buy a tool without hefting it for balance and fit. You can be sure that if it is uncomfortable to handle in the store it will still be so after an hour of working with it in the garden.

As for cutting tools, there is no sure way to tell by inspection in the store whether one pair of pruning shears, for example, will hold an edge better than another. But it is reasonably safe to assume that the more expensive models will be made of better steel than the cheaper ones.

When you buy shovels, rakes, and hoes with wooden handles attached to the metal parts, make sure the handles are set into long sockets (ferrules) and that the two parts are firmly riveted together.

There are some seasonal chores and a few big jobs that are most easily done with relatively expensive power tools and equipment. Fortunately, in most communities, these labor-savers can be rented. Among the most useful ones to keep in mind for making quick work of back-breaking chores are the power tiller and chain saw. For ailing lawns there are machines that will aerify and dethatch. Lawn seeders and rollers are also very useful, though used infrequently.

While the following list of tools that you should own may seem rather long, it would be unrealistic to try to handle the complete range of garden chores without them.

Long-handled round-pointed shovel. For general digging and planting.

Garden fork. The best tool to use for spading a garden or otherwise breaking up the soil.

Iron rake. The level-head kind is handiest. The back can be used for fine-smoothing planting beds.

This garden fork has flat tines that pierce the ground easily and help break up the soil as it is lifted.

The ferrule of this scuffle hoe is long and an integral part of the blade—hallmarks of a sturdy tool.

Hoe. The garden hoe with the blade at a right angle to the handle is indispensable for weeding and planting seeds. The scuffle hoe or Dutch hoe has a double-edged cutting blade and works with an easy back-and-forth motion. It is good for cutting weeds just below the surface of the soil, but it can't be used so easily for chopping clods and such.

Trowel. For planting and transplanting. The fit of the handle and overall balance are most important.

Tined cultivator. A short-handled tool often available as a matched model with the trowel. Useful for loosening weeds and removing rocks and such from small planting areas.

Pruning shears. Almost everything in the garden needs pruning or cutting at one time or another. The kind with a scissor action is less likely to damage stems while cutting than the anvil type.

Lopping shears. If you have trees or large shrubs you'll need these for removing branches. The two long handles provide needed leverage.

Pruning saw. The small curved variety will suffice for most jobs.

Leaf rake. The big bamboo ones are the most attractive and easiest to use, although they don't last as long as those with flexible metal tines.

Lawnmower. If you don't have too much lawn to handle, and enjoy the exercise, get a high-quality hand-propelled reel mower. The standard suburban power mower is the self-powered rotary. For really big areas, riding mowers are favored, though they are expensive to buy and operate and require considerable storage space.

Lawn sprinkler. There are half a dozen different types. If you get one that throws a pattern the shape of your lawn, it can save a lot of hose-dragging. There are also rotary sprinklers that creep along the track of the hose as they go. And, of course, the best of all devices for watering the lawn is a built-in sprinkler system on an automatic timer. These are available in kit form with plastic pipe and require no particular mechanical ability to install.

Garden hose. The plastic kind is lightest, and there are kinds that will not get stiff and unmanageable in cold weather. Even a 50-foot length is not too heavy to handle. For maximum convenience, put quick-release fittings on the hose end and on all faucets.

Sprayers. The trombone type is the easiest to use and to clean and it can shoot a spray to the top of a 25-foot tree. The hose-end sprayer is an inexpensive attachment useful for applying fertilizer, pesticides, and weedkillers in small areas.

Wheelbarrow. The kind with balloon tires is easy to wheel. Therefore, don't be afraid to get a big one.

Pocket knife. You will find all manner of uses for this: minor pruning, cutting flowers, trimming vegetables, sharpening stakes.

Sturdy cotton cord. You might as well get a good-sized ball of this for lining up seed rows, staking out planting beds, and making a straight line for trimming hedges.

This is the scissors type of pruning shears. It must be kept sharp. Only the beveled edges are honed.

A pruning saw on a long handle is much safer than a short-handled tool used from a ladder.

TOOLS

❧ |20| ⚕
Chores to Do
Season by Season

Spring

This is the time of year when you look at the garden and the number of things to be done seems so overwhelming that you might be tempted to throw up your hands and head for the house.

But wait. Let's look at your property and see what really has to be done now and what can be left until later.

Your first impulse to head for the house might, in fact, be right. Before getting carried away with the urge to get an early start, make sure that the soil is not still too wet to work. Digging and then walking on the soil should not pack it down. It will if you are starting too soon. The soil has to be dry enough so that when you pick up a handful it will crumble, even after it has been squeezed.

Don't remove protective mulches on strawberries, boxwood, or perennials until the spring winds have died down and the weather is dependable.

One day spring will arrive in earnest. Then you can test the vegetable and annual garden plots for acidity (see chapter 3) and spread lime if necessary. Then you can dig and turn the ground and leave it to dry

further in its unraked state for a week or two.

Start tubs of water lilies indoors where the temperature is above 60° and there is some sunlight for a few hours a day. They will be well along with several leaves by the time the water is warm enough to plunge the tubs outdoors.

Check the entire garden for branches of trees and shrubs broken by winter winds or those that have died and require pruning.

Where freezing is a problem, if the lawn looks rough and uneven, use a roller to smooth it down and reset all the individual sprigs that might have been heaved out of the ground by the spring thaw. An application of fertilizer would also be in order at this time. In Southern gardens, a top seeding might be necessary to revitalize the lawn.

Organize all flower- and vegetable-seed envelopes in a shoe box according to early, midspring, and successive sowings.

Cut branches of flowering shrubs for forcing indoors. There are few garden pleasures more satisfying than having flowers as well as fruits and vegetables a few weeks earlier than normal.

Propagate chrysanthemums by rooting new growth of last year's plants in coarse sand (see chapter 17 for instructions).

Jot down the date you planted each variety of seeds or plants, in order to make any necessary adjustments in timing the following year.

Dust lilacs as soon as they leaf out with sulfur powder to prevent mildew. It is far too difficult to control mildew when the infestation becomes noticeable in midsummer.

Most annuals, except marigolds and nicotiana, should be grown in a slightly alkaline soil. The addition of 20 pounds of ground limestone per 500 square feet will reduce a slightly acid soil to a satisfactory level of more than pH 6.5.

Trees and shrubs should be given plenty of room when planted. Find out the size that each plant will be when it is fully grown and provide the necessary space for it to develop even if there is a sparse effect for the first few years. Resist the temptation to fill the extra space with temporary plantings. This tends to make all the plants leggy, as they shade one another out. It is better to live with some space around the plant and let it spread out fully and naturally as it develops.

Even if you can buy manure, do not rely on it exclusively for feeding your plants. Unless it is gathered from your own barn you have little control over the number and variety of weed seeds it contains. It also may host a number of diseases, and even with these risks your plants may still need an early-spring and midsummer supplementary application of a complete fertilizer to provide the necessary vigor for flower and vegetable production.

We know that it seems like heresy to downgrade manure. But although it is a valuable soil conditioner, it is far from the panacea it has been reputed to be.

Apply lime to areas where you will plant potatoes. About 40 pounds per 1,000 square feet will bring a mildly acid soil to a slightly alkaline pH in which potatoes do best, and do not develop potato scab.

It is common to assume that soil dug from the woods makes a superior growing medium. While it is high in organic matter and is helpful in creating a good texture for root growth, it is not particularly high in nutritional value. Mixed with garden loam and reinforced with a complete fertilizer, it will be adequately fortified to make a good planting medium.

Crop rotation, a term more familiar to farmers than to home gardeners, can be ignored in the vegetable garden, with the exception of plantings of cabbage, broccoli, cauliflower, and radish. All these members of the *Brassica* genus are susceptible to soil-borne disease. Their planting sites should be switched annually with those of other vegetables to avoid the problems that can be caused by planting continuously in the same location.

Oil sprays to control scale insects on fruit trees, euonymous, and other hosts should be applied just as soon as the temperature warms up to between 50° and 60° F. The best time to spray is midday when moisture is at a minimum.

A GARDEN YEAR

This is the ideal time to separate and transplant some perennials, especially those that bloom in late summer and early fall. The most popular of this group are Japanese anemones and chrysanthemums.

Summer

At this time of year you might well perceive that your garden is gaining on you. This is the season of fullness, and in all likelihood *everything* is gaining.

The annuals and perennials will be in full flower. The vegetable garden, and the inevitable weeds, will be burgeoning, and there are sure to be a variety of hungry bugs in evidence. Hedges will need trimming and the lawn will need frequent watering—and mowing.

The only sensible attitude in the face of summer's lush growth is to enjoy the beauty and the weather to the utmost, list the jobs that must be done, and take them on one at a time in the order of importance. If you can concentrate on just the job at hand and not worry about what's left to be done, your chances for a happy summer will be greatly increased.

Early summer

Prune shrubs that have already flowered. Do not attempt to revive a plant whose growth has been checked by injury or transplanting through the application of fertilizer. This is about as sensible as feeding a steak dinner to a patient immediately after major surgery. Unless a plant has begun active growth, it can not take advantage of artificial stimulants.

After the daffodils have finished flowering and their foliage begins to turn brown, look the planting over to see if any of them failed to flower this year. If any did fail, it was probably due to overcrowding. This is the time to dig them up and replant them immediately. In the new planting allow at least 6 inches of space around each bulb.

Pinch out growing tips of annuals and perennials that should develop a bushier form.

Get in the habit of looking for bugs and evidence of disease. Both are easier to control in early summer than later on when they might take on epidemic proportions.

Be aware of watering needs. If there has been no rain for a week or ten days, give your lawn and garden a thorough soaking.

Thin out all the seedlings that have insufficient space to mature. If this chore is done in the evening or on a cloudy day, the excess seedlings can be transplanted elsewhere and watered in.

Do not cultivate the soil around rhododendrons and azaleas. They are shallow-rooted and easily injured. Use a mulch to keep down the weeds.

If you cut flowers to bring indoors, do it in the cool of early evening. Plunge most of the stem into water and leave in a cool dark place overnight. Then arrange the flowers the next morning. This will provide them with the most possible water in their stems and the longest indoor life.

Do not pull root vegetables too early. Young beets and carrots look appealing but do not begin to store up sugars until they approach maturity. The misconception is that young vegetables are sweeter. While true of peas, potatoes, and corn it is not true of root crops. You do not have to wait until they are large and woody, but do give them the extra few weeks needed to build up their maximum sugar content.

If any of your plants seem malformed or show other signs of damage, inspect them carefully for evidence of disease or insects. There is no point in applying a fungicide when an insecticide is needed.

Spread a 2-inch layer of mulch on planting beds to stifle the further growth of weeds.

Cut iris flowers for use indoors when the buds are fully developed or as they begin to open. This also applies to other flowers that bloom on spikes.

Midsummer

Start biennials such as pansies and English daisies by sowing seeds in shallow pots, and then transplanting. They will flower next spring and serve as fillers to replace the tulips after their foliage has died down.

Apply the all-purpose spray mixture (see chapter 18) as a preventive for insects and diseases.

Use a combined fertilizer and herbicide on your lawn. Several granular forms are available and if applied according to the instructions, they will improve your chances of having a better lawn.

Where summers are hot, adjust your lawnmower so that it will cut no shorter than 2 inches until the beginning of fall.

Stake perennials as they continue to grow. Light twigs, such as birch prunings, will support the stems, and the plant will soon hide them from view.

Continue to pinch out the growing tips of chrysanthemums on stems that are 3 inches or longer until about July 4, to promote more branching and more flowers.

As flowers fade, pick them off the plants so they will not go to seed. Seed production takes energy from the plant. The flowering season can also be extended if seeds are not allowed to develop.

Even when a planting bed is mulched, a few weeds are likely to appear. If you pull them up before they go to seed, your summer will be a lot easier.

Nothing can be more important than frequent close inspection of the plants in your garden. Diseases and insects can proliferate at a phenomenal rate once they get started. A spray every two weeks with an all-purpose spray mixture (see chapter 18) will keep any such problems in control.

Do not apply insecticide and fungicide dusts to foliage when plants are wet. Only when the leaves are completely dry will the coverage be complete.

Immediately after applying fertilizer around plants, it should be lightly worked into the soil and then watered thoroughly to reap the benefits as quickly as possible without injuring the roots.

About a month after flowering is the ideal time to lift and separate iris (see chapter 17). Iris should be separated about every third year to perpetuate healthy growth and good flowering. In replanting, allow at least 6 inches between each new section of root.

Dig a half-cup of bone meal into each square foot of soil where transplanting is to be done. Never apply bone meal to any planting without working it into the soil. If it is not worked in, little of the phosphorus that it contains will be taken up by the plant roots.

Look over your roses, rhododendrons, and azaleas. It is still not too late to pick off any seed pods that may have escaped your eye. Removing seed pods helps conserve the plant's energy.

Late summer

Your garden should still have good flower color. If not, visit your nearest botanical garden for ideas. In all parts of the country there are flowers that thrive in late summer.

The Southeast has marigolds, zinnias, and camellias. In the Southwest, portulaca and petunias are outstanding at this season. The Northeast has cimicifuga, chrysanthemums, dahlias, and cosmos in flower. On the West Coast the fuchsias and tuberous begonias are in their glory.

Make your plans now to ensure a full season of bloom in the years to come. Learn from a visit to the best public and private gardens in your area.

A late planting of lettuce, Chinese cabbage, carrots, spinach, and beets is a must. It is a great pleasure to harvest these vegetables that thrive in cool weather right up until hard frost. Be sure to thin the seedlings to allow space for the remaining plants to mature. Plant the excess elsewhere.

Fall

In regions where the autumn weather turns the leaves to flame, this can be a marvelous time of year. After the pressure to keep up with the lush growth of summer, the noticeably shorter days and diminishing rate of growth effectively reduce the need for work in the garden.

At its most mundane, fall is the cleanup season. It's time to rake the leaves, prune out dead wood, and pick up the remaining debris in the flower and vegetable gardens.

Take advantage of this opportunity to recall what was best about the summer garden and what could be made more rewarding for next year. Now you can also see what end-of-season delights you might be missing, and plan on having them next year. It might be autumn crocus, more chrysanthemums, or a late crop of Chinese cabbage. And, above all, if you have a place for more of anything with the brilliant color for which the season is famous, don't deny yourself the pleasure.

This is the best time to separate and transplant peonies. Space each clump at least 3 feet apart and plant the crown no deeper than it had been previously.

The spacing may seem wide at first, but top growth has twice the spread of the growth at the base of the plant. And the better the ventilation and exposure to the sun, the more bloom there will be.

If you are storing dahlia tubers, put a high-low thermometer with them until you can be certain of the temperature range in the storage area. This kind of thermometer indicates the highest and the lowest temperature in that location since the last setting. A high of 55° F. and a low of 40° provide the optimum conditions.

Cut off all the dead stems and leaves of perennial plants. The annuals can be pulled up roots and all. If late summer was a relatively dry period, this debris can go on the compost pile; otherwise, assign it to the garbage can for removal.

If you live where the ground freezes, do not put a mulch around plants until the ground has actually frozen. The purpose of the mulch is to keep the soil frozen and prevent the damage that is caused by alternate thawing and freezing.

Plant spring-flowering bulbs early enough to allow three or four weeks for their roots to become established before the ground freezes.

Walk around your house and see if any shrubs are vulnerable to breakage from snow sliding off the roof. If so, insert metal snow catchers in those locations. These are L-shaped metal pieces that slip under the shingles at the eaves. They are available at building-supply stores.

Winter

In those benevolent climes where greenery and flowers are to be had the year round, the pleasures of growing favored specimens and displaying them to best advantage need not stop now.

But where there is a dormant season the gardener, too, must take a rest. There will doubtless be some chores to do. Tools need sharpening and oiling before they are stored away, and other such matters of maintenance can be attended to. But most of all, this is a time for dreaming.

This is the season to conjure up the visions of all the things you would like to add to your garden and landscape.

We don't say that dreaming will make it so. But be assured that nothing can come to pass unless it is first conceived.

By January the garden catalogs will arrive and, in your mind's eye, you can start the annual cycle of growth a good two months ahead of nature's schedule.

Making a plant inventory is a pleasant and useful off-season activity. Some of the entries will have to come from memory, since the stems of herbaceous plants will not be visible. Such a list will provide you with a basis for making schedules for pruning, seeding, spraying, and winter storage as well as for planning future additions to the garden.

Feed all your house plants with a liquid fertilizer and inspect the foliage closely for insects and disease.

If you have dahlia tubers in storage, uncover a few of them to see how they are doing. If they are shriveled, water them lightly.

If you made a New Year's resolution to improve the wintertime appearance of your landscape, now is the time to take action. You could start by ordering such winter-flowering beauties as Christmas rose (*Helleborus niger*) for a damp location, witch hazel (*Hamamelis mollis*) for the sun, and jasmine (*Jasminum nudiflorum*) for a place in partial shade. They can all be planted in the spring.

Redwood or cedar planting boxes are easy to nail together in preparation for spring planting of impatiens or begonias for color in shady places or for geraniums or petunias to further brighten sunny spots. Use the planters beside entryways or on a deck or terrace where the flowers they contain will be regularly seen and enjoyed.

If you have ever left a garden tool lying

in the garden for a month or two, you know that metal can rust and the grain of wood handles will raise and crack. If you paint the handle a brilliant color it is less likely that the tool will be overlooked, and even if it does manage to hide out in the grass the paint will protect the handle. This is a good time to do the painting.

In climates where camellias flower, apply an acid fertilizer in late winter, similar to that used for azaleas and rhododendrons. Apply according to the directions on the label and water the area thoroughly to carry the added nutrients down to the roots.

If you garden in a very warm climate, you can plan now for a garden of white flowers for the coming summer. Such a planting can have a great psychological effect. You will actually feel cooler sitting on a terrace surrounded by white than by such hot colors as red, orange, and yellow.

No matter where you live, start a few pots of tuberous begonias in late winter. They can be rooted in slightly damp peat moss in a warm location and transplanted when the foliage begins to show. Plant in shallow clay pots, called bulb pans, and stake the main stem. Feed each pot every two weeks with a 5-10-5 liquid fertilizer according to the instructions on the label.

They will flower in the shade, and the following year you will undoubtedly want to grow even more of them. They can do wonders to brighten a shady place, and are ideal on a screened porch.

Order seeds of vegetables and flowers. Get materials ready for sowing seeds. This includes shallow pots and saucers, market packs (papier-mâché plant containers 6 by 9 inches by 4 inches deep), perlite, vermiculite, and packaged potting mixture.

Consider tools and equipment you might want for the following season. Not very subtle, but effective, is to make a Christmas list of things you'd like to see under the tree: quick hose connectors; a tensiometer to measure the need of water in potted plants; a good plastic hose (not one of those stiff hard-to-handle kinds); a soil-testing kit; a sharpening stone, one large enough for shovels as well as for pruning shears; or even a few 6-foot squares of canvas for collecting clippings or on which to pile soil when digging a planting hole.

Perhaps winter's greatest gift to the gardener is the perspective it imposes. The garden enables us to observe the forces of nature at first hand, to differentiate cause from effect, and to appreciate the virtues of patience, as the seasons set the rhythms to which we must respond.

⚘| Index |⚘

Page numbers in bold type indicate the main reference for the given topic.

A NOTE ABOUT THE AUTHORS

Jerome A. Eaton, formerly the director of such showplaces as Old Westbury Gardens and Duke Gardens, is on the board of the Brooklyn Botanic Garden and of the Horticultural Society of New York. He was born in New York City and now lives in Pine Plains, New York, where he works a 200-acre farm. He is the author of *Gardening Under Glass* and *Greenhouse Gardening.*

Carroll C. Calkins is a photographer and author, and has served as an editor at *Sunset, House Beautiful,* and *Home Garden* magazines. He is the author of *Great Gardens of America* and *Gardening with Water, Plantings and Stone.* A native of Oregon, he now lives in New York City.

A NOTE ON THE TYPE

The text of this book was set in Uranus, a
film version of Melior, a typeface designed
by Hermann Zapf and issued in 1952. Born
in Nürnberg, Germany, in 1918, Zapf has
been a strong influence in printing since
1939. Melior, like Times Roman, another
popular twentieth-century typeface, was
created specifically for use in a newspaper.
With this functional end in mind, Zapf
nonetheless chose to base the proportions
of its letterforms on those of the Golden
Section. The result is a typeface of unusual
strength and surpassing subtlety.

Composed by Superior Printing, Champaign,
Illinois. Printed and bound by Murray Printing Company, Inc., Forge Village, Massachusetts.

Typography and binding design by Karolina
Harris.